John Clare, Politics and Poetry

John Clare, Politics and Poetry

Alan D. Vardy

palgrave
macmillan

© Alan D. Vardy 2003

First published 2003 by
PALGRAVE MACMILLAN
Houndmills, Basingstoke, Hampshire RG21 6XS and
175 Fifth Avenue, New York, N.Y. 10010
Companies and representatives throughout the world

PALGRAVE MACMILLAN is the global academic imprint of the Palgrave
Macmillan division of St. Martin's Press, LLC and of Palgrave Macmillan Ltd.
Macmillan® is a registered trademark in the United States, United Kingdom
and other countries. Palgrave is a registered trademark in the European
Union and other countries.

ISBN 0–333–96617–1 hardback

This book is printed on paper suitable for recycling and made from fully
managed and sustained forest sources.

A catalogue record for this book is available from the British Library.

Library of Congress Cataloging-in-Publication Data
Vardy, Alan, 1954–
   John Clare, politics and poetry / Alan Vardy.
      p.   cm.
   Includes bibliographical references and index.
   ISBN 0–333–96617–1
   1. Clare, John, 1793–1864.   2. Poets, English—19th century—
Biography.   3. Psychiatric hospital patients—Great Britain—
Biography.   4. Clare, John, 1793–1864—Political and social views.
5. Agricultural laborers—Great Britian—Biography.   6. Mentally
ill— Great Britian—Biography.   7. Clare, John,
1793–1864—Authorship.   I. Title.

   PR4453.C6Z955 2003
   821'.7—dc21
                                                    2003049763

10   9   8   7   6   5   4   3   2   1
12   11   10   09   08   07   06   05   04   03

Printed and bound in Great Britain by
Antony Rowe Ltd, Chippenham and Eastbourne

For Shasta, Peter and Elizabeth

Contents

Preface

John Clare, Politics and Poetry could not have been written without the help of many friends, colleagues and institutions. I would like to acknowledge the generous support of the Social Sciences and Humanities Research Council of Canada in providing the Postdoctoral Fellowship that enabled me to complete the majority of the research for this book, and the School of English at the University of St Andrews for their kindness in allowing me to tenure the Fellowship at their institution. I also want to acknowledge the support of a Professional Staff Congress of the City University of New York in awarding a Research Grant that allowed me to complete my research, and Hunter College for the Eugene Lang Junior Faculty Development Award that assisted in the production of the book.

Friends and colleagues have been generous in discussing this book throughout its planning and composition. In particular I would like to thank Tim Fulford, Bob Heyes, Bridget Keegan, Simon Kövesi, James McKusick, Eric Robinson and Nicholas Roe, all of whom read part of the manuscript and provided me with feedback at some stage in the process. I want to especially acknowledge the encouragement of John Goodridge whose thoughtful responses to parts of the work were particularly helpful. I also want to thank Jack Kenigsberg for his help in preparing the manuscript.

The following institutions provided free access to their manuscripts and other research materials: the British Library Manuscript Collection and Rare Book Room, the Colindale Newspaper Archive, the Peterborough Museum, the Northampton Library, the Pforzheimer Collection of the New York Public Library, the University of St Andrews Library Special Collections, the Sheffield City Library, the University of Sheffield Special Collections, and the Spalding Gentleman's Society. I am grateful to the librarians and staff of these institutions who made research a pleasure.

ALAN VARDY
Hunter College, 2003

Introduction

On the occasion of his first trip to London, John Clare described his experience of sudden celebrity as a physical displacement:

> ... seeing people at my old occupations of ploughing and ditching in the fields by the road side while I was lolling in a coach the novelty created such strange feelings that I could almost fancy that my identity as well as my occupations had changd that I was not the same John Clare but that some stranger soul had jumped into my skin.[1]

Not only did he feel a sense of guilty pleasure, 'lolling in a coach', separated from the other members of his rural labouring class, but also a sense of physical transformation. It was as if he had been changed essentially once he had been removed from his life of perpetual drudgery, and he registered this feeling in visceral terms. The 'stranger soul', John Clare the poet, had 'jumped into the skin' of John Clare the labourer. The enduring misery of Clare's life from this point forward was his inability to make this change permanent, make it something more than a seeming. This cultural trap has generated the critical commonplace, 'poor John Clare'. Clare's eventual madness seems to evolve from this unstable identity, and the source of the instability is external to him and imposed. Thus Clare becomes the quintessential victim of circumstances; as the 'peasant poet' he can never be simply a 'poet' and he can never again return to his 'old occupations'. But Clare struggled against the finality of this socially imposed sentence. His poetry addresses the problem of his divided self, eloquently and powerfully. One of Clare's primary aesthetic goals as 'poet' was to accurately represent his 'old occupations', and as a subject for poetry, lift them from the cultural margins. His defence of dialect, vernacular speech and orality in his poetry

1

constituted a cultural intervention fully aware of its social and political implications.

The recovery of Clare's agency, his sense of acting in relation to the cultural forces arrayed against him (some of which purport to help him), mitigates against the tendency of settling for 'poor John Clare' and recovers a measure of his autonomy as an artist that has been assumed away by critics.[2]

*

This book pursues two interrelated goals. The first is the creation of a more specific social, political and cultural context in which to examine and understand Clare's use of language in general, and his defence of vernacular speech and dialect in particular. The second goal is the recovery of a record of Clare's agency, the ways he responded to the powerful cultural formations that surrounded and defined him and his poetry. The four categories, class, aesthetics, politics, and poetry provide an index of the interconnected subjects that the study reveals. None of these categories exists independently of the others. Understanding the aesthetic responses of contemporary reviewers, for example, is impossible without an understanding of the class assumptions that underlie them. Neither is the recovery of the cultural meaning of Clare's status as a peasant possible without understanding the politics of disenfranchisement that he was born into. Nor can the political commitments represented in Clare's poems be understood outside the aesthetic issues of representation that occupied him. Clare lived and worked inside the social upheavals of the 1820s and 1830s, and only through a thorough understanding of this specific context can a record of his agency (his acts of resistance, capitulations, compromises and contradictions) emerge. Historicist approaches to Clare's life and poetry have done much to establish the social context in which Clare lived and wrote. That critical work, indebted to the pioneering work of John Barrell's *The Idea of Landscape and the Sense of Place, 1730–1840: An Approach to the Poetry of John Clare*,[3] has deepened our understanding of the circumstances of Clare's career. The work of John Lucas, John Goodridge, Hugh Haughton, P. M. S. Dawson and others has made it possible to make historically based judgements about Clare's poetry. The Oxford publication of the complete poems has put Clare's poetry before us in a more comprehensive way,[4] and thus enabled a complex expansion in the scope of Clare studies. With these crucial critical developments, the whole range of 'stranger souls', the proliferation of potential selves occasioned by Clare's literary fame, has begun to emerge.

*

Given the new availability of Clare materials to critics and general readers alike, the lamentable tradition of classifying Clare as a 'minor Romantic poet' provides part of the impetus for this study. The most notorious opinion in that tradition belongs to Harold Bloom who opined in *The Visionary Company* that Clare was a 'failed Wordsworthian poet'. Bloom's subsequent edition of the *Oxford Anthology of Romantic Poetry* repeated this view and added the notion that maybe we can also read Clare's 'mad' poems as a kind of weak version of Blake (even though Clare's despair seems much more akin to Coleridge's). While these views are now considered exploded, especially by Clare scholars, they persist in the selections chosen for anthologies. David Perkins's revised anthology of *English Romantic Writers* increases the number of Clare poems, but still relies on the Bloomian line in making its selections. Poems are chosen for their relationship to other Romantic writing. For example, 'Pastoral Poesy' is commonly anthologised despite the fact that it is unrepresentative of Clare's work and probably written to appease the demand of his publisher, John Taylor, that he be more 'philosophical'. Even Duncan Wu, in his *Romanticism: An Anthology*, repeats the same predictable choices, with the exception of the addition of 'The Flitting', likely in response to arguments put forward by John Lucas concerning the radical politics of the poem's conclusion. Jerome McGann's inexplicable decision to include a single, utterly untypical, poem in his *Oxford Book of Romantic Period Verse* represents the nadir of the critical tradition of creating Clare's minor status as a self-fulfilling prophecy.[5] In response to this persistent critical tradition it is crucial to understand its origins, both in the literary taste underlying the reception of Clare's poetry, and in his editor's introductions to his volumes. Subsequent critical opinion is founded on these initial critical leads. I have unravelled these complex aesthetic assumptions, and established Clare's awareness of them, and his struggle both inside and against them. In particular, analysis of Clare's relationship to Wordsworthian and Coleridgean aesthetics shows how he self-consciously resisted those formulations, and positioned his own poetics in opposition to them. While he was a lover of Wordsworth, that love had serious limits and was far from unconditional. Furthermore, it is premature to characterise the Wordsworthian critical response to Clare as simply an outdated vestige of formalism, or Bloom's anxious assertion of his critical model. Even John Barrell's groundbreaking study relies on Wordsworthian assumptions when it decries the vacillation in the early poetry between political and cultural analysis, and an elegiac inwardness. The assumption that the elegiac voice distances the poetic speaker from the social fray is patently Wordsworthian (although this assumption itself is now debatable), and not really applicable to Clare where, rather, the elegiac marks the emotional depth of his involvement in social events.

Thus the history of editing of Clare's poetry presents a uniquely fascinating study in how a poetic career is made and develops, and continues to be at issue. The ongoing Clarendon Press edition of the complete poetry, under the general editorship of Eric Robinson,[6] serves as a direct response to perceived editorial injustices committed by Clare's editor, John Taylor. The decision to return the poems to their manuscript form has produced an extraordinarily rich scholarly resource, but at the expense of an accessible reading text. The rationale for creating a 'primitivist' standard edition is clear enough: the belief that Taylor's editorial imposition on Clare must be reversed. The moralistic tone of the project cannot be avoided. Taylor's moral fitness is at issue, and the principled defence of the culturally powerless Clare the goal. The origins of these beliefs and subsequent editorial goals lie in the careful manuscript work of Robinson and Geoffrey Summerfield in the early 1960s.

Examination of the manuscript materials for *The Shepherd's Calendar* contained in the Peterborough Clare MSS,[7] caused these scholars genuine shock and outrage. Taylor's deletions and emendations were severe, capricious and seemingly arbitrary. Robinson and Summerfield detailed the enormous cuts to which the poems were subjected, and forcefully demonstrated that there was no aesthetic rationale for many editorial decisions: 'one is forced to conclude that Taylor's text is too often a travesty, not only quantitatively but also qualitatively, of Clare's poems'.[8] After detailed examination of Taylor's emendations, the authors conjecture that there were three criteria for the cuts: the rejection of 'low' subject-matter, concern over the political implications of passages that 'bordered too close on discontent and radical disaffection', and 'language and syntax' that were 'too uncouth for publication'.[9] I will come back to this last criterion, but first want to investigate their second criterion in more detail.

Robinson and Summerfield argue persuasively that Taylor sacrificed the chaotic specificity of the rural scene, complete with its disaffected and displaced peasants, public drunkenness and bawdy humour, in favour of more genteel and generalised description. They demonstrate that the cuts that produced this effect fundamentally distort the poems and weaken their aesthetic and political force. As regards 'The Memory of Love', they rightfully complain about Taylor's elimination of many of Clare's references to the social upheaval and destruction caused by enclosure. Indeed, they show that references to enclosure seem to be among the most common subjects cut in Taylor's editing practice. Such editing, they argue, had disastrous effects on the poem in question:

> The melancholy sense of loss which is central to the meaning of Clare's poem ['The Memory of Love'], and close indeed to his abiding preoccupation with the sorrows of deracination, associated as it was, for Clare, with the effects of enclosure, has been expurgated in the interests of that 'joy' which seems to us to be more of Taylor's making than of Clare's.[10]

All in all, Robinson and Summerfield produced a persuasive indictment of Taylor's editing practice on political, social and aesthetic grounds. That Taylor expurgated much of the politics and social disaffection from the poems is beyond dispute. The matter that remains is determining Taylor's possible motives for having done so. The primary motive offered by Robinson and Summerfield is an overriding concern on Taylor's part not to upset Clare's conservative patrons, specifically Lord Radstock. They pointed out that: ' – references liable to cause Radstock to fall into a state of apoplexy – are methodically expurgated by Taylor's sanguine and utilitarian pencil'.[11] The obvious problem with this line of argument is that Radstock had died, true to character, of an apoplectic fit in August 1825, at least a year before Taylor began slashing Clare's manuscripts. Even if Robinson's and Summerfield's assertion is read figuratively, with Lord Radstock standing in for conservative elements in the reading public, it is difficult to consider it a sufficient explanation for Taylor's editorial excesses. Taylor did not have a history of deferring to Radstock, and their relationship had been strained from the beginning. The oft-cited example of Taylor removing the offending stanza attacking 'accursed wealth' from 'Helpstone' when reprinting *Poems Descriptive of Rural Life and Scenery* is an isolated event, and one that he resisted, first declaring that he and Clare should 'remain obstinate',[12] and subsequently assuring the poet that: 'When the Follies of the Day are past with all the Fears they have engendered we can restore the Poems according to earlier Editions'.[13] Certainly the radical sentiments in *The Village Minstrel* survived Taylor's editing the following year. Furthermore, Taylor and

Radstock were active enemies. Radstock spent considerable effort trying to convince Clare that he should quit Taylor. In a letter of 5 February 1822, Mrs Emmerson communicated Radstock's antipathy:

> . . . the conduct of certain persons, has so thoroughly displeased Lord R. that he cannot take one step to serve you, without feeling he is at the same time serving those who have acted most unbecomingly to him—this reflection necessarily abates the ardour of his Lordships exertions—though very much against the desire of his kind and liberal heart—particularly as far as your welfare is concerned—and I know it is the wish of Lord R. that your future productions should be brought out through another & a higher channel in which case he could more freely serve you—But all this must depend on yourself.[14]

This bullying would not have been a surprise to Taylor, and I will come back to it in evaluating claims about Clare's publishing options. Given the history of the Taylor/Radstock relationship, it is difficult to believe that any deference to Radstock's feelings or influence motivated Taylor to remove the radical sentiments from *The Shepherd's Calendar*. The argument that Taylor feared the harm such sentiments might have on sales is counter-intuitive to begin with. From every indication, Taylor was fully aware that the market for single-author volumes of poetry had collapsed. In such a climate, he was free to publish the book he thought was right, regardless of public taste, precisely because nothing he did would affect sales one way or the other. He was publishing the book, as he told Clare in the cruelly haranguing letter of 28 January 1826 out of a sense of honouring his commitments despite 'whatever Pains it cost' him.[15]

Of course, it is impossible to know Taylor's motives for the cuts. It is possible that he had none. Most critics now agree that the cuts were largely arbitrary, although opinion is still divided over whether any cuts were necessary. In this debate two issues get confused: the condition of the original manuscript that Clare had sent Taylor years before, and that had simply been neglected at the press, and the corrected manuscript that Clare finally provided and that Taylor subsequently slashed. Even Robinson and Summerfield suggest that the original manuscript was a disaster, and they quote Taylor's exasperated letter of 28 January 1826:

> Look at the Vol. of MS. Poems which I now send you, & show it where you will, & let any of your Friends say whether they can even read it—I can find *no one* here who can perform the Task besides

myself. Copying it therefore is a Farce for not three words in a Line on the Average are put down right, & the number omitted, by those I have got to transcribe it, are so great, that it is easier for me at once to sit down & write it out fairly myself. But suppose I attempt to do this, here I encounter a greater Difficulty:—the Poems are not only slovenly written, but as slovenly *composed*, & to make good Poems out of some of them is a greater Difficulty than I ever had to engage in your former Works,—while in others it is a complete Impossibility.

It is surprising that critics have been willing to take Taylor's tirade at face value as a justified complaint. The condition of the manuscript was woeful, but it had been so for years as it languished unread at the press. Taylor's fury may be understandable, but cannot be excused. His problems with the *London Magazine* were the cause of the delays in preparing the book for the press. To lash out at Clare was cruel and dishonest. Once Clare received the returned manuscript, he quickly made the necessary corrections to allow Taylor and Hessey to commence work on the volume. The delays in publishing Clare's third book were entirely caused by Taylor. No number of tirades about 'slovenly' work can erase his culpability. Furthermore, the condition of the manuscript itself was a function of the author–editor relationship between Taylor and Clare that the publisher had always maintained was necessary in order to capture the wildness, the uncultivated energy, of Clare's poetry. From the outset Taylor had stressed that he receive the poems unrevised. Clare, as a result, became unusually reliant on Taylor's judgement. He was simply following their normal pattern of book preparation, and any complaint concerning the problem of copyists is disingenuous. Clare could have found another publisher. As I indicated above, he had powerful friends that urged him to do so. The intimate nature of the editorial relationship held Clare, even though as J. W. and Anne Tibble write: 'Clare could have done his own copying and correcting long before if he had been allowed to do so – or perhaps if he had been less filially acquiescent with Taylor'.[16]

The editing of *The Shepherd's Calendar* therefore represents a crisis in the poet/editor relationship, and Taylor's expurgation of radical references to enclosure cannot be seen as continuous with an ongoing concern with conservative opinion, but rather more likely, indicate a shift in Taylor's own socio-political commitments. The crisis of this volume is simply a piece of the comprehensive crisis of the collapse of his hopes for the *London Magazine*, the dissolution of Taylor & Hessey, the erosion of the market for poetry, the aftermath of his serious attack of brain fever, and his subsequent nervous breakdown. Taken together, all of these events paint a portrait of personal crisis that marks the end of Taylor's career as an important literary publisher and his transformation into a pedestrian publisher of textbooks in his role as the bookseller and publisher to the University of London.[17] Taylor's possible motives in editing *The Shepherd's Calendar* are important to critics working today because of evidence of bad faith, imposition, incompetence, and arbitrariness, which Robinson and Summerfield demonstrate have ultimately been used as the means of understanding the whole of the Taylor/Clare relationship. But the editing of *The Shepherd's Calendar* shows a marked change in that relationship perhaps triggered by psychological trauma and quite outside any aesthetic or political issues inherent to the poetry. In other words, we must deplore the mess Taylor made of the volume, and the cruelty of his tone in shifting responsibility away from himself, but to argue that he had a plan for the volume that violated Clare's intentions gives him too much credit. The arbitrariness of his editorial decisions points to the incompetence of a desperate and shattered man. By using the 'Taylor's Editing' article as a de facto mission statement for the Clarendon Press edition, and the decision to return to manuscript versions of the poems, Eric Robinson has read Taylor's crises of 1825–7 back into the editorial process of *Poems Descriptive*, and *The Village Minstrel*. How much he is justified in doing so is the subject of ongoing critical debate, and it is particularly important to evaluate given the second criterion he and Summerfield offered as motivating Taylor in 1827: the elimination of 'uncouth' language.

Tim Chilcott, who argues that the cogency of their general claim does not tell the whole story, has challenged this part of the Robinson and Summerfield thesis:

> ...Taylor either through misreading or deliberate policy, clearly did reduce the force and sharpness of Clare's dialect by substituting more commonplace and more immediately comprehensible expressions. Yet to seize upon these alterations without examining what he did not excise is, equally clearly, a distortion of his position regarding the poet's language.[18]

Chilcott offers a long list of dialect words and phrases that survived Taylor's pencil in the title poem alone as evidence that: 'far from consistently suppressing Clare's dialect words in the interests of propriety or comprehensibility, on many occasions Taylor retained his earlier perception of the importance of such language to Clare's work, and he did support frequently his use of provincialisms.' Given that Taylor's alleged antagonism to dialect words is one of the foundational principles of the Clarendon Press editions, this critical controversy cannot be avoided in attempting to understand the ways in which Clare's critical reputation has been constructed and shaped.

*

The following study, then, consists of two parts: Chapters 1 to 3 offer fresh perspectives on the controversies over Clare's reception history, and Chapters 4 to 7 reconstruct a sense of Clare's agency by examining his relationship to Radstock's social vision, his various publication efforts outside the confines of his 'peasant poet' persona, his efforts to produce a 'natural history' volume in response to market conditions, and his relationships with various patrons. Chapter 8 takes up the vexed question of his political views through the lens of the overcharged environment of the 'Swing Riots', including his response to Cobbett's political agitation (Cobbett's career intersects Clare's life at crucial political moments). A concluding Epilogue presents a revised version of Clare's agency.

The first part of the book seeks to establish the social, cultural and political landscape into which Clare's poetry appeared, and, further, to make clear what forces and conditions Clare resisted and why. Chapter 1 explores Clare's poetic 'difference' and demonstrates the poverty of the critical tradition of reading him through the lens of Wordsworthian and Coleridgean aesthetics. Clare knew and admired much of Wordsworth's poetry, and by examining what he admired in it, and via a close reading of Clare's poetry in relation to Wordsworthian and Coleridgean aesthetic categories, we can see the ways in which he attempted to self-consciously develop a poetics that resisted many of the goals and operations of so-called Romantic aesthetics. Chapter 2 narrows the focus of the discussion of the politics of language to the areas of poetic taste and aesthetics at the time of Clare's early publications. By examining Hugh Blair's influential essay on the 'pastoral' in poetry and Taylor's use of Georgic pastoral and Romantic aesthetics in introducing Clare, we can recreate the presuppositions of his reading public. By deducing the aesthetic assumptions of the initial reviews of Clare's poems, we can uncover the class implications of those assumptions. Chapter 3 evaluates the debate about the implicit and explicit class politics of Taylor's editing, and describes the 'politics of language' that developed through the introduction of grammar books and Johnson's *Dictionary* in the eighteenth century, cultural events that confined Clare and the other members of his class in the social margins, outside 'polite' society.

Once the cultural and political stakes inherent in questions of language, popular taste and aesthetics have been established, it becomes possible to evaluate Clare's actions within his contemporary literary and social milieus. His poetic actions become recognisable as social and political interventions. Attending to the ways Clare managed to assert his agency in relation to powerful cultural forces arrayed against him, challenges the traditional view of 'poor Clare', the eternal victim, passively buffeted by the actions of others. Instead, a portrait emerges of a writer fully aware of the cultural stakes in his poetry, holding distinct and clear political and aesthetic views, and possessing a powerful integrating mind that enabled him to formulate a coherent position out of these seemingly disparate materials.

The second part of this book recovers Clare's agency by, first, investigating the specific structures of several of Clare's relationships to important patrons by reconstructing the terms under which they patronised 'contented' peasants. A brief history of the stakes involved in being 'discontented' illuminates Clare's responses to the inference he regarded as the work of 'medlars'. Even the imperious Lord Radstock, to whom Clare was deeply grateful for creating a subscribers list, could be and was resisted.

The idea of Clare's passivity is also undermined by a careful reading of his activities during the trying period in the 1820s when he weathered the delays in publication of his third book, *The Shepherd's Calendar*. Clare did not idly stew during these delays, but rather broadened his range of interests and artistic skills to include formalised studies of botany and archaeology, drawing and watercolouring. He was active in publishing poems in the magazines, in selling songs, and in developing new poetic voices and strategies. Cognisant of the decline in the market for single-author volumes of poetry, he worked at developing a new genre, the poetic natural history, in which his detailed knowledge of the 'natural history of Helpstone' would be supplemented by occasional poems and illustrations. Clare's use of established models that were proven publishing ventures, Gilbert White's *Natural History of Selborne* and Elizabeth Kent's *Flora Domestica*, shows that he was capable of pragmatically shaping his poetic output. Furthermore, such shaping extended the range of his social and cultural aims rather than diluting them to please fickle tastes.

The penultimate chapter of this book offers a view of Clare's political investments by focusing on the intense period of 1830–31. Clare appears to equivocate between the two established political camps, conservative Tories and radical reformers of various kinds (including the radical Whigs represented by the Fitzwilliams), as witnessed by his publication in both Tory and radical newspapers. Using Cobbett's political career over the same period as a baseline, and by discussing his intellectual relationship to Marianne Marsh in detail, a position that is uniquely Clare's emerges. Clare had many social aims in common with Cobbett as well as many well-defined disagreements, usually to do with ideology and/or method. Clare's engagement with a variety of Cobbett's texts, in a number of very different social contexts, reveals a subtly evolving and complex political position outside the definitional confines hitherto employed to discuss his politics. The uniqueness of Clare's positions constitutes his political agency. In the past critics have, with some justification, seen such positions as eccentric and isolating. But, in conjunction with the other chapters in the 'agency' section of this volume, Clare's politics, in all their subtle shadings, represent the means by which he attempted to connect himself to the social world. As such, they also reflect the profoundly integrated textures of his political and aesthetic positions. By better understanding Clare's actual political commitments, it is possible to analyse a complex literary event like his anonymous publication of the satirical poem 'The Hue & Cry', and his subsequent hopes of interesting Cruikshank in producing an illustrated edition of it, and the subtle politics the poem embodied (and that apparently alarmed Cruikshank). Such readings place Clare firmly and simultaneously in both the marketplace and the political world.

The book closes with a brief summary of Clare's agency as reconstructed over the course of the volume as a whole.

1
Clare's 'Minorness'

In order to understand how Clare came to be considered a 'minor' poet in the Romantic canon, it is necessary to investigate the aesthetic assumptions that form the bases of such judgements. In part, Clare's status is a continuation of assumptions concerning his class identity. The social and political nuances of the earliest aesthetic claims made for and against Clare[1] and his poetry persist. This troubling persistence of the original terms of the critical debate demands that we examine what we mean by Romantic poetry, and what we mean when we identify Clare's poetry as a 'minor' variant. Attitudes towards class have changed sufficiently that Clare can be admitted as a poet without any special pleading on class grounds, yet the view of him as a naïve rustic, simple-mindedly in love with the objects of the natural world, continues to have currency. David Simpson provocatively addresses this puzzle in his essay, 'Is the Academy Ready for John Clare?'.[2] Simpson puts the problem in succinct historical terms:

We would not expect to see much of Clare in the pages of M. H. Abrams's *The Mirror and the Lamp* or *Natural Supernaturalism*, for these were at the forefront of the 'old' Romanticism of complex high philosophic consciousness whose avowed displacement has been the task of so much recent criticism. But neither does Clare figure (except in two brief mentions) in Marilyn Butler's *Romantics, Rebels and Reactionaries*, the book that best represents the 'new' Romanticism's commitment to placing its writers in forgotten social and historical environments; and he is completely absent from Jerome McGann's *The Romantic Ideology*, which has received even more attention than Butler's book for its claim to set right the theorization of the Romantic period and its legacies. (p. 70)

Simpson suggests several reasons for this critical omission. The reason may be as simple as a lack of space in anthologies for all the new poetic voices that could be included. But why omit Clare? Simpson makes a trenchant observation when he points out that Clare's class position as a rural labourer 'is in the constellation of received classes no class at all' (p. 73). In the 'identity politics' that underwrites so much current critical discourse, Clare simply has no constituency (p. 73). He is not subject to traditional Marxist definitions focusing on an industrial 'working class', and the class to which he did belong has all but vanished. Whatever the causes of Clare's relative neglect in the 'new' Romanticism, the purpose of this chapter is to make clear the ways in which he challenges the 'old' Romanticism, and thus to establish beyond all doubt 'the potential of Clare's work for articulating the preoccupations of the contemporary critical moment' (p. 77).

*

As we have seen, the eighteenth-century taste for pastoral poetry, exemplified by Hugh Blair in his lecture on the subject, provided the reading public with a critical guide to reading Clare that was simplistic and inaccurate. The more complex version of a rural poetics offered by Wordsworth, and critiqued by Jeffreys, Coleridge and others, slowly displaced that older taste in establishing a critical idiom in which to assess Clare's poetry. It is this later historical development in critical attitudes that needs to be addressed if the puzzle of Clare's designation as 'minor' is to be unravelled. The cause of this pervasive judgement can be summarised, in James McKusick's phrase, as 'the normative use of Wordsworthian categories'.[3] Chapter 2 demonstrates how the ideas on which these categories are based were already present in the critical debate via Taylor's introduction, and the various critical controversies raging at the time. In order to see how current critical evaluations of Clare derive from the critical edifices of Wordsworthian and Coleridgean aesthetics, and, further, to understand how these critical assumptions are ill suited to the task of reading Clare, this chapter pursues three tacks. The first section looks at Clare's attitude towards Wordsworth's poetry through examining his correspondence and journal. By understanding how Clare read Wordsworth, and other poets, we can begin to differentiate his poetics from those typically employed by critics in reading him. The second section provides a detailed comparison of Clare's aesthetic beliefs in relation to Wordsworth's by producing close readings of several of their poems. In the past, critics have employed such comparisons to define Clare's 'minorness'. The final section of the chapter resituates Clare inside the critical debate concerning Romantic aesthetics by using his poetics as the means to construct a new critical vantage point from which to view the conflict between Coleridge and Wordsworth over the legitimacy of the use of 'low' rural subjects and diction. The many nuances of that debate create the most complex version of the Romantic aesthetic that has traditionally defined the field, the 'old Romanticism', and which has come under so much fire from historicists, feminists and others in the past fifteen years.[4] Clare's marginal position, paradoxically, provides an excellent vantage point to evaluate these unfolding critical debates.

Clare's reading

A sonnet composed between 1837 and 1841 captured Clare's attitude towards Wordsworth, in brief.[5] This homage described the poetic values that Clare found in Wordsworth's poetry:

> Wordsworth I love, his books are like the fields,
> Not filled with flowers, but works of human kind;
> The pleasant weed a fragrant pleasure yields,
> The briar and broomwood shaken by the wind,
> The thorn and bramble o'er the water shoot
> A finer flower than gardens e'er gave birth,
> The aged huntsman grubbing up the root—
> I love them all as tenants of the earth:
> Where genius is, there often die the seeds;
> What critics throw away I love the more;
> I love to stoop and look among the weeds,
> To find a flower I never knew before;
> Wordsworth, go on—a greater poet be;
> Merit will live, though parties disagree![6]

No mention was given to the presumably crucial poetic value of reflection. The growth of the poet's philosophic mind appears not to have interested Clare. Instead, Wordsworth was admired for his careful delineation of the natural world and its human inhabitants. The flowers to be admired were not cultivated, but fragrant weeds entangled in 'briar', 'thorn and bramble'. The emphasis on the humbleness and the inextricability of the plants and the human inhabitants from their environment dominated the poem. These sturdy, tenacious 'tenants of the earth' were precisely the parts of Wordsworth that critics disparaged. Coleridge went to great length in admonishing Wordsworth for his use of 'low' subjects. The humble rustics like Simon Lee 'grubbing up his root', were attacked as absurd caricatures and examples of Wordsworth's unevenness: what Coleridge called his 'inconstancy'.[7] Clare defended these natural objects and humble figures as inherently valuable, and the source of natural beauty. His use of the word 'tenants' was telling in its self-consciousness of the class rhetoric embedded in attacks on Wordsworth. Clare loved what critics threw away, and argued for a minute examination of the seeds of beauty in the common weeds. New poetic knowledge was found in the discovery of the beauties hidden from everyday view.

From his earliest readings of Wordsworth's poetry Clare valued not only the quality and variety of natural description, but also the apparent spontaneity of the verse. In a letter to Markam Sherwill of 12 July 1820, Clare wrote asking if he had met Coleridge and Wordsworth, and for Sherwill's opinion of Wordsworth's sonnet on 'Westminster Bridge'. Clare's extravagant praise of the sonnet was based on its power of description, and he made his point by way of a comparison to Milton (and against critical opinion):

> I think it (& woud say it to the teeth of the critic in spite of his rule & compass) that it [the sonnet] owns no equal in the English language Miltons I reckon little of keeping the 'Paradise lost' in view—one might have expected far better but he sat down to write to the rul[es of][8] art in the Sonnet just as a architect sets about a building while wordsworth defies all art & in all the lunatic Enthuseism of nature he negligently sets down his thoughts from the tongue of his inspirer[9]

Clare vehemently defended Wordsworth against the formal enclosure of 'rules of art'. In a witty turn, Milton's 'Paradise Lost' was lost when he composed his sonnets because it was displaced from his mind by superficial formal concerns. Wordsworth's greatness was his spontaneous composition in the moment of inspiration. Clare's language insisted both on the intensity of that moment; the 'tongue of his inspirer' suggested a physical transport, and its escape from the confines of formal concerns. The act of poetic composition was 'negligent', and nature herself, as a source inspiration, was uncontrollable, a 'lunatic Enthuseism'. Clare's vocabulary dramatised the issues of formal and critical enclosure that I will discuss in Chapter 2, and emphasised the essential spontaneity of Wordsworth's art. And, furthermore, the passage excluded philosophical reflection as a source of poetic value. The conclusion of the letter made it clear that Clare understood the crucial divide in Wordsworthian poetics, a divide that contributed to the reception of his own poetry: '...dont think I favour his affected fooleries in some of his longer pieces theres some past all bearing'.[10] For Clare, reflection was equated with affectation, and marked the loss of poetic inspiration in pursuit of the extraneous; it indicated the failure 'of keeping the "Paradise lost" in view'.

Clare defended Wordsworth against himself. In resisting the move to reflection, he hoped to preserve the moment and force of inspiration, its 'negligent' freedom, and also hoped to preserve the objects of nature from displacement by poetic self-creation, the 'growth of the poet's mind' as Wordsworth famously called it. The stakes for Clare, as Chapter 2 indicates, were enormous. He needed to resist calls to purify his language of its 'real defects', and hoped in the process to develop an aesthetic practice that represented the natural beauties of the landscape for their own sake.

Clare's poetic taste for unaffected representations of nature developed through his reading of poetry in general, and led to a general theory of poetic value quite against the grain of most of his contemporary critics. In one of the earliest entries to his 1824 journal Clare stated his belief in the intrinsic value of the landscape, and his antipathy to affectation, in his appreciation of Izaak Walton's *The Compleat Angler*:

> what a delightful book it is the best English Pastoral that can be written the descriptions are nature unsullied by fashionable tastes of the time they are simply true and like the Pastoral Ballads of Bloomfield breath of the common air and the grass and the sky one may almost hear the water of the river Lea ripple along and the grass and flags grow and rustle in the pages that speak of it[11]

The 'best' pastoral poetry was that freest of 'fashionable' affectations, and that closest to the ideal of representing the natural world as it was. According to Clare, the poet should strive to come as close as possible to the thing itself, to 'almost' recreate the experience of that thing for the reader. In this aim, the poet, of necessity, must disappear in order for the landscape to emerge 'unsullied'. Clare's observation of this poetic value in Walton and Bloomfield does not surprise, but the predominance of it as a poetic principle becomes clear in a journal entry a few weeks later. This time Clare discussed his aesthetic responses to Milton, and after praising the sublime grandeur of the beginning and ending of 'Paradise Lost' he stated his reading preferences:

'Comus' and 'Allegro' and 'Penserose' are those I take up Oftenest
what a beautiful description at the shut of evening is this

> '—What time the labourd ox
> 'In his loose traces from the furrow came
> 'And the swinkt hedger at his supper sat'[12]

Again, Clare valued the accuracy and trueness of the description above
all else. The adjective 'swinkt', used to describe the physical weariness
of the farm labourer, is the precise dialect word. This is exactly the kind
of diction that reviewers of Clare's poems objected to as 'low' or vulgar,
yet here it is in Milton. Wordsworth's anxiety that such diction be
'purified' of such defects seems terribly misplaced in this context, the
context of Clare's reading. So slippery is the matter of cultivated versus
'low' poetic diction, that even Eric Robinson and David Powell, probably the most vocal defenders of Clare's use of dialect words, become
confused. They include Milton's word 'swinkt' in their glossary of Clare's
dialect words in their edition of the autobiographical prose.[13]

*

Central to Clare's poetic principles was the idea that an interrelationship
existed between the aesthetic issues of 'low' diction and self-creation.
He believed that the ethics of representation per se was at stake in discussions of his use of local vernacular speech. Clare's defence of idiomatic speech was based on the assumption that only through local
language could local objects be accurately, and truthfully, represented.
Calls for the purification of Clare's language, besides being couched in
class condescension, threatened the very objects Clare wanted to preserve
and elevate. His poetic representation of the landscape established the
aesthetic value of its constitutive objects and resisted the commercial
values that threatened its destruction.

Crucial to aesthetic judgements of Clare's lack of sublimity, judgements
which contributed to his canonisation as a 'minor' writer, was the
assumption that his diction was trapped in a landscape that failed to
attain sufficient poetic heights. But it was precisely Clare's deliberate and
spirited defence of the intrinsic value of the local against the affectations
of poeticisms that provided one of the driving forces of his poetry. When
The Village Minstrel was published in 1821 the critics predictably groused
about Clare's use of 'provincialisms' (rustic speech unpurified of its
defects), and about the lack of sublimity in his landscapes. These two

complaints were interdependent, and together they constituted an aesthetic judgement about the nature of the sublime and the beautiful that threatened Clare's chosen landscape, his locality, by labelling it poetically 'deficient'.[14] In retrospect, it seems absurd to praise Clare's careful observation of nature, while criticising the variety of natural objects he had to choose from (was the anonymous critic in the *Literary Gazette* suggesting a grand tour of the continent?). And, it seems equally absurd to praise his 'naturalness', the source of his genuineness, while demanding that he purify his 'natural' speech into the elevated language of *the poet.*

This returns us to Wordsworth, and the crucial distinction between Wordsworthian and Clarean aesthetics. In Wordsworthian poetics the aesthetic categories of the beautiful and the sublime are the ultimate ends of the poem; the objects of nature are the means to those ends not ends in themselves. And ultimate poetic value therefore lies in the aesthetic expansion of the poet (and vicariously of the reader) – what he, Wordsworth, called 'abundant recompense' in 'Tintern Abbey', or the growth of a poet's mind. Clare, on the other hand, resisted this self-referential system of value in his poems by striving for what might be called a truthful representation of the natural objects around him. They were in themselves 'the beauties', not the source of an intellectual achievement called 'beauty'. This was not an accident. It was a deliberate choice. Clare's refusal to recuperate the objects of nature into the aesthetic construction of the self cannot be read simply as a sign of a naïve poetics; and yet, it is precisely this assumption that defines him as a 'minor' poet. Clare, in manuscript marginalia of 1821, made his poetic intentions clear in his response to the critics' complaints about his unpurified language in *The Village Minstrel*:

> [the] observation that Poets should conform their thoughts or style to the taste of the country by which he [the anonymous critic being challenged] means fashion—is humbug.

And in another note he took a precisely contrary view to that of the critics of the shortcomings of the second book:

> I...often feel sorry that I did not withhold it a little longer for revision. the reason why I dislike it is that it does not describe the feelings of a rhyming peasant strongly or locally enough...[15]

Clare's search for the 'genuine word' was a deliberate aesthetic choice, and raised questions about the very ethics of representation.

Clare took the issue of 'genuine' representation one step further by arguing that *all* poetic language was finally unequal to the task of capturing the intrinsic value and pleasure of the natural scene. In the sonnet simply entitled 'The Scene', from *Poems Descriptive of Rural Life and Scenery*, Clare illustrated the impossibility of representing aesthetic value. The poem begins with a list of the natural objects that can be viewed from a single point: 'The landscapes stretching view that opens wide.' Within this expanse the poet's gaze seems to fall on a disconnected series of things:

> The steeple peeping just above the trees
> Whose dangling leaves keep rustling in the breeze
> —& thoughtful shepherd bending oer his hook
> & maidens stript haymaking to apear
> & hodge a wistling at his fallow plough
> & herdsman hallooing to intruding cow[16]

The accident of the steeple being framed by the trees is the only thing that connects the first two lines of this passage, and the human inhabitants of the scene are of the most humble, and presumably unpoetic, character. Yet, it was the aesthetic value of precisely this sort of landscape that Clare wished to establish. The homeliness of the 'herdsman hallooing to intruding cow' was transformed by the aesthetic pleasure it afforded. Clare made the most extravagant possible claim:

> All these [objects viewed] with hundreds more far off & near
> Approach my sight—& please to such excess
> That Language fails the pleasure to express

The poet was overwhelmed by the 'excess' of the scene. Such an experience answered both critics of the humbleness of the landscape, and those conditioned by Wordsworthian aesthetic assumptions. The failure of the poet to represent the surfeit of pleasure inherent in the scene caused a cognitive crisis characteristic of the sublime, a crisis of perceptual excess, and thus demonstrated that sublimity could be located in the most humble natural landscape. Clare's Northamptonshire landscape was as aesthetically valuable as the Alps. But, unlike Wordsworthian versions of such overwhelming moments, no effort was made to recuperate the perceptual excess of the scene, and the poet's failure, into personal growth; its value was purely intrinsic and remained unassimilated. Contrary to critics who claimed Clare's chosen landscape was incapable of creating sublime transport, the poem argued that such transport was dependent on the quality of perception, on attention to detail. Furthermore, Clare demonstrates the value of the scene by refusing to exploit it.

In the early 1830s, Clare presented the aesthetic notion of the unrepresentable in simple and eloquent terms. A margin note to a prose fragment in which Clare had tried and failed to transcribe the song of the nightingale expressed the unrecuperable power of the objects of nature:

> ... many of her [the nightingale's] notes are sounds that cannot be written the alphabet having no letters that can syllable the sounds.[17]

The extraordinary use of 'syllable' as a transitive verb captures the sheer physicality of the poet's failure. Yet in this failure Clare discovered a potential sublime via his careful contemplation of his sensual experience of his place within the natural world (as the hearer of the nightingale). Clare is transported by the nightingale's song, and his failure to represent either the song or his experience of it need not devalue its aesthetic import.

*

Normative Wordsworthian categories

I want to develop some of these aesthetic arguments further by looking at two sonnets from later in Clare's career, specifically in relation to Wordsworth's poetry. The first, from around 1835, is 'The Vixen':

> Among the taller wood with ivy hung,
> The old fox plays and dances round her young.
> She snuffs and barks if any passes by
> And swings her tail and turns prepared to fly.
> The horseman hurries by, she bolts to see,
> And turns agen, from danger never free.
> If any stands she runs among the poles
> And barks and snaps and drives them into holes.
> The shepherd sees them and the boy goes by
> And gets a stick and progs the hole to try.
> They get all still and lie in safety sure,
> And out again when everything's secure,

And start and snap at blackbirds bouncing by
To fight and catch the great white butterfly.[18]

In the note to this poem in the Robinson and Powell *Oxford Authors* edition of Clare, the editors explain that it is from a group of poems concerned with the theme of human cruelty to animals.[19] While I agree that many readers are led to reflect on this theme, I would suggest that such reflection is the result of the reader's aesthetic and emotive responses to the poem, rather than the poet's intention. The poem does not make moral pronouncements. Much of the pleasure in the poem is in its images of spontaneous animal behaviour. The stunning final image of the foxes leaping in an effort to catch 'the great white butterfly' depicts the animals' behaviour as its own ends. The young foxes do not find their value as part of an illustration of the evils of the hunt, or of the wantonness of the boy in the poem, but in an action that we, as humans, cannot comprehend. It is partly this final incomprehensibility of their behaviour that we translate into spontaneous joy. However, this affective response is not recuperated into the systematic self-expansion of the poet. Rather, it remains inexplicable, refusing to serve as an uncognisable negative stage in a sublime moment. The poem insists on the intrinsic value of the foxes, not on their potential as a moral lesson. After the fact, if we accept the value of the foxes as objects of nature per se, then we can conclude that cruelty towards such objects is unethical and perhaps immoral. But even the reader's recuperation of the poem into their personal moral education is resisted by the final inexplicability of the poem's action. Clare insists that ethics and aesthetics are intertwined in this way: in order to represent the intrinsic value of the objects of nature, the poet and the audience must recede as the ultimate centres of aesthetic value. There is strong evidence in poems like 'The Vixen' that Clare believed that the conversion of nature into the self, by poetic means, or through the self-interest of enclosure, or his landlord making 'use' of his favourite elms, exploited the objects of nature by converting their intrinsic value into purely human value. He knew at first hand what it was to be menaced as an object of nature. The collapse of the traditional relationships of rural labour had taken a physical, emotional and material toll on Clare, and, as I indicate at length in Chapter 2, others hotly contested his very identity as a peasant poet beyond his own power of self-determination.

Clare's refusal to affect such a conversion of value in his poetry defines his 'minorness', according to the critical tradition (from Taylor's echoes of the Preface to Harold Bloom's 'failed Wordsworthian'). Compare, for example, Clare's total lack of concern about the boy in 'The Vixen' to the famous Wordsworthian boy of 'The Prelude', Book First. Both are engaged in acts of transgression against nature, but in Wordsworth the boy's transgression is the site of moral learning made meaningful as evidence of a kind of primitive sensibility necessary to the growth of a poet's mind. When Wordsworth purifies these humble recollections he intellectually converts them into 'abundant recompense'[20] and redirects all value into the poet. The child's moral terror is taken as early evidence of the poetic capacity for the sublime:

> ... but after I had seen
> That spectacle [the 'huge peak'], for many days, my brain,
> Worked with a dim and undetermined sense
> Of unknown modes of being; o'er my thoughts
> There hung a darkness, call it solitude
> Or blank desertion. No familiar shapes
> Remained, no pleasant images of trees,
> Of sea or sky, no colours of green fields;
> But huge and mighty forms, that do not live
> Like living men, moved slowly through the mind
> By day, and were a trouble to my dreams.[21]

This is the familiar structure of the idealist sublime[22]: a crisis, or negative stage, based on the uncognisability of the sublime object, followed by the supersession of the object into the expansion of the poet's mind. As evidenced by his written views on Wordsworth in his letters, Clare was deeply suspicious of this idealist structure precisely because it collapsed any intrinsic value of the object into the purely human value of self-expansion. He made his feelings about the ethics of this exploitative relationship to the 'pleasant images of trees' abundantly clear (in more prosaic terms) in the letter to Taylor of 1821 lamenting the impending destruction of his favourite elms, and his representation of the foxes in 'The Vixen' repeated this analysis in the realm of poetry. The violence of the terms in the letter, the trees were 'condemned to die' by the 'savage' who owned them, was replaced in the sonnet by a quiet defence of the foxes, but the claims for the intrinsic value of each was consistent over the roughly fourteen-year period between the two.

Clare's stubbornness in his adherence to the many registers of this single principle, the ethical refusal to exploit the objects of nature, whether by physical or aesthetic means, cut him off from the production of true poetic genius according to the dominant aesthetic theories of the day. But that is not to say that his poetic practice did not constitute an aesthetic position. He believed in a different poetic truth, in a strict adherence to truthfulness in the representation of nature and human activity in nature. Even when the poet entered the poem as a human figure, potentially the poem's subject, Clare refused to redirect meaning into the poetic self. This resistance to recuperation is clear enough in another sonnet of around 1835, 'The Mouse's Nest':

> I found a ball of grass among the hay
> And progged it as I passed and went away;
> And when I looked I fancied something stirred,
> And turned again and hoped to catch the bird—
> When out an old mouse bolted in the wheats
> With all her young ones hanging at her teats;
> She looked so odd and so grotesque to me,
> I ran and wondered what the thing could be,
> And pushed the knapweed bunches where I stood;
> Then the mouse hurried from the craking brood.
> The young ones squeaked, and as I went away
> She found her nest again among the hay.
> The water o'er the pebbles scarce could run
> And broad old cesspools glittered in the sun.[23]

The human figure in the poem gives us no clue about what this event might mean. We witness an instinctual response (the poet's running) to an inexplicable sight. We cannot even guess at the cause of this response, much less construct a moral out of it. If this were an incident from 'The Prelude', the poet would meditate on the event and eventually secure its meaning, and the apparent panic attack would be superseded as a necessary negative stage in the growth of the poet's mind. This final meaning would be at the expense of the quality of the moment, and Clare strives to preserve the truthfulness of that visceral moment's inexplicability. The final couplet is a logical non sequitur; the glittering cesspool bears no relation to the mouse, yet it rings true as the next moment in Clare's intense perception and scrupulously accurate representation of the world he viewed. In creating these intensely perceptual poems, Clare is unique as a sonnet writer. Rather than developing an argument through the length of an octave and sestet or three quatrains and a couplet, Clare creates a series of vivid perceptual moments of an almost cinematic quality. The matter of the poems is not formal, and thus the sonnet becomes merely the unit of perception.[24]

Coleridge and the trouble with rustics

Clare's resistance to locating aesthetic value in the process of reflection was deliberate and consistent. His reasons for resisting were complex, and concerned social as well as aesthetic worries about the exploitation of objects. But in another way Clare's poetry seemed in perfect agreement with Wordsworth's poetic aims. Wordsworth argued eloquently for the inherent aesthetic value of the rural landscape and its inhabitants, and this argument legitimised Clare's subject matter. The rural scene was established as a suitable subject for poetry. However, Wordsworth's use of rustics had different goals. He idealised such figures in the process of self-creation, 'Resolution and Independence' being the prototypical example, while Clare represented such figures for their own sake. Nonetheless, as I indicate in Chapter 2, critics were quick to concede that Clare's subjects were poetical, partly on Wordsworthian grounds. Hostility to Clare's humble subject matter, usually by conservative critics, was primarily grounded in class biases, but also appeared in aesthetic debates. Specifically, Coleridge's turn against Wordsworth's *Lyrical Ballads* as a poetic project (partly as the result of his sense of grievance at being excised from the book) supplemented critical concerns about Clare's 'lowness' and vulgarity. It was precisely Wordsworth's claim of the superior authenticity of rustic speech, albeit 'purified of its defects', that Coleridge most fiercely attacked in *Biographia Literaria*. Critical reception inevitably picked up the terms of that attack, and the value of colloquial speech, so crucial to Clare's aesthetic claims, became contested terrain. Coleridge's attack on Wordsworth serves as one of the foundations of Romantic theory, and thus becomes a key piece in the intellectual history of the construction of Clare's place in the Romantic canon.

In chapter 22 of *Biographia Literaria* Coleridge loses his patience with the central conceit of Wordsworth's use of rustics. The idea that rustics were as the speakers of the poems' philosophical truths becomes too much:

> in order to remove all doubts on the subject [the poetical nature of a rustic character], [Wordsworth] had *invented* an account of his birth, parentage and education, with all the strange and fortunate accidents which had concurred in making him at once poet, philosopher and *sweep*![25]

In his attack he makes it clear that he considers the phrase 'peasant poet' to be an oxymoron: '... *one* BURNS, among the shepherds of *Scotland*, and not a single poet of humble life among those of *English* lakes and mountains' (emphasis his, p. 132). Such a figure, then, could only function as a mask for the poet, which Coleridge denigrates as a weak 'ventriloquism'. His objection here is, specifically, to Wordsworth's confusion of the 'high' and the 'low', what Coleridge calls Wordsworth's 'inconstancy', the false 'matter-of-factness' (p. 126) of his choice of characters. This argument runs that the poem is marred by an incongruous combination of 'high' poetic ideas and diction, with 'low' subjects, in this case, rustics. It is absurd, he argues, to pretend that the speaker in 'The Excursion' could be a pedlar. To illustrate this perceived fault, Coleridge selects a particularly bad Wordsworth poem as an example, 'Gipsies'. He employs withering sarcasm to make his point: 'he [Wordsworth] expresses his indignation [over the Gipsies' lack of industry] in a series of lines, the diction and imagery of which would have been rather above, than below the mark, had they been applied to the immense empire of China improgressive for thirty centuries'(p. 137). Here are the offending lines (quoted in full by Coleridge):

> The weary Sun betook himself to rest.
> —Then issued Vesper from the fulgent West,
>   Outshining like a visible God
>   The glorious path in which he trod.
> And now, ascending, after one dark hour,
> And one night's dimunition of her power,
>   Behold the mighty Moon! this way
>   She looks as if at them—but they
> Regard her not:—oh better wrong and strife
> Better vain deeds or evil than such life!
>   The silent Heavens have goings on;
>   The stars have tasks—but these [the Gipsies] have none.
>
>   (pp. 137–8)

It is difficult not to agree with Coleridge that this is absurd diction to apply to a gypsy camp, but what is surprising, perhaps, is his defence of the gypsies against Wordsworth's presumptuous moral judgement. He decries the poet's lack of reflection concerning the actual conditions of the gypsies' lives, that they 'might probably have been tramping for weeks together through road and lane, over moor and mountain, and consequently must have been right glad to rest themselves' (p. 137).

Coleridge persuasively demonstrates that the poem is objectionable on both grounds (the aesthetic and the social). From a social perspective, in particular, Wordsworth, in attempting to assert his moral superiority, inadvertently expressed the opposite.

Coleridge's detection of moral weakness in Wordsworth moves him to object to the characterisation of the gypsies, but his primary motive is not a defence of the gypsies. He is not writing in order to illustrate his sympathy for the plight of the landless. More accurately, he objects to Wordsworth's failure to sympathise, and he believes that this reflects negatively on Wordsworth's capacity for poetic sympathy. Wordsworth's diction is shown to be absurd, and his observations suspect. In short, Coleridge's quarrel is aesthetic.

The best possible illustration of the moral and poetic shortcomings of Wordsworth's poem is provided not by Coleridge's attack, but by an irregular sonnet of Clare's from about 1840, 'The Gipsy Camp'. Written at Northampton asylum, it is a poem of profound identification and sympathy, and treats the same subject as Wordsworth's poem. However, Clare's poem presents a complete antithesis to Wordsworth's in terms of diction and moral sympathy:

> The snow falls deep; the Forest lies alone:
> The boy goes hasty for his load of brakes,
> Then thinks upon the fire and hurries back;
> The Gipsy knocks his hand and tucks them up,
> And seeks his squalid camp, half hid in snow,
> Beneath the oak, which breaks away the wind,
> And bushes close, with snow like hovel warm:
> Their stinking mutton roasts upon the coals,
> And the half-roasted dog squats close and rubs,
> Then feels the heat too strong and goes aloof;
> He watches well, but none a bit can spare,
> And vainly waits the morsel thrown away:
> 'Tis thus they live—a picture to the place;
> A quiet, pilfering, unprotected race.[26]

Not only is Clare not interested in judging the gypsies, the only language of judgement is directed back at the reader as a challenge to his or her habitual notions about gypsies. The fact of their 'pilfering' is not denied, but rather is presented in the context of the description of the camp, and the other descriptive adjectives that surround it, 'quiet' and 'unprotected'. The effect of this is to force the reader to re-evaluate 'pilfering' as an oversimplified view of the gypsies. Furthermore, Clare has no interest in the construction of a moral position for the poet through the agency of the poem. His aesthetics, here as elsewhere, are dedicated to the faithful representation of the object and the resistance of the urge to recuperate the aesthetic process back into the construction of the self. In fact, sympathising as he does with the gypsies' plight, any authorial self-creation would offend his sensibilities as an exploitation of human misery. In stark contrast to the self-congratulation and utter lack of sympathy that Coleridge denounces in the Wordsworth poem, Clare sympathises with the characters in his poem in an intense way. He literally follows the 'pilfering' boy back into the camp by imagining his needs; the boy 'thinks upon the fire', and returns because warmth is momentarily of primary importance in this harsh economy of needs. Clare's sympathy is extended to the extreme point of empathising with the camp dog whose hunger is an eloquent re-expression of the gypsies' own. His imaginative sympathy for the dog recalls 'The Vixen', and, as with that earlier example, Clare resists the construction of his own moral position in favour of a detailed representation of the harsh reality of the world he saw. The realistic delineation of a series of moments, the experiences of suffering in the gypsy camp, is the sole poetic purpose of the poem, rather than the means to a self-aggrandising moral position.

What then would Coleridge have made of 'The Gypsy Camp'? Would he have commended its fierce resistance to the moralising weakness of Wordsworth's poem? It is impossible to say, but it is important to remember that the defence of the gypsies was not Coleridge's motive for writing. Furthermore, the 'lowness' of Clare's subject concerned Coleridge as much as his famous rival Francis Jeffrey, and the conclusion he drew from his attack on Wordsworth's 'Gipsies' was not that Wordsworth had failed to truthfully represent the gypsies, although that was undoubtedly so, but that gypsies were not a fit subject for poetry. As a subject they violated a 'fundamental distinction', made by Coleridge earlier in chapter 22, between the correct objects for art and for philosophy. In that passage, Coleridge objected to Wordsworth's use of rustic characters, even as he admitted that we should consider all persons as equals regardless of their various stations in life; he nonetheless objected because they were, what he called, 'immediate objects', and, as such, better suited to treatment in 'sermons or moral essays'. He made his distinction on these grounds, and as follows:

It [representation of rustics] seems, indeed, to destroy the main fundamental distinction, not only between a poem and prose, but even between philosophy and works of fiction, inasmuch as it proposes *truth* for its immediate object instead of *pleasure*. (p. 130)

Clare's poem takes *truth* for its immediate object. This Coleridgean distinction provides a succinct expression of the aesthetic divide between Clare and mainstream Romantic aesthetics. His insistence on the truth of his poetic representations is in direct opposition of the construction of the poetic self that dominates the poetics of both Wordsworth and Coleridge. What is euphemistically called *pleasure* in Coleridge's distinction refers to the aesthetic process by which the poet affects self-creation through poetic creation. An 'immediate object' is too easily grasped to afford the 'pleasures' of the sublime or the beautiful. For example, the subject of 'Resolution and Independence' is not the leach gather, but rather Wordsworth's harnessing of his personal crisis into a moment of self-expansion – the sublime effect. Clare resists this aesthetic effect on ethical grounds. He sees it as an exploitation of the object being represented, in that case, the leach gatherer. 'The Gipsy Camp' makes this clear enough, I think, in its gestures away from the poet and towards the feelings of the members of the camp (including the dog). Anything outside the accurate description of those represented and their feelings is extraneous to the poem. Clare would call these extraneous additions, as he did in the letter to Sherwill quoted above, Wordsworth's 'affected fooleries', the philosophical pretensions that to Clare's mind marred many of Wordsworth's poems.[27] In order to see how completely integrated this belief is in Clare's mind, one need only recall the angry letter to Taylor complaining about his landlord's plan to cut down his favourite elms and his outrage at 'his arrogant presumption'. This powerful attachment, what he elsewhere calls his love of 'wild things almost to foolishness',[28] forcefully illustrates Clare's respect, even reverence, for the objects of nature and his opposition to the 'presumption' of converting them to our use. This ethical stance is indistinguishable from his aesthetic stance vis-à-vis representation (as I argued above in relation to Wordsworth). Put another way, Clare refuses to differentiate between ethics and aesthetics, and thus refuses to abide by Coleridge's 'fundamental distinction'. It is this refusal, as I have said, that comes to define Clare as a 'minor' poet; the critical judgement of him as 'minor' really means that he does not convert the objects of nature into the grandeur of the self. He is not Wordsworth or Coleridge, and, frankly, he does not share their aesthetic project.

*

The trouble with rustics, then, for Coleridge is first of all that they are 'immediate objects', unsuitable for poetry. They entrap the hapless Wordsworth in confusions about the very aims of art, and into embarrassing examples of uneven diction. Clare is doubly troubling in this regard because not only does he directly resist Coleridge's 'fundamental distinction', he *is* a peasant, and thus functions as an extremely uncooperative, if 'immediate', object; he is a living challenge to Coleridge's original assertion of the impossibility of a 'peasant poet'. He points to the distinct possibility of an 'English Burns', and perhaps a whole tradition of poets who had simply fallen outside the boundaries of Coleridge's critical view.

Another set of assertions from chapter 17 of the *Biographia* brings us full circle in our examination of the critical contexts of Clare's poetry. In describing Wordsworth's notions of the purity of rural speech as expounded in the Preface to *The Lyrical Ballads* Coleridge strikes a familiar note. In his argument against Wordsworth's claims for rural diction, Coleridge alludes to that other trouble with rustics, their use of idiomatic speech. More importantly, he attacks Wordsworth's extravagant claims for that speech in the Preface. Here, again, is the crux of Wordsworth's argument:

> Low and rustic life was generally chosen, because in that condition, the essential passions of the heart find a better soil in which they can attain their maturity, are less under restraint, and speak a plainer and more emphatic language.[29]

Coleridge, of course, will have none of this, and goes on at great length, attacking the very basis of Wordsworth's claims by pointing out that:

> a rustic's language, purified of all provincialism and grossness, and so far reconstructed as to be consistent with the rules of grammar (which are in essence no other than the universal laws of logic, applied to psychological materials) will not differ from the logic of any other man of common-sense, however learned or refined he may be, except as far as the notions, which the rustic has to convey, are fewer and more indiscriminate. (p. 52)

Coleridge's parenthesis raises a question, to be addressed in Chapter 3, about the language theory that underwrote aesthetic judgements in the period. It amounts to a succinct, if very Coleridgean, recapitulation of Harris's theory of 'universal grammar'. Cobbett was actively challenging this theory and its assumptions about class and language at the time, in his grammar, and by parliamentarians through petitions for reform. Coleridge's reliance on such theory serves as a marker of his turn to conservatism and reactionary politics, and reveals him as a political opponent of Cobbett who argued that grammar was a set of rules that did not determine the quality thinking that they shaped. Cobbett argued that grammatical correctness was an arbitrary system imposed in order to exclude the mass of the populace from the political process – and from the ongoing debate about their enfranchisement.

In his attack on Wordsworth, Coleridge deliberately overlooked the political context of Wordsworth's original statements. The vocabulary of levelling implied in the claim that the common man had a more authentic existence than members of the corrupt and decadent urban milieu in London[30] was clear enough, but Coleridge effectively buried it with his reactionary condescension. Coleridge supports his argument with examples from Wordsworth's poetry. The argument works from both directions; he shows that Wordsworth did not really employ rustic speech at all in poems like 'Michael' (in such instances he didn't know what he was talking about when he described his poetic method), and in the real experiments with the rural idiom, in the ballads, he failed precisely because such language contaminated his poetic thinking and representation. The poet's attempt to represent 'maternal affection' in 'The Idiot Boy', for example, had instead produced a portrait of 'morbid idiocy' (p. 51). This is a failure of diction in Coleridge's view, and leads him to conclude that the English peasantry are singularly incapable of poetic beauty or philosophic complexity. According to Coleridge, Wordsworth's experiment with rustic speech had seriously contaminated his poetic thinking, and part of Coleridge's project in the *Biographia* is to expunge this taint, and thus purify Wordsworthian poetics. And, as a noted above, part of what is expunged is the political impetus of *Lyrical Ballads* itself.

Clare again provides a challenge to the basic assumptions of Coleridgean aesthetics. His initial success in London literary circles was, in part, because he fulfilled the requirements of a Wordsworthian type; he was literally a 'peasant poet'. As such, he was nonetheless at odds with Wordsworthian ideals, in that he was not so much representing rural speech 'purified of its defects' as he was naturally employing such speech. He is thus a more extreme case of what Coleridge abhorred in Wordsworth's experiments with idiom. Furthermore, Clare was utterly opposed to removing the 'defects' of the rural idiom, and rather (consistent with his aesthetic and ethical beliefs) took the faithful representation of it as one of his poetic goals. In this he is an extreme example of a poet at odds with Coleridge's pronouncements on Wordsworth's 'defects'. Not only did Clare employ 'unpoetical' rural speech, he refused to 'purify' it to suit literary tastes. In the letter of 1821 quoted above, he answered the critics of 'The Village Minstrel' by making it clear that the need to 'describe the feelings of a rhyming peasant strongly or locally enough' far outweighed any criteria dependent on literary taste. Clare did not want to purify his poem of its 'provincialisms'; he wanted to make sure that they were faithful to nature and that the intrinsic value of those who spoke them was accurately represented. Again, the divide here is over the purpose of poetic representation. Coleridge believed that poetry should provide the 'pleasure' of sublime transport, or the harmony of beauty, while Clare believed it should, as accurately as possible, represent the objects of nature in order to assert first their intrinsic, and secondarily their aesthetic, value.

Relying on Coleridge's statement in chapter 22, then, Clare should be an impossibility other than as a poetic mask for a more cultured poet, a dubious 'ventriloquism'. And, while it is patently false that Clare is the exception that proves Coleridge's rule – the *one* English Burns, (the tradition of self-taught English plebeian poets was extensive and over half a century old by Coleridge's writing), part of the profound sadness of Clare's life is his exceptional status, which removed him from the labouring class of his birth and yet failed to allow him membership in the London literary class. Despite this, it is crucial, I believe, to examine what kind of poetic exception he is to Coleridgean aesthetics. This is important both for what it shows us about the divergence of various practices of Romantic poetics and traditions, and for what it tells us about the conformity of subsequent critical judgements. The critical view of Clare as a 'minor' Romantic poet has been constructed from the materials of Wordsworthian and Coleridgean aesthetics, yet these materials are wholly unsuited to the task of reading Clare's poems. Any thorough re-examination of Romanticism and its cultural assumptions must take into account the ways in which Clarean poetics directly challenge and subvert the 'old Romanticism', and thus contribute to our critical understanding of the 'new Romanticism'.

The 'stranger soul'

To return briefly to the summer of 1820 and Clare's departure for London, his feeling that a 'stranger soul' had 'jumped into' his 'skin' not only made it difficult for him to imagine who he might be as an individual following this seminal change in circumstances, but it also indicated that it was difficult to know who he was in class terms. He had been removed from the landless labouring class into which he had been born, by virtue of his literary gift, but, as is clear in the prose fragment, he was not yet the member of any other class. He felt a sense of displacement when he saw others 'ditching', one of his 'old occupations', and he experienced the guilty pleasure of 'lolling' in luxury in the moving coach.[31] And this displacement was complete in that he felt his old self had been usurped and a new John Clare put in its place. While it is too simple to suggest that this ambivalent class identity was the root cause of Clare's eventual madness, the overwhelming feeling of isolation that dominated his life did, in part, have its source in his inability to find stable membership in any class. Over the following ten years Clare made something of a virtue of his isolation in the village as it drove him to expand his range of contacts, both in his immediate neighbourhood and nationally.

Clare, of course, had always felt estranged from village life even as he chronicled it. *Poems Descriptive* is marked both by its deep commitment to the rural way of life that it sees threatened by the progress of the system of enclosure, and by a refined sensibility in delineating the objects of nature. In other words, the sensitivity that created his political commitments *and* his desire to represent the beauty of the countryside simultaneously connected him to his native landscape and marked his alienation from its other inhabitants. John Barrell argued that Clare's faithfulness to his 'locality' (Barrell's term), and the dependence on a 'sense of place' produced the poetry. In an unpublished early poem, 'Lamentation of Round Oak Waters', the specificity of the landscape underwrites the poem's force. In that and other poems, he was not discussing enclosure as a general social ill, but rather demonstrating its physical effects on the topography of a specific tract of land. Clare's vocabulary redoubled this discreet 'sense of place' by naming it in 'local' terms: 'the bawks and Eddings are no more' ('bawks' were the green strips between cultivated fields and 'eddings' are the green margins at the ends of fields). However, the same poem, that on the one hand so intimately represented Clare's connection to his landscape, also proclaimed his essential alienation from its other human inhabitants. The personified voice of Round Oak spring observes of the poet's agonistic relationship with the other local 'swains':

> 'The sports which they so dearley lov'd
> Thou could's't not bear to see

> And joys which they as joys approv'd
> Ne'er seem'd as joys to thee
> The joy was thine couldst thou but steal
> From all their Gambols rude
> In some lone thicket to consceal
> Thyself in Sollitude[32]

This feeling of separateness was severe enough to be a subject of gossip in the village, and a concern for Clare's mother as he himself reports: 'I grew so fond of being alone at last that my mother was fain to force me into company for the neighbours had assured her mind into the fact that I was no better than crazy'.[33] We are left then with a paradox concerning Clare's perception of himself as a member of the rural labouring class. He was doubtless a member of this class, his poetics are founded on the minute perceptions of the experiences of a rural swain and on the 'sense of place' those experiences engendered in him, but he was unable to feel any intimate relationship to the other specific members of his class. The quotation above from his journal even suggests a certain amount of alienation from his mother. Despite this, he was still able to understand and sympathise with the economic plight of those around him, and he was careful in his analysis of the effects of enclosure to exempt the other local 'swains', the other members of his specific class, from ultimate responsibility in the destruction of the landscape:

> 'But sweating slaves I do not blame
> Those slaves by wealth decreed
> No I should hurt their harmless name
> To brand 'em wi' the deed
> Altho their aching hands did wield
> The axe that gave the blow
> Yet 't'was not them that own'd the field
> Nor plan'd its overthrow (p. 23)

During his early village life then, he is a class of one, the peasant poet, and this designation becomes a name for belonging to two classes, peasant and poet, and to none. Once he embarks on his trip to London and his career as a published poet, he is forever alienated from full membership as a peasant (his status as a poet contaminates him), and, as we shall see, sociability becomes one of his key literary values as he develops a network of friends and correspondents across class boundaries.

Clare argued for the intrinsic value of nature as opposed to its use value, whether that use value was seen as the destruction of the trees lining the banks of Round Oak brook or in the aesthetic production of Wordsworthian 'spots of time'. John Barrell makes an analogous point at the very end of *The Idea of Landscape and the Sense of Place*, when he argues that Clare's refusal to suppress the specificity of the objects in his poetic landscapes put him at odds with eighteenth-century landscape aesthetics, in particular with the emphasis on the creation of harmony via the arrangement of the objects of the visual field. The aesthetics of the beautiful, of course, demand this visual harmony as their very definition, but the picturesque is no less dependent on a constructed harmony, and is under considerably more psychological pressure to achieve it. The picturesque risks including jarring elements in the visual field so that their assimilation can create greater aesthetic pleasure than the overly-domesticated beautiful can achieve, and without engaging in the potentially dangerous attachments of the sublime. Clare's refusal to assimilate the jarring details of the 'local' made him literally dangerous (his landscapes were outside the confines of aesthetic and ideological certainty, harmony in the broadest sense); and this refusal thus resulted, in Barrell's memorable phrase, his 'writing himself out of the main stream of European literature'.[34] Thus efforts to understand Clare as a peasant or a rustic, whether in the tradition of picturesque aesthetics or of Wordsworthian poetics, end by further marginalising him as not only as a peasant, but also as a 'minor' writer.

2
Viewing and Reviewing

When John Clare's first volume of poetry, *Poems Descriptive of Rural Life and Scenery*, appeared in 1820, it was reviewed in aesthetic terms familiar to contemporary readers of magazines and reviews: the Georgic tradition of the unspoiled rustic poet. During this period Wordsworth's adaptation and revision of pastoral traditions in his Preface to *Lyrical Ballads* and Coleridge's re-interrogation of them in *Biographia Literaria* were gaining currency. Those formulations founded one of the most influential varieties of what we now call Romanticism,[1] and much of present-day criticism of Clare's poetry relies more on Wordsworth and Coleridge's refinements than on the older Georgic tradition itself. The initial reviews of Clare's poems occurred before such adaptations of the Georgic had become ubiquitous, and they clearly demonstrated a powerful gentlemanly taste for new poetic 'discoveries' among the labouring classes. Reviewers sought after images of a pastoral world where peasant poets could represent a rural landscape lost them in their hectic urban milieus – 'represent' both in the sense of composing the images of nature that constituted that landscape and in the sense of standing for that lost pastoral world. John Taylor, Clare's publisher, was keenly aware of this immediate aesthetic context as he attempted to situate Clare's poetry in his introduction to the volume, and his intellectual lead shaped much of the critical response. Taylor's own tastes were highly refined. He had incorporated the Wordsworth/Coleridge debates into his aesthetic views, and those complex considerations colour his advice to prospective readers of Clare. Echoes of Wordsworth's Preface occur throughout Taylor's introduction, and define Clare in several Wordsworthian ways.

Clare was, wrote Taylor, 'the Poet as well as the Child of Nature'.[2] In other words, Clare, like Wordsworth, drew poetic inspiration directly from the objects of nature. As we will see, while this reliance on the natural world was shared in Wordsworthian and Georgic poetics, the distinctly Wordsworthian idea that philosophical reflection was necessary in order to give form to the finished poem produced anxiety in Taylor's account of Clare's poetic practice. Clare also conformed to a Wordsworthian type, the rustic, who provided not only the model of the natural unaffected artist, but also a source of inspiration. Clare was himself an object of poetic contemplation for a Wordsworthian poet, and, more conventionally, a prize for the discriminating patron.[3] Discovered as a detail in a picturesque natural landscape, he was a kind of living leach gatherer. Taylor's introduction moved between these two views, the declaration of Clare's poetic genius, and an insistence on his exceptional status as an object of nature: 'a young Peasant, a day-labourer in husbandry, who has no advantages of education beyond others of his class' (p. i).

How were reviewers reliant on established versions of pastoral poetry and on Taylor's intellectual lead in defining Clare's genius, how did the issue of class penetrate aesthetic discourse and critical judgements about Clare, and how did Clare attempt to resist such judgements?

Viewing

Hugh Blair's 'Lecture Thirty-nine, Pastoral Poetry' from his *Lectures on Rhetoric and Belles Lettres* [4] provides the most concise statement of the aesthetic and cultural values of eighteenth-century pastoral poetry. Blair's history of the classical invention of pastoral poetry made it clear that pastoral was not rural poetry produced by rustics, Clare's idiom, but a pleasing mode of urban nostalgia:

> It was not till men had begun to be assembled in great cities, after the distinctions of rank and station were formed, and the bustle of Courts and large Societies was known, that Pastoral Poetry assumed its present form. Men then began to look back upon the more simple and innocent life, which their forefathers led, or which, at least, they fancied them to have led: they looked back upon it with pleasure; and in those rural scenes, and pastoral occupations, imagining a degree of felicity to take place, superior to what they now enjoyed, conceived the idea of celebrating it in poetry. (pp. 115–16)

Pastoral poetry was an urban affectation, quite unlike Clare's faithful record of a rural landscape meticulously viewed and represented.

In order to satisfy this particular taste, a peasant poet had to become a part of his or her own pastoral world and thus a living evocation of the nostalgia the reader sought. Blair wrote that the purpose of pastoral poetry was to: 'banish from our thoughts the cares of the world, and to transport us into calm Elysian regions' (p. 116). Clare's poetry could hardly fulfil this need while the 'Elysian regions' that he represented in his poems were being torn up and enclosed. The stark realism of many of Clare's descriptions of rural hardship and privation challenged readers, and potentially produced the opposite effect to the one Blair described. Blair made it clear that neither actual peasants nor over-idealised ones made good poetic subjects:

> Pastoral life may be considered in three different views; either as it now actually is; when the state of Shepherds is reduced to be a mean, servile and laborious state; when their employments are become disagreeable, and their ideas gross and low: on such as we may suppose it once to have been, in the more early and simple ages, when it was a life of ease and abundance; when the wealth of men consisted chiefly in flocks and herds, and the Shepherd, though unrefined in his manners, was respectable in his state: or, lastly, such as it never was, and never in reality can be, when, to the ease, innocence, and simplicity of the early ages, we attempt to add the polished taste, and cultivated manners, of modern times. Of these three states, the first is too gross and mean, the last too refined and unnatural, to be the groundwork of Pastoral Poetry. Either of these extremes is a rock upon which the Poet will split, if he approach too near it. We shall be disgusted if he give us too much of the servile employments and low ideas of actual peasants ...; and, if ... he makes his Shepherds discourse as if they were courtiers and scholars, he then retains the name only, but wants the spirit of Pastoral Poetry. (pp. 117–18)[5]

As we shall see, the anxiety that Clare's status as an 'actual peasant' might be a source of 'disgust' to his potential audience permeated Taylor's introduction to *Poems Descriptive*, and he constantly responded to fears that Clare's ideas were 'gross and low'. Clare's vulgarity became an important subject for reviewers, and the most bawdy of his early poems met with calls for censorship. In short, the critical terrain that Taylor had to negotiate, and the gentlemanly taste it represented, was full of pitfalls seemingly designed to ensnare Clare, and, more importantly, critical taste was directly at odds with many of Clare's own poetic principles. Clare could not always be persuaded to walk this impossibly fine line. He was asked on the one hand to be exceptional, not an 'actual peasant', so he would not be contaminated by 'gross and low' ideas, and on the other hand he had to guard against affecting philosophical airs beyond his station. When readers objected to the 'low and gross' subjects of some of the early poems, Clare bitterly resented being asked to conform to genteel, and in his view false, taste. His exchanges with Taylor and Hessey over 'Dolly's Mistake' and other bawdy poems illustrate both Clare's frustration at having to submit to polite society, and the expectations that society placed on peasant poets.[6] These expectations were clearly in Taylor's mind as he introduced Clare to the reading public.

Clare's class identity as 'the peasant poet' was integral to Taylor's construction of poetic genius in the introduction, and informed his discussions of Clare's poetic practices. Aesthetic judgements were inseparable from class judgements in the introduction, and that conflation produced a double bind that continues to constrain our understanding of Clare. Taylor's argument that Clare was a natural genius whose work was of intrinsic interest was undermined by a special pleading based on class origins. Taylor's rhetorical strategy, while successful in shaping public opinion and securing sales, guaranteed that Clare be viewed and reviewed with condescension. His background, making it impossible for him to aspire to true poetic genius because, as a peasant, he lacked the philosophical education necessary for Wordsworthian reflection, limited his genius. And furthermore, in the view of the dominant critics of the day, such reflection represented fatal overreaching. For a critic like Francis Jeffrey,[7] for example, following Blair's lead, the peasant poet could only be admitted as an object of condescension, and pretence to philosophical reflection was seen as a threat to the poet's 'natural' simplicity. As a result, in his contemporary milieu, Clare would be considered a failure if he aspired to a version of poetic genius beyond his class. The antithesis is true in present-day criticism. For Harold Bloom, Clare becomes a 'failed Wordsworthian poet'[8] precisely because of his lack of a suitable reflective mode, the same poetic mode that would have been decried as overreaching by Jeffrey. Taylor was left with the unenviable task in his introduction of attempting to please both the conservative Georgic tradition of the unaffected natural genius, and the emerging, and contradictory, Wordsworthian emphasis on philosophical reflection. The remainder of this chapter quarrels with the cultural assumptions of these views by analysing Taylor's introduction, and by evaluating its impact on public reception in the magazines and reviews, tracing the influence of both the conventional taste for Georgic pastorals and the emerging Wordsworthian aesthetic of reflection. These aesthetic formulations, as echoed by the reviewers, betray a clear, and for Clare debilitating, set of cultural assumptions in relation to questions of class. Class-bound aesthetics dominate critical judgements of Clare's career and poetry from the beginning. Yet despite his almost total lack of cultural power, Clare developed a poetics that both confounded the conservative aesthetics that authorised his career, and challenged the very assumptions that reviewers claimed were integral to an appreciation of his work.

*

Clare's peasant background inevitably played a part in Taylor's account of the typical composition of a poem: 'Most of the poems were composed under the immediate impression of this feeling [the love of nature], in the fields, or on the roadside' (p. xv). The emphasis on 'immediate impression' echoed Wordsworth's most famous formulation; according to Taylor the poems were the natural result of 'the spontaneous overflow of powerful feelings', but unlike Wordsworth they were recorded as immediate impressions of those feelings rather than conforming to the second half of Wordsworth's dictum: 'Poems to which any value can be attached, were never produced on any variety of subjects but by a man who being possessed of more than usual organic sensibility had also thought long and deeply' (pp. 774–5). Taylor argued that special allowances should be made for Clare. Circumstances did not allow for the full expression of the Wordsworthian ideal, but Clare's poems should be valued anyway because of the special 'circumstances under which they were written' (p. i). A critical paternalism was therefore deemed necessary in order to extract the aesthetic value from the work; the critic could complete the poetic equation and provide the products of Clare's 'organic sensibility' with the philosophical reflection that they lacked. The critic or reader could reflect on the meaning of the landscape that Clare artistically supplied. This was a well-established strategy in marketing peasant poets; patronage was integral to the creation of poetic meaning. Taylor's rhetorical strategy was largely successful, but the cost was an abundance of self-congratulatory condescension on the part of reviewers, and ultimately the foundation of the false view of Clare as a 'failed Wordsworthian'. The persistence of this view is ironic given that Clare was suspicious of the self-dramatisations of Wordsworth's poetics, and attempted to resist their focus on poetic recuperation through reflection – the self-reflexive quality he was judged by many critics to lack.[9] In his references to Wordsworth in letters from this period Clare clearly values spontaneity in Wordsworth's poetry over reflection: 'wordsworth defies all art & in all the lunatic Enthuseism of nature he sets down his thoughts from the tongue of the inspirer.' In his discussions of Wordsworth with Taylor, he commented in December 1821 that Wordsworth's recent efforts at philosophical poetry were 'ridiculous' and gave him an 'itch after parody'. Clare's were not a naïve poetics of place, incapable of philosophical reflection, but rather an insistence on the ethical representation of objects for their own sake. In other words, Clare's poetic defence of the objects of nature was not an incomplete Wordsworthian gesture, apprehension without reflection, but a deliberate choice that implicitly, and often explicitly, contained ethical and political commitments. Taylor's sanitised version of Clare's origins and the origins of the poems was careful to disclaim any knowledge of such poetic principles.

Taylor's introduction also drew on Wordsworth's poetics in establishing the poetics value of rustic or idiomatic language, and this was subsequently reflected in reviews. I am not arguing that Taylor relied on Wordsworth's ideas, but his letters indicate that he was familiar with them, and any perceived resemblance to Wordsworthian poetics has been crucial to subsequent critical constructions of Clare's poetic career. Harold Bloom's view, for example, depends on normative Wordsworthian categories, and Taylor unwittingly authorised that reading strategy. Evidence of the pervasiveness of the Bloomian position, surprisingly, extends even to John Barrell's historical account of the early poems in *The Idea of Landscape and the Sense of Place*. Barrell persuasively argues that the poems of the Helpstone period vacillate between specific attacks on enclosure and an elegiac sense of loss. He concludes that these two modes are at odds, and his identification of a sense of ambivalence in the poetry has been influential in readings of Clare's political investments. However, Barrell's conclusion depends on a Wordsworthian version of the aesthetic use of the elegiac voice. Yet, Clare's poetics of loss do not seek to stage a series of crises that can be recuperated through the construction of the poetic self, the Wordsworthian procedure decried by many recent Historicist critics as a conservative retreat from the political world. Rather, Clare places the self amongst the field of objects affected by enclosure. There is no recuperation of his crises. This difference means that the two poetic modes identified by Barrell are complimentary rather than competing: Clare's sense of loss in an intimate instance of the effects of enclosure, not a shift to a disengaged subjectivity. Barrell's critical assumptions are formed by normative Wordsworthian categories of which he is suspicious, but which he nonetheless misapplies to Clare.

Wordsworth valorised rustic speech as authentically representing human experience, free from the taint of decadent urban acculturation manifested as faddish 'social vanity' (p. 744). This argument was a clear source of aesthetic value that Taylor could exploit in constructing Clare's poetic pedigree. Wordsworth had claimed that rural life created 'a plainer and more emphatic language' integrated as it was into a natural scene where 'the passions of men are incorporated with the beautiful and permanent forms of nature' (pp. 743–4). He further claimed that the rural idiom best served the contemplation of these natural forms:

> The language too of these men [rustics] is adopted (purified indeed from what appear to be its real defects, from all lasting and rational causes of dislike or disgust) because such men hourly communicate with the best objects from which the best part of language is originally derived. (p. 744)

Clare was the most authentic of poets in these terms, yet Wordsworth's parenthesis suggested that Clare, as a rustic, required purification lest his language inspire 'dislike or disgust'. In his introduction to *Poems Descriptive*, Taylor attempted to serve, in his role as editor, as the purifier of Clare's work, removing its 'real defects' of grammar and spelling. More importantly, he attempted to answer potential criticism of Clare's vulgarity.

Taylor ingeniously argued that Clare, naturally enough given his background, lacked the language to communicate the poetic conceptions that arose during his intense observations of nature. His poverty of language was explicitly connected to his physical poverty: 'his vocabulary would have been too scanty to express even what his imagination had strength enough to conceive' (p. vii). Had John Turnill not taught Clare to write, presumably, such inchoate conceptions would have remained pre-linguistic – a powerful sensibility without expression. Taylor's argument made two important claims: first, that Clare was the true 'Child of Nature' endowed with the 'simplicity' Georgic taste craved and the extraordinary 'organic sensibility' that Wordsworthian aesthetics demanded (*Preface*, p. 745), and second, that Clare was a special case whose impoverished circumstances had to be taken into account before he was dismissed as vulgar and lacking in the philosophical depth to be gained by reflection. Taylor's solution was to turn on its head the argument that Clare was restricted by his linguistic poverty. After concluding that the poet 'seems to labour under great disadvantages' (p. viii), he attacked the idea as a mere 'seeming'. Clare, Taylor argued, turned his disadvantages into a new source of poetic value:

> On the other hand, his want forces him to extraordinary exertion of his native powers, in order to supply the deficiency. He employs language under his command with great effect, in those unusual and unprecedented combinations of words which must be made, even by the learned, when they attempt to describe perfectly something which they have never seen or heard expressed before. And in this respect Clare's deficiencies are the cause of many beauties. (p. viii)

This was an ingenious argument in that it took advantage of Wordsworth's claim that rural folk expressed themselves in a 'more emphatic language', while it claimed that Clare's search was for new knowledge and that his language, which at first may have appeared crude, was actually the only language capable of representing what had hitherto been unrepresented and thus unknown (this claim appealed both to the conventional taste for the primitive and to Wordsworth's formulations). Clare's native speech was the only possible source of aesthetic value in that landscape. Indeed, Clare himself argued the point more forcefully in a manuscript note to Taylor concerning the use of the invented word 'twitatwit' in the poem 'Helpstone':

> The word 'twitatwit' (if a word it may be calld) you will undoubtedly smile at but I wish you to print it as it is for it is the Language of Nature & that can never be disgusting.[10]

Clare's resistance to having his language 'purified from what indeed appear its real defects', and his forceful denial of the potential 'dislike or disgust' inherent in such language challenged the Wordsworthian conception of a natural rural poetics, and insisted on the inherent beauty of 'deficient'[11] idiomatic speech.

As we will see, reviewers followed Taylor's lead in noting the special circumstances of the poet's life; his class position became a key to a proper reading strategy, and an extraordinary ambivalence about the value of Clare's presumably vulgar language coloured most reviews. Provincialisms were alternately decried as coarse or vulgar, and celebrated as the source of startling poetic beauty. But, before turning to the reviews, it is important to remember that Wordsworth's ideas, on which

Taylor drew, were still being contested, by Coleridge, and, more importantly for reviewers of the time, by Jeffrey. Coleridge was unwilling to
accept claims of a greater authenticity for rustic speech, and, in chapter 22
of *Biographia Literaria*, characterised Wordsworth's use of colloquial speech
in *Lyrical Ballads* as a weak 'ventriloquism' (p. 135), and a failed poetic
experiment. Even with philosophic reflection as part of the poetic process,
Coleridge remained sceptical of the value of such works. Worse, he argued,
was the predominance of Wordsworth's imitators, both poetic and theoretical. In chapter four, Coleridge bitterly complained:

> But that a downright simpleness, under the affectation of simplicity,
> prosaic words in feeble metre, silly thoughts in childish phrases, and
> a preference of mean, degrading, or at best trivial associations and
> characters, should succeed in forming a school of imitators, a company
> of almost *religious* admirers,—and that this bare and bald *counterfeit*
> of poetry, which is characterised as *below* criticism, should for nearly
> twenty years have well-nigh *engrossed* criticism, as the main, if not
> the only, *butt* of review, magazine, poem, and pamphlet;—this is
> indeed a matter of wonder. (p. 75; emphasis his)

This passage provides abundant evidence of the perceived influence of
Wordsworth's poetics at the time of Clare's first publication, and the
heated nature of the ensuing debate. Jeffrey was, of course, even harsher
in his estimations. Taylor went to some pains to rationalise Clare's idio-
syncratic grammar and diction in response to the possibility of such
attacks; he was especially sensitive to Jeffrey's antipathy to affected
'lowliness', and wary of his cultural power as a critic. The aesthetic
value of Clare's poetic vocabulary was at stake in these attacks, and
therefore a careful counter-argument about the aptness of rural diction
in Clare's poetry was required.

The claim that such language was inherently 'deficient' could not go
unanswered. Taylor's response certainly could be accused of arguing
that the verse was '*below* criticism', in Coleridge's phrase, exempt owing to
the author's class status. Taylor's constructed view of Clare as a 'natural'
and necessarily naïve poetic genius risked identifying him as one of
Wordsworth's many 'simple' imitators, and, despite Taylor's apparent
awareness of this risk, that view became widespread once the reviews
appeared. According to Taylor's introduction Clare was a genius, but one
severely limited by the deprivations of his class. As a result, he was
believed to be incapable of philosophic reflection, and that lack of
reflection was partly converted into a poetic virtue both by Taylor, for

strategic reasons, and by conservative critics suspicious of philosophical affectations. Taylor related that Clare had to record the poems immediately because: 'He could not trust his memory, and therefore he wrote them down with a pencil on the spot, his hat serving him for a desk; and if it happened that he had no opportunity soon after of transcribing these imperfect memorials, he could seldom decipher them, or recover his first thoughts' (p. xv). In describing Clare as completely dependent on the moment of sensation, the power of his sensibility excited by nature, Taylor painted a portrait of a brilliant child for whom even the act of memory was a puzzle beyond his grasp, let alone the careful meditation required by a more philosophical poetics. Such then were the hazards of the critical terrain that Taylor negotiated in his introduction, and the real effects of his efforts, for good and ill, were soon revealed by the reviewers of *Poems Descriptive*.

Reviewing

As I have indicated, Taylor's preparation of the public[12] conformed to pre-existing critical notions, and made Clare's class identity, his exceptional status as the 'peasant poet', integral to public consumption of his poems. The responses of reviews and magazines of different political stripes revealed how the meaning of Clare's peasantness shifted to meet specific preconceived political and cultural assumptions and expectations. Clare's unusual strength of sensibility, for example, was taken as evidence of dramatically different ideas about rural life and labour depending on the political orientation of the reviewer. While the reviews recapitulated most of Taylor's aesthetic leads, they drew varying cultural meanings from that material. Was Clare's genius evidence of the inherent rightness of rural relationships of power and patronage, or a challenge to class-bound social assumptions about the source of genius?

One of the most curious events surrounding the initial reception of *Poems Descriptive of Rural Life and Scenery* was the delayed reaction of one of Clare's patrons to radical elements in the poetry. This delay tells us much about the motivated reading strategies of various segments of Clare's audience. Lord Radstock, a conservative Evangelical landowner and naval hero, reacted angrily to what he called 'radical and ungrateful' sentiments in the very first poem in the collection, 'Helpstone'. The offending lines offered a succinct analysis of the effects of enclosure on Clare and those like him, and named 'accursed wealth' as their ultimate cause.[13] It was not until the third edition[14] that Radstock noticed these lines and demanded their removal. How could such sentiments have escaped notice? The answer may lie in the power patronage bestowed on the reader. Radstock had taken the decision to patronise Clare after *Poems Descriptive* had appeared, and apparently without reading the poems. He was, in fact, patronising an idea of what Clare might represent, and was shocked to discover his error after the fact. Various versions of this kind of self-confirming patronage, prepared for by Taylor, and obligatory to gentlemanly taste, permeated the reviews. The critics' power created blind spots as they attempted to reconfirm their own tastes and cultural values through the vehicle of Clare's poems.

The 'radical and ungrateful' stanza from 'Helpstone' had a similar spectral existence in many of the reviews. Perhaps simply because it was the first poem in the volume, it was almost always quoted, but Clare's dangerous piece of political analysis was never commented on. The conservative *British Critic* provides a good example. Their June 1820 review quoted three stanzas from 'Helpstone' in support of the view that 'the tendency of his [Clare's] book [was] moral'.[15] This abridged version of the poem had several effects. The radical passage on enclosure was omitted. Coupled with the fact that Taylor had already edited out the final stanza describing:

> ...when the Traveller uncertain roams
> On lost roads leading every where but home,

before publication, the result was a poem that began with a conventional evocation of place, 'Hail, humble Helpstone' (p. 3), moved through a catalogue of the natural beauty found in the place:

> Where golden kingcups open'd into view;
> Where silver daisies in profusion grew; (p. 7)

and concluded with a nostalgic hope that the speaker could return to this 'happy Eden' to end his days:

> And as reward for all my troubles past,
> Find one hope true—to die at home at last! (p. 11)

In short, the edited version of the poem that appeared in the review became a sentimental encomium on the natural 'delights' of the countryside, and of the peasant speaker's contentment in that scene. The fact that the poem was an elegy on the irrevocable loss of that landscape, a 'paradise lost' at the hands of the local 'improving' gentry, was replaced by moralising about rural pleasures. It is impossible to know whether the review was a deliberate attempt to constrain Clare's subversive potential through careful omission, or whether, like Lord Radstock, the reviewer's paternalistic assumptions about Clare's peasant identity blinded him to the 'radical and ungrateful' sentiments of the poem's political analysis. On the one hand, the reviewer's condescension towards Clare, prompted by Taylor's special pleading concerning the poet's circumstances, made it possible to read both for evidence of Wordsworthian natural genius and for confirmation of the critic's social superiority. The review deferred judgement because the poet's 'peculiar situation effectually disarm(ed) – criticism', yet went on to claim that if any vulgar coinages, 'which cannot fail to offend every reader', managed 'to creep in', they could be set aside as the inevitable result of the poet's simplicity. The 'principal merit of the poems' *was* 'the circumstances of the writer'. Confirmed in his social power and reading to locate a humble Arcadia, the reviewer, conceivably, could have missed the radicalism of the poem.

On the other hand, the brief note introducing a lengthy quotation from 'The Village Funeral', suggests that political anxieties were provoked in the writer of the *British Critic* review. Overall, he viewed the poem as 'common-place', but for 'two stanzas which redeem it'. The redeeming stanzas describe the fate of two orphans who have just buried their father, and the quality of human compassion that they inspire moved the critic to pity despite his reservations. He stated that the lines were, 'breathed, we fear, in too genuine a tone of feeling'. He had reason to 'fear' the 'genuine' tone of the stanzas because it exposed the hypocrisy of the institutions of charity that conservative critics supported, and the value of which they hoped to find confirmed in Clare's poems. The readers of the *British Critic*, conservative self-styled gentlemen like Lord Radstock, would have done well to be uncomfortable with the ungrateful candour of the stanzas:

> Yon workhouse stands as their [the orphans'] asylum now
>   The place where poverty demands to live
> Where parish bounty scowls his scornful brow,
>   And grudges the scant fare he's forc'd to give.
>
> Oh may I die before I'm doom'd to seek
>   That last resource of hope, but ill supplied;
> To claim the humble pittance once a week,
>   Which justice forces from disdainful pride!

These lines threatened conservative notions of altruism by exposing the self-motivated source of charity and its economic inadequacies. The workhouse was exposed as a horrific form of servitude rather than an expression of altruism, and wealthy landowners would not have found the spectacle of their unseemly psychological motives and hypocrisy suitable subjects for poetry. Despite this, the critic included the stanzas because of their affective power, thus trapping himself in a contradiction between his aesthetic response to the poem's emotional resonance and his search for confirmation of his own social values. The review ended by recuperating the social values the critic sought by quoting from 'To Religion', a poem where he could take 'pleasure, from its unaffected piety'.

Other conservative journals praised the poems in less conflicted terms. The reactionary *Antijacobin Review* enthused:

> This little volume is the production of a second Burns; a poet in humble life, whose genius has burst through the fetters with which his situation had surrounded it; and astonished the neighbouring villages with the brilliancy of his song.[16]

The anonymous reviewer picked up the vocabulary of natural genius from Taylor's introduction and re-presented it in class terms. Clare had risen above his station, but what made the poems praiseworthy was the ability of the critic to retain his position of authority over the poet. Genius could 'burst fetters' to a point, but the review itself represented a new social containment of the peasant poet. Conservative readers found comfort in the paternalism occasioned by making an exception for Clare, and by following a cultural version of the Wordsworthian dictum that rural speech should be 'purified of its defects'. The review quoted the final two stanzas of 'Helpstone', apparently oblivious to the radical analysis of the effects of wealth on the countryside in the previous stanzas, and ended by calling for greater care in avoiding vulgar diction in future poems. The poems were finally recommended to readers as instances of 'honest simplicity, and natural genius', and for their 'unaffected piety'. Clare was a 'discovery' and capable of improvement via the instruction of the critic in matters of taste.

More liberal publications were cautious in their praise. The *Monthly Review* recapitulated Wordsworth's Preface in refusing to grant Clare the status of a true poet:

> To attempt the sublimer provinces of song, a mind stored with the philosophic treasures of the past and with the wisdom and beauty of

antiquity is requisite, as well as a heart that is alive to the sublimity of the highest feelings of our nature; but to achieve a description of the external beauty of the creation requires no knowledge that gazing will not give.[17]

The double bind implicit in Taylor's aesthetic claims strikes home here. Clare could never be a true poet because of the simple fact of his peasant identity. Lack of formal education made philosophic reflection impossible, and Clare was left to write in a lesser poetic mode.[18] The review ends by repeating this premise in an unflattering comparison with Burns. Clare was judged to possess 'but a small share of the acquirements of Burns, whose mind was well stored with much useful knowledge'. Given Clare's class-determined lack of access to sublimity, praise was limited to condescending liberal moralising:

> To extend judicious encouragement, however, to a man who has so laudably displayed the wish for advancement, and the powers and energies which distinguish the writer of these poems, is only an act of justice.

This plea amounts to little more than the aesthetic equivalent to Lord Radstock's sense of charity.

Not all reviewers were willing to grant Clare charity. Deeply suspicious of the rhetoric of natural genius, the review in *The Guardian* dismissed Clare as, 'simply a tolerable versifier' who had, 'exhibited nothing of the spirit, feeling, or original views of genius'.[19] Rural subjects were ridiculed, and the reviewer called on Clare's patrons to ensure that Clare remained a peasant, 'the best preservative of his health, humility and happiness'. The equating of 'humility and happiness' underlines the ubiquity of the class judgements that dominated the reviews. J. G. Lockhart's reference to Clare in *Blackwood's Edinburgh Magazine*, alluded to *The Guardian* review as the 'best view'[20] of the promotion of Clare. Lockhart, who admitted that he had 'never seen Clare's book', nonetheless dismissed it with the unsolicited advice that: 'a respectable peasant is a much more comfortable man, and always will be so, than a mediocre poet.' This fantasy of happy peasants rather confirms the view of Lockhart as an alienated urbanite, and is notable only for the traces of class anxiety it exhibits, and that found fuller expression in his notorious 'Cockney School' tirades.

The *Eclectic Review* alone resisted Taylor's efforts to shape the reception of the poems. All the other reviews either celebrated Clare's rise through his natural genius, took comfort in his depiction of the pastoral world, or warned against the hollowness of the rhetoric of genius. In any case, they responded directly to the terms of the aesthetic debate Taylor dictated. The reviewer[21] for the *Eclectic* resisted the association of Clare's peasant origins and natural genius. He adhered to a general Romantic definition of genius by quoting from Coleridge's *Biographia Literaria*, chapter 4, to the effect that the 'most unequivocal mode of manifestation' of genius was: 'to represent familiar objects as to awaken the minds of others to a like healthy freshness of sensation concerning them'.[22] Coleridge was describing the essence of Wordsworth's genius in relation to the natural world, and this passage followed the warning against the vulgar imitators of Wordsworth's style. The reviewer in the *Eclectic* picked up on both the Wordsworthian aesthetics in the introduction, and on Coleridge's suspicion of idealised rustic verse in *Biographia Literaria*. More importantly, he challenged the class determinants of Taylor's introduction by appreciating the poet's gift of awakening fresh sensations on its own terms: ' ... there can be no hesitation in classing the Author of these poems, to whatsoever rank in society he should prove to belong, among the most genuine possessors of this dangerous gift.' I will take up the dangerousness of Clare's gift in a moment, but first want to indicate how thoroughly this particular review resisted Taylor. A forthright statement of poetic value replaced the tone of apology that accompanied the defence of rural speech in the introduction, and the range of attitudes towards it, from mild condescension to ridicule, of other reviews:

> Colloquialisms and provincialisms abound in his poems, and attest its substantial originality; but of the grosser vulgarity of affected expression, of all attempt at fine writing, he has steered most commendably clear.

This wonderful inversion of poetic values, poetic affectation not idiomatic speech as the source of vulgarity, exploded the class basis of aesthetic judgements of Clare's diction. The review completed the logic of this line of reasoning by asserting the genius of the verse independent of any reliance on making an exception because of Clare's class impoverishment:

> instead of thinking them [the poems] *very clever considering they are by a day labourer*, our readers agree with us in conceding to them a high degree of poetical merit quite independent of the circumstances of their Author.

The idea that it was a 'dangerous gift' to be able to provide fresh 'sensations' in relation to familiar objects suggests a political approach to understanding the power of poetic sympathy, Clare's strength of sensibility. The *Eclectic Review* printed the majority of 'Helpstone', including the radical stanza attacking enclosure that the other reviews quoted around. The workhouse passage from 'The Village Funeral' was also quoted. In neither instance was reference made to the explicit political resonances of the passages, but rather attention was called to the poet's power of 'feeling'. His sensibility, his sympathy for the inhabitants and objects of the countryside, was judged to be the essence of his poetic gift. It was made 'dangerous' by what it could show readers about their society and themselves. The response of Lord Radstock and conservative reviewers had been a wilful blindness to the social insights of Clare's 'dangerous gift'. They read in order to find self-confirmation, not to discover potentially dangerous new insights that might threaten their social complacency. That the *Eclectic Review* recognised and promoted the political implications of poetic genius became clear in the following year with their review of Clare's second volume, *The Village Minstrel*. In that review, the attack on enclosure in Clare's poems finally makes an appearance in the public discourse:

> ...the Poet's indignant deprecation of that mistaken policy which has pushed the system of enclosure to so vexatious and ruinous an extent. Poets are not always sound political economists...; but it is our firm persuasion, that the changes deplored by Lubin [the poem's protaganist], have, in a large proportion of instances, been decidedly prejudicial.[23]

Clare's poem played a role in persuading the reviewer of the 'prejudicial' nature of enclosure by describing its effects:

> There once were lanes in nature's freedom dropt,
> There once were paths that every valley wound,—
> Inclosure came, and every path was stopt;
> Each tyrant fix'd his sign where paths were found,
> To hint a trespass now who cross'd the ground:
> Justice is made to speak as they command;
> The high road now must be each stinted bound:
> —Inclosure, thou'rt a curse upon the land,
> And tasteless was the wretch who thy existence plann'd.[24]

The specificity of Clare's descriptions of the effects of enclosure on the inhabitants of the countryside doubtless contributed to their power to persuade. The disruption of traditional rural patterns extended to the physical destruction of liberty as the peasantry was confined to the 'bounds' of public roads. As if to make the point himself that politics and aesthetics were inseparable, Clare characterised this abuse of power ('justice' was a thing owned by tyrants), as 'tasteless'. The disfiguring of the landscape was an assault on beauty itself. In real and aesthetic terms, this destruction was precisely the social and physical force that conservative readers were loath to see in the world around them, or in Clare's poems, and in fact hoped to escape via their nostalgia for an ideal pastoral world.

*

The final question to address, then, is how did Clare resist the various efforts to 'enclose'[25] his poetry, aesthetically and politically. He reacted with fury at Taylor's suggestion that they appease Lord Radstock by dropping the 'radical and ungrateful sentiments' from the third edition of *Poems Descriptive*[26], but relented and allowed the change. Despite resenting 'that canting way of being forcd to please', Clare and Taylor had little power to resist Lord Radstock whose threats to ruin Clare had to be taken seriously. After some initial bravado in which he declared they should 'remain obstinate'[27], Taylor adopted a more pragmatic line in which they would rely on Lord Radstock's short memory and lazy reading habits. It had taken until the third edition for him to notice the passage after all. Taylor promised: 'When the Follies of the Day are past with all the Fears they have engendered we can restore the Poems according to earlier Editions'.[28] This shift in Taylor's response caused him to be scorned by some of Clare's supporters at the time. Edward Drury, the Stamford bookseller who had brought Clare to Taylor's attention, quipped that Taylor was 'firm in council but weak in purpose & doing'.[29] Subsequent criticism has been equally harsh. John Lucas, for example, declares in a footnote that he is 'not trying to demonise Taylor'[30], yet his essay consistently equates Taylor and Radstock. Lucas follows Johanne Clare in arguing that: 'Taylor...and Lord Radstock... between them emasculated much of his [Clare's] early work' (p. 150), and suggests that the relationship between publisher and poet was antagonistic: 'Taylor always had the upper hand' (p. 158). While this last statement is doubtless true in a strictly literal sense, its tone makes it sound as if Taylor habitually abused his power to Clare's disadvantage, a view that underplays the necessity of a pragmatic approach to publishing, and that inadvertently creates a false impression of Clare as a passive victim.

The real test of Clare's resistance to calls for self-censorship, and of Taylor's attitude towards the radical elements in the poems, came with the publication of Clare's next volume of poems, *The Village Minstrel*. Far from conforming to the political views and wishes of conservative patrons, the long title poem provided detailed realistic views of the happenings in village life during the immediate aftermath of the Napoleonic Wars. Disabled soldiers, homeless and unemployable, pass through the village and make their appearance in the poem. They and the gypsies that pass by appear with a harsh realism that makes them unassimilable to a conventional picturesque landscape. They would have represented jarring and undesirable elements, so far as Lord Radstock was concerned, and clearly violated Blair's foundational dictum that we readers should not be subjected to feelings of 'disgust' at the 'mean' employments of 'actual peasants'. Most significantly, attacks on enclosure continued to appear. Stanzas 90 to 97, in particular, denounced the effects of 'oppression's power'.[31] In Clare's view enclosure created a desert:

> There once were days, the woodsman knows it well,
> When shades e'en echoed with the singing thrush;
> There once were hours, the ploughman's tale can tell,
> Where morning's beauty wore its earliest blush;
> How woodlarks carol'd from each stumpy bush;
> Lubin himself [the poem's speaker] has mark'd them soar and sing:
> The thorns are gone, the woodlark's song is hush,
> Spring more resembles winter now than spring,
> The shades are banish'd all—the birds have took to wing. (p. 49)

The destruction of the local landscape, witnessed by Lubin, the peasant poet standing in for Clare, saw the inherent value of nature betrayed. The outcome was an affront to the very rhythms of nature, spring resembled winter, and the loss was final. The destruction of 'the thorns' would have been a common sight; they would have been considered of no economic value, and grew in the hedges that were destroyed as the land was 'improved'.[32] The conflict between the economic value of the landscape, and its inherent and poetic value came to a head in these stanzas. The 'woodlark's song' was lost, and, as an inhabitant of this landscape, Clare's song was clearly threatened as well. His poetic gift was dependent on the existence of the natural variety of rural scenery, and he was unwilling to falsify the record of economic destruction in order to protect his patrons from discomfort. If they were implicated in this destruction they deserved their share of guilt. And, if they wanted to maintain a paternalistic relationship to this 'child of nature', they first must recognise the essential conflict between their economic and aesthetic interests. Clare had promised as long ago as 'Helpstone' that he could 'be content' within the existing relationships of power, provided they truly were benevolent rather than hypocritical and destructive.

Taylor did not attempt to censor this material even though it was certain to anger Lord Radstock. In fact, over time Taylor came to have little use for Radstock, and ceased being interested in appeasing him.[33] Instead, he used the introduction to the volume to attempt to rationalise Clare's 'vehement' attachment to the objects 'in nature'.[34] He cautiously described the passage as 'some apparently discontented stanzas about the middle of the poem', and claimed that even if the stanzas truly were (as opposed to 'apparently') 'discontented' they should be excused as: 'some of the most vigorous and beautiful ebullitions of true poesy that can be met with in our language' (pp. xix–xx). Their political content should be forgiven for the sake of their aesthetic value. This line of reasoning was disingenuous to say the least, and Taylor constructed a more substantial defence to bolster the aesthetic argument. He appealed to readers' understanding and sympathy in judging Clare's vehemence: 'allowance ought to be made for the passionate regard of poor Clare for things which were the landmarks of his life, the depositories of almost all his joy' (p. xx). The stanzas themselves were unequivocal in denouncing the immorality of enclosure on economic *and* aesthetic grounds, but Taylor buried the 'political economy' in a call for tolerance for the poet's childlike attachments. This was doubtless an astute reading of the psychology of conservative patronage and the public taste, but hardly true to the spirit of the poem. In order to support his construction of the innocent poet grieving over his lost objects of nature, Taylor included an excerpt from a letter from Clare decrying the destruction of his favourite elm trees[35]:

> My two favourite elm trees at the back of the hut are condemned to die—it shocks me to relate it, but 'tis true. The savage who owns them thinks they have done their best, and now wants to make use of the benefits he can get from selling them. O was this country Egypt, and was I but a caliph, the owner should lose his ears for his

arrogant presumption; and the first wretch that buried his axe in their roots should hang on their branches as a terror to the rest. (p. xx)

The violence of this outburst seems unlikely to have provided much comfort for any 'improving landlords' among readers, but Taylor included it precisely because Clare was unable to sustain the violent tone and the letter ended in utter deflation:

A second thought tells me I am a fool: were people all to feel as I do, the world could not be carried on,—a green would not be ploughed—a tree or bush would not be cut for firing or furniture, and every thing they found as boys would remain in that state till they died. This is my disposition, and you will laugh at it ... (p. xx)

Taylor's intention then was to comfort conservative readers with the assurance that any 'apparently discontented' sentiments would be moderated by 'the reflection of a wiser head' (p. xx). Radical passages could be explained away as the products of childlike nostalgia. The 'child of nature' was finally granted the central poetic power of 'reflection' only as a means of undoing the affective force of his poetry. In fact, Clare's defence of his favourite elms proclaimed the conflict between the intrinsic value of nature, the value that he struggled to preserve in the poems, and the crass economic value of the 'benefits' to be gained from 'selling'. Taylor misrepresented Clare's resignation at his lack of power as the 'wiser head' reflecting on the earlier statements in the letter. The language of absolute power in the letter defined what Clare lacked. He was not a 'caliph', nor was this 'Egypt'. The violence of his temper marked the severity of his sense of powerlessness, and the collapse into a mood of deflation and assumed ridicule ('you will laugh at it') followed from the inability to effect any meaningful change to the exploitative status quo.

Clare's stubbornness in including accurate analyses of the effects of enclosure in his poems despite the threat it posed to the continuation of his patronage pointed to more than a fierce political independence under the most difficult of circumstances. His deep commitment to the inhabitants and natural objects of the landscape defined his poetic practice and his aesthetic beliefs. Despite Taylor's belated effort to attribute the power of reflection to Clare, in the form of sentimental nostalgia, the peasant poet deliberately resisted becoming a philosopher of nature. In order to ensure that poetic value remained in the objects of nature he represented, Clare refused to divert aesthetic power into the creation of the poet's philosophic mind. He would not sacrifice nature's intrinsic value in the service of his own poetic self-fashioning. The consistency and vehemence of this belief were evident whether the exploitation he decried was the economic force of enclosure, the act of destroying a tree, or the aesthetic conversion of the landscape into the self.

*

The aesthetic and political terms of Clare's patronage, and the reliance on those terms in the reviews, provide us with insights into the powerful cultural forces that surrounded him, and which attempted to define the meaning of his poetic gift. Clare's struggle to resist such apparently overwhelming forces throws light on his lifelong feelings of isolation, and bears witness to the strength of his aesthetic and political convictions.

3
'Grammer in learning is like Tyranny in government'

In order to fully understand the political resonance of Clare's use of 'vulgar' dialect words it is necessary to establish the history of 'grammatical correctness' as it originated in the eighteenth century, and to explore the various ways in which political and class assumptions were embedded in its rhetorical formulations. This chapter sets out, first, to show how Clare found himself in the midst of a complex cultural controversy, and how current arguments about editing his poems indicate that he remains trapped in the original terms of that controversy. Second, it establishes the ways in which Clare was subject to grammatical 'instruction', and explores the social meaning of that 'instruction'. And the final section explores the counter-tradition of 'radical grammar' that was founded by Horne Tooke at the end of the eighteenth-century, and subsequently developed into an integral part of the radical movement for reform by William Cobbett during the same period that Clare was composing his first two volumes[1].

Editorial 'meddling'

Clare's letter to John Taylor of 22 February 1822 has long been used as the prime exhibit in debates about Taylor's alleged editorial interference. Tom Paulin cites it to denounce Taylor as a meddler who abuses his position of power and imposes his own blinkered notions of 'correctness' on Clare:

> Taylor edits, shapes and sometimes rewrites Clare's poems, sends them back, and Clare replies, 'your verse is a devilish puzzle I may

alter but I cannot mend   grammer in learning is like Tyranny in government'.[2]

Paulin characterises this exchange between author and editor as a part of the 'hegemony of Official Standard' English (p. 47), but as Zachary Leader has demonstrated this view is too easy. Through a meticulous rereading of the correspondence of 1820–21, Leader clearly demonstrates the close collaboration between Clare and Taylor in producing the first two volumes. Of necessity, there was considerable mutuality in the relationship; Taylor could not revise by himself without running the risk of losing the aesthetic power of the original, and Clare could not be relied on to 'mend' spelling mistakes or grammatical solecisms.[3] Leader does well to correct the impression Paulin gives that Taylor was the author of the 'verse' referred to in the letter, and that it was an instance of Taylor's 'rewriting'. The practical problem that the letter addresses is what to do about the following stanza:

> And, fairest daughter of the year,
> Thrice welcome here anew;
> Tho' gentle Storms tis thine to fear
> The roughest blast has blew.

As Taylor says in his letter of 18 February to which Clare is responding: 'Blew ought to be blown.'[4] The question to be addressed by critics is whether or not the phrase, 'ought to be', constitutes imposition or mere editorial correction. When he responded to suggested revisions, Clare differentiated between diction, which he saw as expressive of the integral value of the local names of things, and grammar, which he saw as a necessary feature of publication. Indeed, he and Taylor acted in concert to resist Radstock's 'meddling', as Taylor himself called it, in matters of presumed radical or vulgar content.[5] And, there is little evidence that Clare permitted 'meddling' with his diction, or that Taylor attempted to 'meddle' in an intrusive way in preparing the first two volumes.[6]

The worst that can be said of Taylor's editing of the first two volumes is that he was confused about the value of dialect words, and struggled to come up with a rationale for his editorial suggestions. In reference to 'The Village Minstrel' in a letter of 23 January 1821, he wrote:

We have few Provincialisms in the poem, & I should be glad if we could get rid of One that is left *himsen*, but if it cannot be easily done never mind.—Real English Country Words are different in my mind

& should be judged differently from those which are only peculiar to a district, & perhaps *himsen* & *shanny* are of the latter class.—Shanny is not used beyond the Trent, tho' himsen is common enough I know.[7]

The attempt to base his aesthetic judgements on the distinction of 'Real English Country Words' foundered immediately, and given his conceptual confusion he deferred to Clare's judgement. In a letter a few weeks later, Taylor suggested possible changes: 'I have turn'd the swopping Kite to *swooping* (a Word us'd in that sense by Shakspeare)—& the swopping Crows to *flopping* (heavy winged)'.[8] As swopping refers to pouncing, neither of these suggestions was acceptable, and swopping was retained. Given his struggles, Taylor, in the same letter, expressed much relief at being able to take guidance from Clare: 'Your Explanation of the Provincialisms suits me Capitally for the glossary. I have a general but not a true Sense of their Meaning—so I think I shall get you to interpret a few more—*Grains* for instance I had quite mistaken'. Taylor's difficulty points to a serious editorial conundrum: how to distinguish between 'low' coinages and precise expressions of the thing itself. He was unable to find a solution. Even Leader in his defence of Taylor's editorial decisions and judgement concedes that many if not all decisions regarding diction were strangely arbitrary: 'individual choices remain puzzling'.[9] The arbitrariness of editorial decisions raises a different set of questions which I will address in Chapters 5 and 7, but at this juncture it is safe to say that critics need not pillory Taylor on the grounds of linguistic insensitivity or imposition. While he was certainly culpable in the delays in publishing *The Shepherd's Calendar*, and the excessive cuts to that manuscript (although Chilcott and Leader would challenge the latter assumption), he harboured no intentions to regularise Clare's language to Standard English.[10]

Clare's frustration at being thrust into the role of grammarian explodes in his outburst to Taylor:

> grammer in learning is like Tyranny in government—confound the bitch Ill never be her slave & have a vast good mind not to alter the verse in question—by g–d Ive tryd an hour & cannot do a syllable so do your best or let it pass the last way woud please me the best[11]

Leader argues that 'Clare's exasperation' is not with 'editorial meddling', but with 'grammatical complication' (p. 217). However, this interpretation is itself too easy. Clare has not admitted, in the letter, the authority of the grammatical rule. He is frustrated at having written a stanza that violates Standard English, and that cannot be mended after the fact. That he accepts Taylor's role in identifying such grammatical problems does not mean he himself believes them to be anything but arbitrary. He chafes at being made grammar's 'slave', and stops just short of insisting on the verse being published as is. When he consents to Taylor trying to 'mend' it (something which, to Taylor's credit, he did not attempt), Clare makes it clear that his preferred choice would be to 'let it pass'. Leader assumes this meant to lay the stanza aside, but it is more likely Clare meant that it be published in its 'uncorrected' form. Clare's anger vacillates between frustration at failing to conform to standard grammatical convention, and the belief that such conventions were impositions.

As an example of a specific editorial problem, the stanza demonstrates how difficult it is to make a stable distinction between questions of diction and questions of grammar. Clare's line, 'the blast has blew', *is* Standard English in northern Northamptonshire and Lincolnshire. His anger is partly directed against being asked to change a coinage that is true to his local speech. So, far from being simply an instance of 'grammatical complication', the task of 'mending' the stanza moves towards what Paulin calls Official Standard English at the expense of the inherent value of local dialect. To Leader's rhetorical question, 'Would Taylor have been doing Clare a favour by publishing "the blast has blew"?' (p. 217), Paulin's response would likely be an emphatic yes. The assumption that Clare's problem was technical, a grammatical solecism, rather than cultural, the imposition of rules that divided the population into literate and vulgar, shows how completely internalised is the notion of a natural grammar, and rather proves Paulin's wider point that 'a dead official language and a centralising conformity have worked to obliterate individual speech communities' (p. 47). In order to understand how this occurred, how it persists and how it constrained Clare, it is necessary to review the development of 'Official Standard English' over the course of the eighteenth and early nineteenth centuries.

Grammatical 'instruction'

The development of standardised English grammar during the eighteenth century has been brilliantly summarised by Olivia Smith in her Introduction to *The Politics of Language: 1791–1819*. Smith notes that the treatise that informs all influential books of grammar and the dictionaries of the period is James Harris's *Hermes*. Harris contends that language is transparent to mind, and, therefore, the more complex a language the more complex the mind it images. This theory of 'universal grammar' initiates the scholarly tradition of looking to classical languages for models and guides in theorising English grammatical conventions. Hugh Blair's view is typical: 'if speech be the vehicle or interpreter of the conceptions of our minds, an examination of its structure and progress cannot but unfold many things concerning the nature and progress of our conceptions themselves, and the operation of our faculties'.[12] The unintended, but inevitable, result of this theory is the idea that only those educated using classical models can be credited with having complex minds. Latinate vocabulary is preferred to Anglo-Saxon words because of its abstractness. To recognise a 'house' is considered simply an act of recognising a thing found in the world, but to recognise a 'habitation' demands the conceiving of an abstract category. Thus, 'habitation' is to be preferred because it causes the mind to reflect on itself, rather than simply recording sense data. Anglo-Saxon vocabulary is denigrated as 'vulgar', and a class divide opens that a vernacular poet like Clare cannot hope to bridge. As Smith shows, even those grammarians interested in defending Old English coinages do so from a 'primitivist' position that concedes the superiority of cultivated English: 'Concrete terms, emotional expressions, syntactical simplicity, an abundance of metaphors, and a paucity of terms are the distinguishing features of primitive language.'[13] While these features are seen as admirable in ancient literature, and are particularly praised in defending the Bible against charges of 'vulgarity', they are nonetheless seen as inferior to the cultivated neo-classicism of eighteenth-century prose conventions. Blair, for example, defends the Hebrew poets, but as Smith makes clear, he does not believe their good qualities can supersede their linguistic limitations: 'Although he [Blair] admires the emotional intensity and metaphorical character of primitive literature, he considers such traits as a necessary sacrifice to the advance of reason, the grammatical march of civilisation.' This culturally dominant view of language leaves Clare outside the bounds of social power, and his defence of the concreteness of local names ensures that he be viewed as an atavistic outsider at best, or, more likely, as a 'vulgar' peasant incapable of reflection.

Lord Radstock gave Clare a copy of Blair's *Lectures* along with an edition of Blair's *Sermons* in February 1820. They were among the earliest of the many volumes Radstock sent to Clare during his patronage. Like most of the books Radstock chose, these volumes were sent to him with an eye towards instruction and improvement, and groups of books often contained both grammatical and religious treatises. The Blair volumes arrived via John Taylor and came with instructions as to their use: 'I send with this a copy of Blair's Sermons which Lord Radstock makes you a present of, and he particularly recommends to your perusal 3 sermons in the collection, vis. those on prosperity, on adversity, & on humility from which he states himself to have derived very valuable instruction.'[14] 'Instruction' means very different things depending on social status. The lessons Radstock drew on 'humility' and on learning from 'adversity' translate as calls for quietism from someone as socially marginal as Clare. During a re-perusal of Blair's *Sermons* in October 1824, Clare recognised that the primary interest of the *Sermons* was not religious at all, but rather stylistic: 'Blair's [sermons] are queit & cold & his study seems more in the eloquence & flow of Style then in the doctrine of religion for the language is beautiful but it is studied like Dr Johnsons musical periods.'[15] Johnson, like Blair and the other grammarians who relied on Harris's theory of universal grammar, denigrated native English words in favour of the presumed sophistication of Latinate vocabulary. An edition of Johnson's *Dictionary* was also among the earliest gifts Clare received from his patrons, arriving from Lord Milton in 1820. The 'Preface' to Clare's edition lists the reasons why it is to be preferred to other dictionaries available. The third of the reasons is instructive here: 'Many barbarous terms and phrases by which other dictionaries may vitiate the style, are rejected from this.'[16] This principle placed Johnson in diametrical opposition to Clare's beliefs about the intrinsic value of vernacular speech, and made the politics of grammatical correctness explicit. To 'vitiate the style' with 'vulgar' words was to be a barbarian.

A religious treatise that Radstock sent the month following the arrival of the Blair volumes ties together the ideas of religious and grammatical instruction. Analogous to the way Blair attempted to rescue the primitivism of the Hebrew poets, Joseph Addison's *The Evidences of the Christian Religion*[17] attempted to rescue 'pagan' and 'Jewish' authors by deducing evidence of Christian revelation from their writing, an ambitious effort at expanding the tradition of typological reading. This parallel project harboured similar hopes for social improvement and progress to those espoused by grammarians eager to find a means to rescue the ancient Hebrew authors from charges of 'vulgarity'. Radstock made his own hopes for Clare's instruction and betterment clear in the homily he inscribed on the flyleaf of the volume:

> This most admirable and exquisitely beautiful reflection is presented by Admiral Lord Radstock to his friend John Clare, not only as

a testimony of his high esteem for his character, and of the delight he has received[?] from the perusal and reperusal of this charming and *instructive* little volume, but still more from the conviction that the author will truly appreciate the book now presented to him and that, by its constant study, it will enrich and expand his mind, as to open to him the gates of an earthly paradise, which, if only *cultivated*, cannot fail to yield such fruits as to ensure him (through the merits of our blessed Saviour and only Redeemer, Jesus Christ) the entrance into that heavenly one, where alone true joys are to be found, and where our happiness will be as perfect as everlasting[?].[18] (emphasis mine)

Radstock's homily fascinates for several reasons. The connection of the aesthetic and didactic purposes of the book ('charming and instructive') is followed to its logical conclusion. While Clare learns to 'truly appreciate the book', he will simultaneously, 'by its constant study', have his mind enriched and expanded. Just as abstract, cultivated prose will create intellectual improvements in the reader/writer's quality of mind, study of the intellectual arguments for the typological relationship of 'pagan' texts to Christian revelation will improve the hitherto uncultivated poet. Radstock's choice of simile makes this clear: the wildness of Clare's natural genius will be superseded by an 'earthly paradise' which must be 'cultivated' in order to gain access to the still greater perfection of Christian revelation. The fact that Clare is a peasant, and familiar with a more prosaic form of cultivation seems lost on Radstock at this point. Issues of 'cultivation' and agricultural 'improvement' became an important point of contention between poet and patron. Indeed, 'cultivation' understood as either religious, grammatical or (metaphorically) agricultural 'improvement' represent, to Lord Radstock's mind, the very terms and goals of patronage. Clare's language was seen as rhetorically equivalent to his religious beliefs – each in need of instruction. The class assumptions embedded in eighteenth-century theories grammar made Clare's 'vulgarity' a challenge, and an opportunity, for the civilised and civilising patron.

'Radical grammar'

Assumptions concerning the vulgarity of vernacular speech, though presented by grammarians as dispassionate discourses on the progress of human language and thought, confined the vast majority of the population to linguistic powerlessness, beneath the consideration of polite, civilised society. Nor was there any real possibility of acquiring the linguistic manners necessary to move up into the realm of public discourse. Olivia Smith argues persuasively that the intimate connection between class identity and language use made participation in public life impossible for most:

> Because both suffrage and ideas about language depended on the question of who was considered to be capable of participating in public life, the two were vitally connected. The ability to define simultaneously a class, its moral worth, and its language presented a formidable stumbling block to the possibility of discussion between classes.[19]

In analysing Hansard's *Parliamentary Debates* from the 1790s, Smith shows that petitions for the extension of suffrage and other 'radical' causes were rejected not on merit, but stylistically as too 'vulgar' to be considered. Political power then, was intimately tied to a classical public school education. Given this socio-linguistic context, Clare's insistence not only on his right to local dialect words, but on their necessity, must be seen as a 'radical' position. It was also alienating, misunderstood, and made him the subject of patronising (in both senses of the word) condescension. Current critical controversies suggest that these issues have yet to be completely resolved.[20]

*

However, Clare's insistence on the intrinsic value of local names, his defence of their concreteness, their truth value, is not as eccentric as it at first appears. While it is true that political radicals were slow to recognise the politics of grammar, eventually a critique of 'correctness' emerged. Joseph Priestly provides a good example of the hegemony of Harris's ideas, and of how they entered the public discourse as mere instruction, presumably free of political bias. He adopted most of the assumptions of Harris's theory of 'universal grammar', and its elevation of abstraction over concreteness, as given, as the signs of civilised and progressive argument:

> Such writers [students], moreover, are in less danger of debasing their style, by vulgar words and phrases, or such as have long been associated with, and, in manner, appropriated to vulgar and mean ideas; than which, nothing can be more unworthy of the mind, much

more the compositions, of a gentleman, or a person of liberal education.[21]

The conspicuous exception to this assumption that grammar was apolitical was the committed radical John Horne Tooke. Unlike his radical friend Priestly, Horne Tooke used his treatise, *The Diversions of Purley*, to attack the grammatical consensus at its fundamental bases, and he was self-consciously aware of the political weight of his analysis.[22] His first target was Harris. As the author of *Hermes*, Harris had founded the tradition of preferring abstract Latinate words, a tradition that had been taken up by the early grammarians like Bishop Lowth,[23] and transmitted forward by Blair and Johnson to Lindley Murray, the author of the standard Grammar book during Clare's lifetime. Horne Tooke produced a telling quip in his introduction to Part I of the treatise: 'Hermes you know, put out the eyes of Argus: and I suspect that he has likewise blinded philosophy: and if I had not imagined so, I should never have cast away a thought upon the subject. If therefore Philosophy herself has been misled by Language, how shall she teach us to detect his tricks'.[24] Horne Tooke equated abstraction with subterfuge, and made the politics of this charge explicit in the title of the first chapter of Part II, 'The Rights of Man'. By choosing Paine's still notorious title, he displayed both political courage and wit, for the 'Rights' of the title did not simply refer to political rights, but rather to the variety of the word's usages. The purpose of the chapter was to mount an attack on Johnson and particularly on what Horne Tooke saw as the arbitrary absurdity of Johnson's definitions:

> Let us see how Johnson handles it [defining 'rights']. He did not indeed acknowledge any RIGHTS of the people; but he was very clear concerning Ghosts and Witches, all the mysteries of divinity, and the sacred, indefeasible, inherent, hereditary RIGHTS of Monarchy.[25]

He observed that Johnson offered no explanations for the uses of 'right', other than defining 'Right hand' as meaning: 'Not the Left'. The rest of the meanings for the term were presented as bald assertions without explanation. What Horne Tooke demonstrated was the essential arbitrariness of Johnson's project. Johnson could not justify his claim that 'right' means 'true' because he relied on his own political biases, couched in abstract categories, themselves arbitrarily derived. The next 400 pages of the treatise are taken up with a series of chapters called 'Of Abstraction', and exhaustively attack the practice of abstract definition and attempt to replace them with a theory of language based on the concrete origins of words in things and actions. By investigating the etymology of 'rights', for example, Horne Tooke claimed that all the senses of the word can be derived from words meaning 'ordered'. He immediately politicised his claim with the example: 'Thus, when a man demands his RIGHT; he asks only that which it is *Ordered* he shall have'. He then listed all of the senses of 'right' that Johnson provided in his Dictionary, thus demonstrating his point; 'A RIGHT conduct is, that which is *Ordered*. To do RIGHT is, to do what is *Ordered* to be done'[26], etc. By recovering the concreteness of 'right', Horne Tooke demonstrated, by comparison, the inevitability of corruption in Johnson's unqualified assertions of meaning. Johnson's *Dictionary* introduced the reactionary Tory politics of the 1750s into the social fabric via his specific definitions, and Horne Tooke exposed the arbitrary and duplicitous nature of this dubious intellectual practice. It was not just a matter of occasional absurdities like defining 'right' as 'not wrong', and 'wrong' as 'not right' that Horne Tooke exposed, but rather a systemic reliance on intellectually ridiculous tautologies. The scope for corruption is almost limitless in a system where 'true' is defined as 'not false', and 'false' as 'not true'.[27] The political, as well as linguistic, goal of *Diversions of Purley* was to recover the concrete nature of language, and thereby make such corruption more difficult, and certainly more easily exposed. Consequently, he elevated Anglo-Saxon words over Latinate vocabulary. The concreteness of Anglo-Saxon words resists efforts at distorting their meaning, and linguistic distortion was endemic in political discourse. Horne Tooke's position matches almost exactly Clare's defence of the truth-value of local, vernacular speech. The very orality of such speech marks it as free of the corruption inherent in the imposed standards of written eloquence, the domain of the grammarians.

Given this historical context, it is not surprising to read accounts of Clare's rage against the ridiculous pronouncements of Lindley Murray, the so-called father of English Grammar.[28] Clare's stubborn defence of his Northamptonshire dialect should be understood as a radical position, not as part of a radical political agenda, but rather in the sense of direct opposition to political authority and the status quo. The most intellectually damning aspect of John Taylor's editorial relationship to Clare is the arbitrary nature of his allegiance to Clare's use of dialect, something that even Taylor's defenders admit. What Taylor's unevenness in treating dialect words shows is his inability to recognise the truth value that Clare ascribed to the specificity and concreteness of such words, the honest effort after the thing itself. This is a position that Horne Tooke shared, and while there is no evidence that Clare was directly familiar with *The Diversions of Purley*, the similarity of the views of the two authors is apparent. Clare need not have read Horne Tooke to understand his struggle against the conservative social force of grammarians. Clare inherited that struggle.

*

The radical English Grammar that Clare undoubtedly did know well was William Cobbett's *A Grammar of the English Language in a Series of Letters*. Cobbett offered the first English Grammar intended for members of the general population rather than public schoolboys. He makes this difference clear in a statement of intention that prefaces the volume:

> Intended for the Use of Schools and of Young Persons in general; but more especially for the Use of Soldiers, Sailors, Apprentices, and Plough-boys.[29]

The reasons for reaching this hitherto unrepresented audience are twofold and entirely political. First, Cobbett wants to undermine the cultural assumptions of grammatical correctness, and in so doing, undermine the systems of social authority derived from a reliance on classical models and Harris's theory of 'universal grammar'. Second, he wants to empower a broad range of the public in their drive for a 'Reform' of parliament by providing them with the rhetorical means to present their ideas and political analyses in a culturally acceptable form. If the charge of 'vulgarity' were eliminated from the state's attack on such analyses, then the petitions of 'Reformers' of all classes would have to be considered according to their merits. An essay addressed: 'To the Blanketteers.[30] On the Utility of Grammar', in *Cobbett's Weekly Political Register* of 21 November 1818 makes these motives abundantly clear:

> The labouring classes were full of information as to the great object on which they dwelt [political reform]: and on this subject they spoke, urged by zeal, warmed by feeling, and unchecked by rules and forms: reason, which is the common gift of God to man, gave arrangement to their thoughts, and all nature furnished them with figures of rhetorick wherewith to enforce their arguments and to ornament, or enliven, their discourse.

But when the same persons came to *put their thoughts on paper*, which was necessary in the case of resolutions and petitions, there appeared, in their writings, many things very ridiculous for the want of good grammar. As to logic and rhetorick, they are found in men's *thoughts*: nature gives them, in a greater or lesser degree, to all persons who are not idiots; but *grammar*, which is a thing proceeding from there having taken place among men a tacit convention that letters and words, used thus and thus, *shall mean* this and that, must be acquired by the learning of those principles and rules which form the basis and the terms of this tacit, or understood convention, or agreement: and, it was this sort of learning that the labouring classes in England stood in need.[31]

Cobbett's distinction between written words and thoughts (writing and discourse) takes apart the foundational principle of Harris's theory by arguing that grammar and writing are not simple reflections of mind. Rather, grammar is purely conventional, a set of habitual agreements limited to the conventions of writing and utterly irrelevant to reason, logic or rhetoric. This distinction also removes the basis for the eighteenth-century bias towards Latinate diction and classical models, and reveals them as mere social conventions, albeit ones that exercise enormous cultural influence. The labouring classes are seen as eloquent and capable, and their exclusion from public discourse as an unfair result of 'tacit convention'. Whereas correct grammar tells us nothing at all about the quality of reasoning, the charge of 'vulgarity' is simply a social slur employed for political purposes. Cobbett hopes his grammar will provide a simple guide to these 'tacit conventions' and thus end political exclusion on the basis of formal language requirements.

Cobbett offers several examples of the pressing need for such a book. He tells the story of 'a journeyman stocking weaver' who had come to London to petition the Commons for electoral reform. Cobbett was asked to read the petition before it was presented, and reports:

The ideas were correct; the judgement sound; the reasoning clear and conclusive; and the figures of speech apt, consistent, beautiful and striking. (*PR*, p. 254)

However, the grammatical shortcomings of the piece were such that the effectiveness of the arguments was undermined. There was 'such discord amongst nouns and pronouns and verbs' that the writing, as writing not as argument, would 'have excited the ridicule' of the 'learned' in 'ninety-nine persons out of every hundred' (pp. 254–5). Cobbett is the one person in a hundred who can see past the grammatical irregularities and note the quality of both the intellectual argument of the petition and its aesthetic qualities ('aptness' of figuration, beauty, consistency). The dominance of the sloppy cultural habit of judging written prose by grammatical conventions instead of intellectual merit inevitably led to frustration on the part of those attempting to find a public voice. Cobbett intends his grammar as a means to overcome this problem.

In reviewing how the unenfranchised came to be so confused about grammatical conventions he needed to look no further than the standard grammar available, Lindley Murray's woeful mishmash of the earlier grammars of Bishop Lowth and Hugh Blair. Murray had taken up the neo-classical biases of these books without a thought, and the predictable result was that his book was unusable by anyone who did not have a public school education in Latin and Greek, the model for all English grammars then available. Cobbett specifically sets out to debunk the notion that the 'Latin and Greek languages' had 'exclusive claim to the epithet "learned"' (*PR*, p. 257). Together with Johnson's *Dictionary*, these books constituted a body of knowledge that was of 'no use' and, as a waste of time, was '*worse than useless*' to new learners (p. 257). He sets out to demonstrate that: 'even a thorough knowledge of those "*learned* languages" does not prevent men from writing *bad English*' (p. 257). He proved his point: 'by citing errors committed by really *learned* men: *Hume, Addison, Doctor Hugh Blair, Judge Blackstone, Doctor Johnson*, and *Doctor Watts*' (p. 263). In addition, he chose: '*specimens of bad grammar* from the *Rambler* of Doctor Johnson', and exposed the 'bad grammar and nonsense of a *King's speech*' (p. 264). He concludes by returning to the current source of grammatical confusion, Clare's nemesis, Lindley Murray. Cobbett notes that the success of Murray's grammar rests solely in its availability, 'booksellers are in possession of his book' (p. 265). An analysis of the opening address of Murray's book reveals all the faults it ostensibly intends to treat: 'poor and feeble thoughts, trying to creep forth, are stifled in the confusion of bad grammar, worse logic, and still worse rhetorick' (p. 268). Cobbett, then, is addressing a pressing social need with the publication of a 'useful' grammar, and the political implications of this act are foremost in his mind:

> I now derive great satisfaction from the hope that, by these my exertions many a private soldier, and many a plough-boy, will be able to shine amongst those who are destined to root out from the minds of

men the base and blasphemous notions, that wisdom and talent are
confined to what is called high-birth, and that the few possess a right
divine to rule, oppress, and plunder the many. (p. 269)

Clare, as a 'plough-boy' and poet, is precisely the kind of figure Cobbett
wants to empower, and Clare's arguments for the use of the English
vernacular and dialect words follow logically from Cobbett's assumptions
about the 'aptness' of true English diction (as opposed to the false value
of 'learned' languages). Clare's antipathy to false notions of grammatical
correctness finds its fullest expression in a note on grammar that begins
in praise of Cobbett's revisionist approach:

> ... such a one as Cobbet who has come boldly forward and not only
> assailed the outworks of such a pedantic garrison but like a skilful
> general laid open its weakness to all ... he plainly comes to this
> conclusion—that whatever is intellig[i]b[l]e to others is grammer
> and what ever is commonsense is not far from correctness[32]

His summary of Cobbett's central arguments indicates how clearly he
understood both the rhetorical and political implications of attacking
conventional grammars:

> A man who learns enough of grammer to write sufficiently well as to be
> understood by others as well as to understand his own consceptions
> himself and trys out the way to make his consceptions correct think-
> ings rather than the correct placing of particles and stops and other trif-
> ling with which every writer on grammar seems to be at loggerheads
> about with each other—such an attainment will get the possessor an
> enlightened and liberal mind and if he attain not with this broad prin-
> ciple an excellence in composition the niceties of intricate Lectures on
> grammer with its utmost perfection will not attain it for him

The goal of attaining an 'enlightened and liberal mind' points to the
social stakes in the debate, and suggests a keen awareness on Clare's
part of the politics inherent in Cobbett's project. Zachary Leader challenges this assumption, arguing that this passage and James McKusick's
claim that Clare 'became more stubbornly resistant to the attempts ...
to correct his poems' notwithstanding, the notion that:

> his grammatical mistakes and misspellings were political, an expres-
> sion of conscious resistance, as opposed to what Johanne Clare calls

'indifference' (also fatigue, growing anxiety, unsettledness) is not clear at all.[33]

While Clare's phrase 'other trifling' clearly indicates 'indifference' to the task of grammatical correctness, Leader too narrowly defines 'political' and makes a false distinction between the 'political' and Clare's 'indifference'. His 'indifference' is a mark of his contempt for the social assumptions driving conventional notions of correctness, and as such is nothing if not political. To argue the narrow point that Clare did not intend his writing to be incorrect as a political gesture is to misconstrue McKusick's general point that Clare was interested in promoting a different set of linguistic values – values of a piece with those expressed by Cobbett. It is condescending to assume that Clare fully understood the rhetorical content of Cobbett's grammar but did not pick up its political resonances. Such a reading strategy risks becoming credulous. It searches for direct evidence for a 'political' reading that is everywhere apparent. Clare could readily place himself and his poetic practices inside the current politics of language, and had a clear understanding of the social stakes involved in defending vernacular speech.

*

The complex biases that constituted language as a social phenomenon become apparent when we remember the critical assumptions brought into play in Taylor's efforts to create an audience for Clare's poetry, and in the reviews that responded both to the poetry and to Taylor's critical prompting.

4
The Cottager's Friend

When Eliza Emmerson wrote to her influential friend Lord Radstock in 1820 recommending Clare as a suitable beneficiary of his Lordship's patronage, she concluded with a poem in praise of Clare ending with the assurance that: 'He'll put up with distress—and be content'.[1] Part of the appeal of Clare was the perception that even if his poetic aspirations ended in failure he would not turn his disappointment into anger and bitterness. His capacity for 'contentment' in the face of adversity made him an ideal representative for a peasantry whose fealty to landowners and farmers was being severely challenged by the socially destructive forces of agricultural enclosure. Mrs Emmerson took her line directly from Clare's poem 'Helpstone', and she hoped that the promise of rural 'contentment' would convince Radstock that Clare was worthy of support. The line in Clare's poem ends a description of 'little birds' buffeted by harsh winter conditions. Clare makes an explicit comparison between the birds and himself, 'like to me these victims of the blast', and thus suggests that current conditions in the countryside were analogous to perpetual winter. By removing them from their context, Mrs Emmerson extracted a sense of stoic calm from the lines and offered them to Radstock as a reassurance. She neglected to draw his attention to the passage later in the poem that attacked 'accursed wealth' as the cause of 'every evil' plaguing the countryside and its inhabitants:

> Accursed Wealth! o'er-bounding human laws,
> Of every evil thou remain'st the cause:
> Victims of want, those wretches such as me,
> Too truly lay their wretchedness to thee:
> Thou art the bar that keeps from being fed'
> And thine our loss of labour and of bread;

Thou art the cause that levels every tree
And woods bow down to clear a way for thee.[2]

This forthright expression of rural 'discontent' calls into question the accuracy of the portrait of Clare Mrs Emmerson promoted to Radstock, and eventually became a point of bitter contestation in the poet/patron relationship.

The word 'content' was politically resonant in the period as was its opposite 'discontent'. Both terms denoted Tory anxiety about the forces of reform. To be 'discontented' was to be subversive, dangerous, and any promise of a 'contented' peasantry was bound to appeal. Radstock's patronage was founded on the belief that Clare represented a stable, even idyllic, set of relations between the gentry, their tenant farmers, and landless day-labourers like Clare. Radstock enthusiastically threw himself into the task of increasing sales of *Poems Descriptive* despite his unfamiliarity with the actual poems beyond Mrs Emmerson's character-isation of them. His notorious demand that Clare 'expunge the ungrateful sentiments' from 'Helpstone' came a full two printings after he had begun promoting Clare. It must have come as a terrible shock when the passage was called to his attention, but perhaps his previous oversight was not so surprising when we remember the powerful social discourse on being 'content' to which Radstock himself had contributed, and that he assumed Clare reconfirmed and validated.

*

The political battle over the hearts and minds of the peasantry had been raging for many years. As I have already noted, William Cobbett included 'plough-boys' among the list of those to whom he dedicated his Grammar. The stated intention of his treatise was to empower the unenfranchised classes of British society by providing them with the verbal means of engaging in political debate, thus setting the stage for inevitable political reform. On the other hand, the peasantry was seen as naturally conservative in its values by the Tory establishment and landowners, and the government attempted to bolster feelings of 'king and country' in the countryside as a means of resisting the forces of subversion and 'discontent' represented by the radical Cobbett and his sometime allies among the radical Whigs. Sir Francis Burdett and Major John Cartwright, the champions of parliamentary reform, had long held a place in the imaginations of the peasantry as the potential cham-pions of their cause. The leaders of the Yorkshire Luddites, for example, hoped that Burdett in particular might take the lead in their revolt and bring about a new republic in the disaffected north that could spread throughout the country. Such fantasies now seem sadly comical, but nonetheless they mark the level of 'discontent' that potentially existed.[3] The crisis in the north of 1811–12 was still fresh in the public mind, and, in the wake of Peterloo, anxiety over the level of 'contentment' in the countryside was palpable.

Cobbett included rural cottagers as part of the audience in his general agitation for reform. *Cottage Economy* set out to instruct cottagers on how to become self-sufficient. Cobbett focused on basic subsistence farming as well as the brewing of beer. At first glance the book does not appear to be particularly radical; it imagines each cottager as a smallholder and attempts to instil the value of economic independence. As such, it employs the rhetoric of rural 'contentment' as a natural state derived from the existing distribution of property. For Cobbett, the peasantry would be 'content' provided they were inculcated with the idea of the sanctity of their material possessions, meagre as these might be, and conditional upon a rural society that made such aspirations possible. For example, Cobbett was contemptuous of the movement to educate the peasantry:

> The taste of the times is, unhappily, to give children something of book-learning, with a view of placing them to live, in some way or other, upon the labour of other people. Very seldom, comparatively speaking, has this succeeded, even during the wasteful public expenditure of the last thirty years; and, in times the times that are approaching, it cannot, I thank God, succeed at all. When the project has failed, what disappointment, mortification and, misery, to both the parent and child! The latter is spoiled as a labourer; his book learning has only made him conceited: into some course of desperation he falls; and the end is but too often not only wretched but ignominious.[4]

This passage makes an argument strikingly similar to those of conservative critics like Lockhart who cautioned Clare's patrons against raising him above his station thereby risking his happiness as a 'contented' peasant. Indeed, it is difficult to see how Cobbett's view could be taken as radical. In place of such reckless notions of education, he argued for the dutiful instruction of children in their allotted station in life:

> The education I speak of consists in bringing children up to labour with steadiness, with care, and with skill; to show them how to do as

many useful things as possible; to teach them to do all in the best manner; to set them an example in industry, sobriety, cleanliness, and neatness; to make all these habitual to them, so that they never shall be liable to fall into the contrary, to let them always see a good living proceeding from labour, and thus remove from them the temptation to get at the goods of others by violent or fraudulent means, and to keep far from their minds all the inducements to hypocrisy and deceit. (p. 8)

The final few phrases of this entreaty begin to hint at the radical potential in what is otherwise indistinguishable from a conservative quietism in the Burkean tradition.

The fact of the matter was that the peasantry was not able 'to see a good living proceeding from labour', and Cobbett's treatise becomes political agitation in that social context. The seemingly conservative rhetoric of contented self-sufficiency serves as bitter contrast to the actual state of affairs in the countryside. In a passage in which he exhorts cottagers to be frugal in the acquisition and use of house-hold implements, Cobbett's political purpose appears to emerge as an afterthought:

Good management [of household goods] in this way leaves the man's wages to provide an abundance of good food and good raiment; and these are the things that make happy families; these are the things that make a good, kind, sincere, and brave people; not little pamphlets about "loyalty" and "content". A good man will be contented fast enough, if he be fed and clad sufficiently; but if a man be not well fed and clad, he is a base wretch to be contented. (p. 147)

Cobbett's description of the value of rural frugality suddenly veers into the current pamphlet wars over the hearts and minds of the peasantry. His description of the 'conservative' values of a settled stratified rural economy becomes radical provocation in the context of their utter absence. He ends by exhorting cottagers to be 'discontented' with current conditions. To be otherwise is to consent to your own debasement. Critics have been too quick to characterise Clare's espousal of a rural economy based on stable class relations and the sufficient circulation of wealth to create 'contented' peasants as 'conservative' nostalgia, but seen in relation to Cobbett's treatise it is clear that such 'conservative' social values contain the seeds of radical political attitudes.

Placing Cobbett's attitudes alongside a range of more typical conservative views provides a sense of the political terrain that he and Clare had to negotiate. Among the multitude of pamphlets on rural contentment in circulation in the period when Clare composed and published his first two volumes was a reprint of *Reasons for Contentment Addressed to the Labouring Part of the British Public* by William Paley.[5] We know Paley better as the author of *Natural Theology*, a key text in the intellectual development of rational dissent. It initially comes as a surprise then to find him on the other side of a political issue often associated with calls for institutional reform. However, the pamphlet was originally published during the Terror in France, and its immediate political goal was the prevention of the spread of violent anarchy to the English countryside. That the pamphlet was reprinted and redeployed in 1819 provides a gauge of the level of dissatisfaction that existed. The pamphlet's immediate rhetorical goals were twofold: to describe the advantages of being a member of the 'lower orders' of society, and the introduction of a religious sanction against 'discontent'. Paley wrote: 'So long as a man is intent upon the duties and concerns of his own condition, he never thinks of comparing it with any other' (p. 1). In other words, idleness breeds class-consciousness. The crises in 1793 and in 1819 concerned the collapse of the living conditions of the working poor, affording them the opportunity to reflect on class disparities. Paley tried to pre-empt the spread of discontent by asserting that the laws must be maintained because they 'protect and guard the poor man' along with the rich (p. 4). Radical reform endangered everyone as it threatened to destroy the very basis of 'content'. Paley's reasoning on this point seems laughable now. He argued that land reform would not result in more food being produced or more people being fed (p. 5), but such an argument ignores the unequal distribution of that food and so implicitly justifies resistance in cases where people are not being well fed. This is the fault line in much of the conservative rhetoric of the period: to argue for an ideal rural economy of contented peasants and productive landlords runs the paradoxical risk of exposing the real inequities that shifts in the rural economy caused. Agricultural 'improvement' had shown the vast majority of peasants that the rewards of rural labour were under threat, and it was this potential source of discontent that Cobbett hoped to tap. It did little good for Paley to argue in favour of 'the advantages of those laborious conditions of life' (p. 5), when those conditions were in fact under threat from enclosure, bad harvests, and foreign wars. In a sentiment later echoed by Cobbett, Paley stated that: 'Frugality itself is a pleasure. It...produces pleasure' (p. 7), but such a sentiment rings false when frugality is confused with privation. It was cold comfort indeed to be reassured by Archdeacon Paley that the children of the poor could look forward to a life of honest labour while the children of the wealthy run the terrible risk of falling into a life of meaningless dissipation (pp. 6 and 11). The fact was the children of the poor could not look forward to settled employment. Clare's life as a 'catch labourer', picking up seasonal work as it became available testifies against the basis of conservative arguments for contentment. Paley underwrote his sociological justifications of the status quo by asserting the religious basis of class disparity. 'When we bring religion into view', Paley opined, 'it unfolds a prospect which makes all earthly distinctions nothing' (pp. 11–12). As social station was an accident of birth, Paley concluded:

> I contend that the man who murmurs and repines, when he has nothing to murmur and repine about, but the mere want of independent property, is not only irreligious, but ill-founded and unreasonable in his complaint; and that he would find, did he know the truth, and consider his case fairly, that a life of labour, such I mean as is led by the labouring part of mankind in this country, has advantages in it, which compensate all its inconveniences' (p. 12).

The problem with redeploying Paley's anti-Jacobin rhetoric in 1819 lay in the increasing unlikelihood of locating the opportunities for labour he described, let alone their 'advantages'.

Arguments for the religious basis of class disparities were commonplace, including a strident contribution by Lord Radstock in the ongoing the pamphlet war for the contentment of the peasantry. Before turning to that document, however, I want to explore a different kind of religious intervention: the Reverend Patrick Brontë's poetic representation of conservative values in his 1811 *Cottage Tales*. Brontë's volume not only provides a typically conservative portrait of a contented peasantry succoured by religion, it also trades on a quasi-Wordsworthian poetics, and, by a fortunate historical accident, is set amongst the most 'discontented' valleys in England. Self-published in Halifax, the poems were an expression of their author's faith, and a public effort to have the depth of that faith recognised by an audience of like-minded (and socially powerful) churchmen and government officials. The poems function as a sort of aesthetic calling card. In particular, two poems, 'The Happy Cottagers' and 'The Cottage Maid', offer portraits designed to reconfirm conservative values, especially class deference and the sublimation of material demands to 'rewards' in the next life. These poems show the poet/minister circulating among the neighbouring cottages and observing the devoutly contented inhabitants within. 'The Happy Cottagers' begins with a familiar pastoral description:

> One sunny morn of May,
> When dressed in flowery green
> The dewy landscape, charmed
> With Nature's faintest scene,
> In thoughtful mood
> I slowly strayed
> O'er hill and dale,
> Through bush and glade.[6]

The value of the scene, as with Wordsworth,[7] shifts from the objects described to the poetic speaker. He is 'charmed' and transformed into a 'thoughtful mood'. The process of poetic transference becomes complete several stanzas later:

> A sympathetic glow
> Ran through my melting soul,
> And calm and sweet delight
> O'er all my senses stole;
> And through my heart
> A grateful flood
> Of joy rolled on
> To Nature's God. (p. 198)

Brontë easily equates his aesthetic transport with recognition of the presence of God in His creation. The objects of Nature affect a deep calm, and in creating 'a sympathetic glow' prepare him for his 'pastoral' duties. The double meaning of 'pastoral' is striking in these poems. In aping pastoral conventions, he creates a rhetoric of power and authority in the landscape, which in turn becomes a sign of his moral authority as pastor to his small flock of cottagers. Brontë was just beginning his career and had been given a church that had fallen into disuse, and was thus in search of a congregation as he wandered the local moors.[8] What he purports to find there is hardly surprising:

> I turned me round to view
> The lovely rural scene;

> And, just at hand, I spied
> A cottage on the green;
> The street was clean,
> The walls were white,
> The thatch was neat,
> The window bright. (p. 198)

The inhabitants of this immaculately tended cottage reflect its physical order. The 'aged man' discovered within looks and sounds the part:

> His coarse attire was clean
> His manner rude yet kind:
> His air, his words, and looks
> Showed a contented mind; (p. 199)

Brontë's goal, however, is not a simple portrait of a contented peasant, but rather of a contented peasant who has fallen victim to the physical privations inherent in the age. Characterised as 'affliction's meagre child', the cottager has suffered a life representative of many in the rapidly changing countryside:

> His loving wife long since
> Was numbered with the dead
> His son, a martial youth,
> Had for his country bled;
> And now remained
> One daughter fair,
> And only she,
> To soothe his care. (p. 200)

With his son dead in the war with France, and his wife dead as well, the cottager attempts to survive without the means of doing so. He and his daughter provide a site of nobility in the midst of such privation as they share what 'meagre' fare they have with the poet narrator. Somehow they have transcended their material suffering, and the scene of tidy self-sufficiency they present comforts the narrator and confirms his religious views. They appear 'devoid of care' and refuse to 'env[y] kings'. Instead, they spend the afternoon singing hymns and exalting their 'great Redeemer'. When the old man prays it is not for release from their suffering, but for their reward in heaven:

> He prayed long for all,
> And for his daughter dear,
> That she, preserved from ill,
> Might lead for many a year
> A spotless life
> When he's no more;
> Then follow him
> To Canaan's shore. (p. 202)

Brontë's depiction disconcerts with its mood of resignation. The 'fair daughter', of marriageable age, is the household's only present and potential resource. To pray for her perpetual chastity is a sentence of slow death. Indeed, it is difficult to see how father and daughter can survive in their cottage in the foreseeable future. Praying for his death represents the old man's only chance of escaping the poorhouse and life as a parish case. The poet's denial of their suffering by declaring it irrelevant to the greater goal of spiritual devotion implicates him in that suffering. He literally exploits their suffering as a means of constructing an aesthetic portrait of devout contentment. It is difficult to think of another purpose for the poem. After all, the narrator neither eases their material condition nor provides them with their faith. Their self-sufficiency is spiritual, and has no need of the young Reverend Brontë. It is his faith that the poem constructs, and pays for with their willingness to suffer physical privation.

The greater irony of this poem, and the others in the volume, results from the location of the cottage Brontë leased while composing the poems. The lonely moorland above the Spen and Calder river valleys was inhabited almost entirely with workers in the local wool industry, who, with few exceptions, were participants in the Luddite rising of 1812, the year following the publication of *Cottage Tales*. In short, the portrait of 'The Happy Cottagers' is absurd, and reflects the level of anxiety with which local landed interests feared discontent. The small Luddite army that took part in the notorious Rawfolds Mill raid passed within twenty feet of Brontë's window, but apparently beyond his gaze. This was a necessary blindness. He could little afford to alienate the cottagers he hoped to serve as minister, and dared not offend the powerful local interests who had provided him with his church.[9] While it may appear that the representation of religiously devout cottagers presupposes an emphasis on the promise of the next life, Clare's own early narratives of cottage life demonstrate that this need not be the case.

Clare's poem, 'The Fate of Amy', resembles both 'The Happy Cottagers' and Brontë's encomium to chaste maids, 'The Cottage Maid'. The material conditions of the various characters are similar. Amy is the surviving daughter of an aged widow, and as in 'The Happy Cottagers' the loss of a spouse has caused the collapse of family prosperity:

> The tender father, now no more,
>   Did for them both provide;
> The wealth his industry had gain'd,
>   All wants to come supplied.
>
> Kind heaven upon their labours smil'd
>   Industry gave increase;
> The cottage was contentment's own
>   Abode of wealth and peace.[10]

Clare explicitly connects their religious faith (they work under heaven's benevolent gaze) and their physical labour. Contentment is a function of both. The faith allows them to be happy in their lot, provided their material needs are met. The material basis of contentment recalls Cobbett, and Clare will not elide it in favour of the next life. The death of the father creates terrible uncertainty which Clare shares syntactically with the reader: 'Tomorrow's met with blinded eyes;/ We know not what's to come' (p. 9). The 'we' refers to mother and daughter voicing their fears, and also describes the state of readerly anticipation. We have a stake in the narrative's outcome and are implicated and drawn into village life. The father's absence makes them vulnerable. Brontë denied this social vulnerability in 'The Happy Cottagers' by effacing physical privation. Father and daughter were to somehow live out their chaste existences as if bodily desires did not exist. Clare's Amy falls victim to her sexual innocence and the 'artful ways' of a young 'swain'. Soon village gossip swirls around her, and she sinks into despair. Her concerned mother suspects the worst and turns to her faith:

> And oft she [the mother] hinted, if a crime
>   Through ignorance beguil'd—
> Not to conceal the crime in fear,
>   For none should wrong her child.
> Or, if the rose that left her cheek
>   Was banish'd by disease,
> 'Fear God, my child!' she oft would say,

And you may hope for ease.'
And still she pray'd, and still had hopes

There was no injury done;
And still advis'd the ruin'd girl
The world's deceit to shun.

The mother's psychologically complex response to her daughter being
'ruin'd' demonstrates a realistic version of morality. She does not deny
the change in her daughter's status, being pregnant and unmarried
truly is to be 'ruin'd', but refuses to find her morally culpable. Her innocence produced the 'crime' and she is as much the aggrieved party as
the criminal. The mother's concern is not with blame, but rather that
her daughter not compound the problem by becoming fearful of village
gossip. If Amy can recognise that her mother will defend her, and that
they can seek God's forgiveness, she may escape her fate. It was a common enough fate as testified by Wordsworth's 'The Thorn' and Brontë's
anxiety. In the end, the power of prayer proves insufficient in the face
of village moralising; Amy would inevitably be condemned as a sinner
despite her moral nature. Religion does not provide a transcendent
realm where the social cannot reach. The poem closes with Amy's
suicide, and the mother's premature death from grief.

Brontë's desire to transcend the brute facts of existence and proclaim
the sufficiency of spiritual contentment separates him from Clare and
starkly illuminates the reactionary nature of his social views. He would
be quick to judge Amy even as he denied the human desires that were
her undoing. The maid in 'The Happy Cottagers' prays and sings hymns
in spiritual contentment. The only hint of her humanity, and potential
vulnerability comes, paradoxically, as a response to his male gaze:

With vegetable store
The table soon she spread,
And pressed me to partake;
Whilst blushes rosy-red
Suffused her face— (p. 201)

The power of the poet narrator, as both pastor and from authorial point
of view, sometimes creates the disconcerting impression of Brontë wan-
dering the moors, leering into cottages at unprotected maids. His poem,
'The Cottage Maid', presents a situation even more extreme than the
two we have examined: an unmarried young woman who has lost both

parents, living alone in isolation. The poet observes her as a voyeur: 'She sung by a clear crystal fountain/ (Nor knew I was near)' (p. 231). The conspiratorial tone of the parenthetical aside inadvertently creates a sense of her vulnerability, and his menace. The psychological instability of denying the facts of the body, of desire, of hunger creates a covert portrait of the young vicar full of libidinal drives barely suppressed. Witness another poem, 'Winter-Night Meditations', in which he reveals a psychologically absurd portrait of a sexually wronged village maid, not unlike Amy:

> A blithesome youth of courtly mien
> Oft called to see this rural queen:
> His oily tongue and wily art
> Soon gained Maria's yielding heart.
> The aged pair, too, liked the youth,
> And thought him naught but love and truth.
> The village feast at length is come;
> Maria by the youth's undone:
> The youth is gone—so is her fame;
> And with it all her sense of shame:
> And now she practises the art
> Which snared her unsuspecting heart;
> And vice, with a progressive sway,
> More hardened makes her every day.
> Averse to good and prone to ill,
> And dexterous in seducing skill; (p. 213)

Brontë's self-justification for judging the wronged maid is difficult to take seriously; her seduction does not create shame and suffering, but rather transforms her into a wanton. The preposterous idea that a village girl could be suddenly transformed into a prostitute as a result of her seduction presents a deeply neurotic version of the virgin/whore dichotomy. The phrase, 'dexterous in seducing skill' verges on pornographic and reveals the turmoil driving the author, but little else. The sexual disturbance embedded in Brontë's paternalism aside, the comparison of his cottage poems to Clare's reveals an implicit political divide. Clare defends Amy even as he shows her to be powerless in the face of social forces beyond her control; Brontë denies the importance of social forces, attempts to elide them in the name of religious certainty, and causes them to become covert. If, as Cobbett suggested, the material conditions for contentment did not currently exist in the countryside, then Clare accurately represents the effects of privation on the cottagers, while Brontë denies the seriousness of privation by declaring it irrelevant to the cottager's appropriate goal, spiritual salvation. The proposition that discontent reflects a lack of religious faith and feeling conveniently justifies the suppression of rural dissent and calls for reform, and depends on a false distinction between material and spiritual values. The critical notion that Clare's religious beliefs signify conservative social views cannot be sustained, especially when they are compared with the extreme paternalism of reactionary Christians like Brontë and his patron Lord Radstock.

The early poem, 'The Village Funeral', provides an excellent point from which to observe the social nuances of Clare's political beliefs. The pathetic description of children orphaned by their father's death, marching to solemnly to the graveside evokes feelings of 'anxiety' among their neighbours in equal measure to the narrator's declarations of simple Christian faith:

> But that providing Power, for ever nigh,
>   The universal friend of all distress,
> Is sure to hear their supplicating cry,
>   And prove a father to the fatherless.

This genuine expression of religious faith, and specifically in God's mercy (as substitute 'father') provides a potential source of comfort for the children, and hope for the community at large. The rest of the poem problematises these religious expectations without ever finally losing faith. The anxiety of the village community occasioned by the social realities created by the poem's events creates a dramatic tension with the belief in and desire for religious dispensation:

> While, as they nearer draw in solemn state,
>   The village neighbours are assembled round,
> And seem with fond anxiety to wait
>   The sad procession in the burial ground.
>
> Yet every face the face of sorrow wears;
>   And, now the solemn scene approaches nigh,
> Each to make way for the slow march prepares,
>   And on the coffin casts a serious sigh.

Unlike Brontë, who would instruct the reader to seek solace in God and the promise of eternal life, Clare refuses to efface the 'anxiety' and emotional confusion caused by the scene. The poetic purpose of his scene painting is not simply realism, although this aspect is striking when compared with Brontë's maudlin caricatures. By demonstrating the inward questioning of each parishioner, Clare captures the complexity of trying to come to terms with death and holds off any rush towards religious comfort. In the psychological realism of the poem such a move would be immediately recognised as a species of denial. Yet Clare is careful not to allow the scene to degenerate into an occasion for easy irony at the expense of the devout. He describes the funeral service with the utmost respect:

> The church they enter, and adown the aisle,
>   Which more than usual wears a solemn hue,
> They rest the coffin on set forms awhile,
>   Till the good priest performs the office due.
>
> And though by duty aw'd to silence here,
>   The orphans' griefs so piercing force a way;
> And, oh! so moving do their griefs appear,
>   The worthy pastor kneels, in tears, to pray.

The orphans' grief overwhelms the sanctity of the rite, and the pastor's tears become a sign of their destabilising power. The interjected 'oh' sounds the crisis created by the failure of the funeral rite to efface the terror of death, and the poem goes on to describe the villagers considering their mortal fate. In the midst of this description the poet/narrator interjects his own anxiety, including a Keatsian anxiety of dying forgotten:

> O Memory! thou sweet, enliv'ning power,
>   Thou shadow of that fame all hopes to find;
> The meanest soul exerts her utmost power
>   To leave some fragment of a name behind.

Despite the conventional poetic complaint sounded by these lines, they gain poignancy through their context in the village economy:

> Here stand, far distant from the pomp of pride,
>   Mean little stones, thin scatter'd here and there,
> By scant means of poverty applied,
>   The fond memorial of her friends to bear.

The diction of these lines, full of dissolution and randomness, plays against the solemn certainty affected by the 'pomp of pride' (false bravado) of the funeral rite, and introduce rural poverty into the poem in the shape of the 'mean little stones' marking village graves. The reality of material conditions also refuses to be subsumed by religious faith, and redoubles the tension in the poem. The tension finally proves more than the poem itself can withstand, as the violent emotional juxtaposition of two stanzas signals the collapse of the fiction of devout certainty in the face of inconsolable grief:

> The gaping grave now claims its destin'd prey
> 'Ashes to ashes—dust to dust,' is given;
> The parent earth receives her kindred clay,
> The soul starts to meet its soul in heaven.

> Ah, helpless babes! now grief in horror shrieks,
> Nor sorrow pauses dumb: each looker–on
> Knows not the urging language which it speaks—
> A friend—provider—this world's all—is gone!

The first stanza struggles to regain religious composure and overcome its lurid imagery of the 'gaping grave', but the promise of heaven proves fleeting as the 'horror' of grief and the recognition of what the orphans have lost once again exceeds the capacity of religious solace. Taken in purely emotional terms, the grief of the children can be explained as natural, and their incapacity for religious compensation as a sign of their youth and lack of intellectual maturity. But, such a reading does not explain why their grief so destabilises the faith of the other villagers and the poet/speaker. In the end, the undeniable social consequences of the death intrude into the scene and show religious solutions to be partial, insufficient to the reality of the everyday. Human suffering must be recognised, and religious belief cannot function as a reliable, stable, replacement for real contentment.

A description of the material fate that awaits the orphans ends the poem:

> Yon workhouse stands as their asylum now,
> The place where poverty demands to live,
> Where parish bounty scowls his scornful brow,
> And grudges the scant fare he's forc'd to give.

> Oh, may I die before I'm doom'd to seek
> That last resource of hope, but ill supplied,
> To claim the humble pittance once a week,
> Which justice forces from disdainful pride!—

Clare ends with bitterness towards the institution of the 'workhouse', and the systematic humiliation of becoming a 'parish case'. Coming as at it does at the end of a description of the piety and devotion of the villagers, the intrusion of this institution, unambiguously the agent of hypocritical and selfish interests, shocks the reader. Irony, which had been kept at bay throughout the poem, explodes as anger at the presumption of the parish. The harshest irony occurs when the speaker appears to overcome his fear of death, not through an enlarged religious capacity, but as an alternative to the humiliating penury of the workhouse. The poem masterfully negotiates the tensions between faith in religious compensation and the realities of social privation, and is all the more impressive for refusing to reduce to caricature the figure of the pastor. His good faith is not placed in doubt because Clare can distinguish between the power of sincere religious belief and religious cant embodied by the hated workhouse. Given the complexity of a poem that successfully combines the solemnity of religious observance, the primal terror of mortality, village social anxiety, and a trenchant critique of hypocritical religious and social institutions, the proposition that Clare's autobiographical references to his conventional religious beliefs evidence a native conservatism seems absurd. When Clare states in his early autobiographical fragments that he holds conventional religious beliefs no political valence should be associated with the statement. Keeping in mind that Clare's beliefs are bound to appear inconsistent and even contradictory given that they come to us in various letters and prose fragments, it is difficult to uncover the politics implicit in them. One way is to compare them to identifiable religiously inflected politics like those of Patrick Brontë, but perhaps the most complex portrait emerges as Clare negotiates the difficult terrain of Lord Radstock's patronage.

*

William Waldegrave, first Baron Radstock, received his title as reward for a distinguished naval career. Friend to Nelson, one time governor of Newfoundland, his life as an admiral had been eventful and fully deserving of a public reward. As Lord Radstock he founded a new line of inherited power within the already powerful Waldegrave family. *The Dictionary of National Biography* entry concentrates, rightly, on his military career but remains vague on the details of the barony. Whether or not Radstock received a land grant in Ireland as part of this new patrimony remains ambiguous. The question inevitably arises in the context of his patronage of a Northamptonshire peasant, and more specifically in relation to his authorship of the prescriptive pamphlet: *The Cottager's Friend or, A Word in Season to Him Who is so Fortunate as to Possess a Bible or New Testament, and a Book of Common Prayer*. F. C. and J. Rivington of St Paul's Church-yard, the distributors and sometimes publishers of the 'Cheap Repository Tracts' and the didactic tracts of the Society for Promoting Christian Knowledge, published the pamphlet in 1816. The copy in the British Library is the 20th edition, which suggests that like the other tracts produced by the Anglican evangelical movement it was widely distributed, most likely to rural parishioners at their Sunday service. Radstock actively engaged in the activities of such societies, and vacillated in his dealings with Clare between exaggerated reverence for his genius under the influence of Mrs Emmerson, and seeing him as an opportunity to pursue his evangelical calling. Given his vision of patronage, it hardly matters whether Radstock actually had tenants and employed agricultural labourers. His pamphlet remains a chilling document whether its intended motive was the practical regulation of the structure of rural class privilege (economically motivated), or the devout act of an evangelical zealot distributing his religious prescriptions (a religious duty).[11] In either case, the pamphlet attempts to impose 'contentment' on the rural poor, an effort we may find rich in irony, but at the time sanctioned by presumed religious authority.

Radstock's family history must play a part in his self-image, and provides a fascinating insight into the aristocratic pretensions and anxieties of the day. William Waldegrave, first Baron Radstock, was the second son of John Waldegrave, third Earl Waldegrave, who was himself the second son of James Waldegrave, the first Earl. John Waldegrave succeeded his brother who died without an heir in 1763. As second sons, Radstock and his father had pursued military careers, each with distinction. In 1765, in his new role as Earl Waldegrave, John Waldegrave abandoned the opposition to George III and accepted the position of master to the horse of Queen Charlotte, solidifying the family's position as Tory insiders. Radstock identified strongly with this family pedigree. After his decisive role in the glorious victory at the Battle of St Vincent in 1797, he refused the honour of being made a baronet, insisting that it was an inferior rank to his actual rank as son of an earl. He finally

consented to being made first Baron Radstock on the Irish establishment in 1800. Regardless if he received a personal landed interest along
with his peerage, the Waldegraves were powerful landowners, and he
identified intensely with his family's privilege. Radstock's self-image as
the founder of a new dynastic line inside an established tradition of
Tory power finds graphic representation in the Radstock coat of arms,
perhaps his own design, which shows a crown atop two crests wrapped
in laurel. To the right of the crest is a rampant hound, and to the left
a defiant eagle grasping thunderbolts as if they were sheaves of grain.
The Latin motto, 'tria juncta in uno', marks his religious devotion, and,
at the bottom of the design are the words St Vincent, marking his greatest
military achievement. Jervis, the commander of the British fleet at the
battle had coincidentally been made first Earl St Vincent as his reward.
It is difficult not to read the crest as self-invention, and he attached it
to the endpaper of a book of evangelical religious devotion he presented
to Clare presumably in an effort to establish his authority as he sought to
instruct the young poet. Underneath this public surface – Tory, royalist,
Hanoverian, Anglican evangelical – lay surprising family origins. James
Waldegrave, first Earl Waldegrave (Radstock's grandfather) was the son of
Sir Edward Waldegrave and Lady Henrietta Fitzjames, the eldest daughter
of James II. The first Earl was named after his royal grandfather. In 1718,
after the death of his Catholic wife (Radstock's grandmother) James
Waldegrave secured his place in infamy, in the eyes of Jacobites, by
announcing himself a Protestant and renouncing the Jacobite cause
that was the source of his family's wealth and power. He became indis-
pensable to the Walpoles, and as ambassador to Paris was at the centre
of anti-Jacobite intrigues. His son James, the second Earl (Radstock's
brilliant uncle), was a great friend of Horace Walpole and had a remarkable career in which he shunned office while attempting to serve as
a broker between George II and Pitt. His abilities as a negotiator led
Walpole to believe that had he not died he would have become leader
of the Whigs and may have been able to create a coalition of parties. In
comparison to the first and second Earls, Radstock's father can only be
described as dull, accepting a royal sinecure as the pinnacle of public
life. Radstock, the second son of the second son, creates, as first Baron,
a self-image verging on parody. Despite his emphasis on aristocratic
lineage and privilege, he certainly does not inform Clare that he is the
direct descendent of James II and a cousin of the Stuart pretender.[11]

The pamphlet begins with a statement of purpose: 'In order to
instruct, and induce the ignorant and unlearned to search the scriptures,
and implant or confirm in the heart of every true Protestant, the

Principles of the Church of England, as by law established' (p. 1). The rhetorical strategy that follows offers little scope for the 'ignorant and unlearned' to 'search' for themselves. Instead, Radstock selects passages, deduces their didactic meaning, and imposes that meaning on the reader. The most persistent line of argument elaborates the axiom that faith is insufficient without actions. He quotes from St James: 'But will thou know, O vain man, that Faith without Works is dead', and from St Paul: '...return ye now every one from his evil way, and make your Ways and your Doings good' (p. 6). Given that every good Christian must put him or herself in God's hands, the evidence of 'good works' becomes the crux of any hope for salvation. Radstock tells his audience that the only sure means to this end involves bringing 'an honest simplicity of mind, to be guided, instructed, and directed' (p. 3) by reading the Bible. However, his authorial role usurps the reader's autonomy and provides instruction in the pursuit of instruction.

Radstock's wider social goals begin to come into focus as he selects examples from the cottager's life to elucidate biblical passages. He explores the axioms: 'Depart from evil and do good', and 'Consider your Ways' in the contexts of labour and servitude. He conflates 'works' with 'work', and being a 'faithful servant of God' with being a 'faithful servant' (p. 7). The first part of the pamphlet draws conclusions from scripture, and generally provides biblical direction for the reader. In concluding that section, he exhorts his audience to 'obedience':

> Therefore let me now beseech you, to work with that earnestness, constancy, and unweariness in well doing, as if thy works alone were able to save thee; and so absolutely depend and rely on the merits of Christ for justification and salvation, as if thou hadst performed one act of obedience in all thy life. This is the right gospel frame of obedience,—so to work as if we were only to be saved by our merits, and withal so to rest on the merits of Christ, as if we had not wrought any thing. It is a difficult thing to give to each of these its due in our practice. When we work, we are too apt to neglect Christ; and when we rely on Christ, we are too apt to neglect working. But that Christian has got the right art of obedience who can mingle these two together; who can with one hand work the work of God, and at the same time lay fast hold of the merits of Christ. (p. 8)

The cottager's labour is authorised by God, and 'obedience' in his or her tasks signals certain salvation. Lest the cottager draw dangerously near religious enthusiasm, a balance must be struck between 'work' and reliance on Christ's mercy. Any show of 'discontent' would betray a lack of faith in God's providence, and any dissent from existing conditions of labour would constitute sin. The insidiousness of this doctrine lies in its wilful confusion of the cottager's physical labour and 'good works'. Part II develops this convenient doctrine through prescriptive passages on 'Leading a Godly and Christian Life' (p. 12), and by offering 'Prayers for Particular Persons' (pp. 15–20).

As a doctrine of social control the formulations in Radstock's pamphlet make perfect sense: 'Honour all men. Love the Brotherhood. Fear God. Honour the King' (p. 13). The inevitable corollary to these dicta carries an implicit threat. We must submit ourselves to 'governors as unto them that are sent by him [the King] for the punishment of evil-doers' (p. 13). In short, to disobey civil authority is to disobey God's will, and thus the first prayer he offers institutes social and political hierarchy: 'Prayer for the King's Majesty, the Royal Family, &c. &c.' (p. 14). That the King is George III, violently insane and feeble, and that the Royal Family includes the utterly ridiculous Prince Regent, of course has no bearing. They inhabit a God-given position and cannot be dele-gitimised by their behaviour. The subsequent prayer to 'Lord King George' begins by stating that he was 'set over us' by God. It hardly needs stating that Radstock's social status cannot be questioned from this perspective, and that his authority to instruct the 'lower orders' equally becomes an unquestioned 'natural' consequence of the divine will of God. The social force of this divinely ordained authority strikes home in the final section of the pamphlet, 'Prayers For Particular Persons' (pp. 15–20), instructing the labourer to pray:

> Let thy goodness, and thy commands, incline me in all things to obey thy blessed will, and that I may love my neighbour as myself, and forgive and live in charity with all the world. That I may obey such as have the rule over me; be just in all my dealings; true and faithful in my words and promises. That I may be temperate, sober, and chaste; lead an honest and godly life, be content with my condition, and never desire to better it by unjust ways. (pp. 15–16)

'Contentment', as always, was the social value at issue, and the word, 'content', dominates the rhetoric of the remaining prayers: 'That the Lord may bless our honest endeavours, and make us *content* with what His providence shall order for us', or '...give us *contented* minds' (pp. 17–18, italics mine). The series of prayers for labourers culminates in an unflattering portrait of a 'discontented' rustic even as it exhorts him to be 'content': 'Keep me from all self-conceit and petulance, from *discontent* and murmuring, and give me a meek and humble spirit... make me useful and serviceable, and happy and *contented*, in the station to which it hath pleased thee to call me' (p. 21, italics mine). Any 'murmuring' indicated the 'self-conceit' of wanting to improve your lot, and an interest in reform betrayed the sinner who was 'discontented' with 'the station' that God had selected for him.[12] The choice of the word 'murmuring' to describe 'discontent' indicates the level of Radstock's anxiety. Despite the threats of religious sanction, even divine retribution, and his Lordship's relentless imposition of his presumed authority, the pamphlet must be one of the most anxious documents of an anxious age. Radstock feels driven to regulate every member of the rural peasantry and in every task that they might perform; thus housemaids are made to pray that they do not awaken the sexual desires of their masters, labourers must pray that they do not murmur at long hours and starvation wages, and so on. The pamphlet creates a veritable catalogue of rural 'discontent', and comes into being as a neurotic rearguard action simultaneously in denial of, and obsessed by, the mood of near total 'discontent' that permeated the countryside. Perhaps only in London, playing the part of the powerful rural landlord, could Radstock have produced such a pamphlet. Its capacity for self-delusion would be difficult to match, because, unlike most propagandists, Radstock successfully sublimated his reactionary politics in religious cant. Most polemicists of the time recognised that they were making strategic use of presumed religious authority. Radstock's absurdly pious tone suggests he lacked the capacity for such reflection.

*

Clare's relationship to Radstock, of necessity, keeps to a middle course. In his letters and journal he displays a sincere gratitude for what he perceives to be Radstock's role in his literary success. Clare's perception that Radstock's subscribers held the key to his success came from several sources; Taylor and Hessey encouraged deference in order to protect sales, Mrs Emmerson provided constant reminders of his Lordship's influence as a means of securing her own claim to Clare's feelings, and Radstock himself asserted his moral standing at every opportunity (often in the form of homilies included in the books he sent). Clare operated under the assumption that his Lordship's intentions were noble and sincere, and responded with an appropriate sense of gratitude. He did not however simply defer to Radstock's views, and the letters and journal entries reveal a complex and occasionally conflicting set of relations. Clare often referred to Radstock as his 'best friend'[13] for his early support and tireless efforts at expanding his subscriber's list. His Lordship's social contacts went a fair way in guaranteeing a ready audience for Clare's future works, and Taylor himself fostered the impression that Radstock's contributions were crucial to the poetry's success. Taylor provided Clare with the details of the £300 Radstock's subscription had raised by the middle of April 1820, and when Clare exulted in his new-found prosperity at the largesse of the Marquis of Exeter ('15 guineas a year for life'), Taylor made it clear that such generosity was the direct result of Radstock's influence.[14]

Clare's gratitude at the prospect of financial security should hardly come as a surprise. He understandably hoped to write full time, and while Radstock shared this goal he nonetheless confided to his friend Markham Sherwill that Clare's growing financial independence posed risks:

> I consider the money so generously lavished by Lord Milton & his father, upon John Clare as so dangerous a <u>temptation</u>, that I tremble for the consequences. Had his Lordship placed the poor fellow in a comfortable Cottage rent free, and added to that liberally [liberality?] a Cow & a few pigs, his Lordship would, in my humble opinion, have acted more wisely and certainly would have render'd our protigé a far happier man. (emphasis his)[15]

Given his history, Radstock's paternalism comes as no surprise, and the rest of the letter follows the same logic of class intervention, and exudes a deep anxiety lest *their* poet become too independent. He writes Taylor requesting: 'Dury to keep a strict eye upon Clare, that we may have a better chance of keeping him within bounds.' For Radstock, Clare presented a cultural opportunity to instruct the lower orders, and while he sympathised with his poverty, he nonetheless feared it alleviation: 'This poor peasant is certainly vain, and his temper has been sour'd by the neglect which he has till of late experienced. We must, therefore, be cautious not to [?] him further, but, on the contrary, endeavour to soothe his feelings, and restore him to his *natural* character, which, to judge by his writings, I have no doubt was originally good & praiseworthy' (emphasis mine). Radstock acts to recover and preserve Clare's 'contentment', the identical goal of his didactic pamphlet, and he closes the letter with an 'effusion' concerning the potential Clare might fulfil with the moral and artistic intercession of he and his friend Sherwill:

As Clare appears by his letter to look up to you with that respect & attention which he ought to do, I have no doubt that he would attend to your councils with gratitude. Such advice as you would naturally offer to him, could not fail of producing the most desirable effects. Besides, should your generous benevolence lead you into a sort of regular correspondence with this poor fellow, such correspondence must necessarily be attended with countless advantages to him. How it would expand his mind! What edifying instruction would it not afford him! How much would it not add to his present circumscribed vocabulary. What a power of eloquence would he not speedily acquire by having his soul thus unfettered, and all its now dormant beauties drawn forth by those sage councils, that sympathizing pity, that noble & disinterested benevolence which such a correspondence as yours would so assuredly unfold to him!

Pardon this incoherent effusion, my dear Sir, for I find that my heart has been entirely getting the better of my judgement. In a word,—I feel too much at this moment to be rational.

Clare represents ample potential for improvement: artistically, linguistically and morally. His Lordship and Sherwill are the primary beneficiaries of these improvements via their truly extraordinary capacity for self-regard. Even in his 'effusion' concerning Sherwill's moral superiority, Radstock manages to bring the rhetorical purpose of his letter round to his own sensibility – the fineness of his capacity for feeling.[16] At this stage in their relationship, Clare had no inkling of Radstock's desire to meddle and improve – cultivate the peasantry, but he would soon feel Radstock's obsession for keeping him 'within bounds'.

5
'Medlars'

The first manifestation of Radstock's need to control Clare is well known and took the form of censorship. In his letter to Taylor of 16 May 1820, Clare described the pressure that had been brought to bear on him from Radstock via letters from Sherwill and Mrs Emmerson:

> Being very much botherd lately I must trouble you to leave out the 8 lines in 'helpstone' beginning 'Accursed wealth' & two under 'When ease & plenty'—& one in 'Dawnings of Genius' 'That necessary tool' leave it out & put ***** to fill up the blank this will let them see I do it as negligent as possible d——n that canting way of being forcd to please I say—I cant abide it & one day or other I will show my Independance more stron[g]ly then ever you know who's the promoter of the scheme I dare say—I have told you to order & therefore the fault rests not with me while you are left to act as you please.[1]

I quote the entire letter because very often critics only consider Clare's outburst about the 'canting way of being forcd to please', and the letter reveals a complex strategy for resisting the efforts of Radstock, 'the promoter of the scheme', to establish himself as the de facto editorial censor of Clare's work. Critics have been moved by the pathos of Clare's inability to resist his powerful patron, and the letter has long served as a pillar in the construction of the 'poor Clare' tradition. Yet, Clare's resistance is not entirely deferred to some future moment when he might show his 'Independance'. He directs Taylor to simply omit lines, refusing to rewrite the poem 'to please', and, furthermore, making it visually apparent to these meddlers that he has been negligent in the face of their demands. By insisting that rows of asterisks take the place of the 'offending' lines, Clare asserts his independence by refusing to recant the radicalism of the original lines. Indeed, any new readers of the poems would immediately be alerted to the fact that the poems had been adulterated. The end of the letter betrays an even more subtle resistance; in reporting these demands to Taylor 'to order' Clare relieves himself of any responsibility should Taylor *choose* to ignore him and reprint with the poems intact. He can claim to acquiesce while passing responsibility to Taylor who is in a less vulnerable social position and better able to see the meddlers off. This proved to be a successful strategy for the present and preserved the lines in the next printing, even though he and Taylor eventually gave in with the subsequent edition.[2] In short, the letter reflects much more than Clare's considerable frustration at his lack of power. He manages that anger and acts to resist editorial interference as much as possible.

The following January found Radstock's efforts at censorship vigorous as ever. Taylor wrote to ask Clare's opinion on possible changes to 'Helpstone' for the fourth edition in an effort to appease his Lordship in the short term, and to alert him that success as a censor had increased Radstock's appetite for interference:

> ...what are we to with those 8 lines L[ord] R[adstock] marked out of Helpstone? I cannot print the 4th Edit. From not thinking it right to omit them—you must determine for yourself. Taking 8 away, the preceding Lines end too abruptly; send 2 more af[ter] them, & 2 more after them, and the Pause is li[ttle] better. —Shall we alter the Word 'Accursed' to *Insa[tiable]* or *Despotic*? I dislike all comparison with the original. —To print the passage in X X X X X would look too pointedly reproachful of those who had rendered it necessary. —Again, in The Peasant Boy, Lord R. has put his Mark 'This is radical Slang' against 2 of the best Stanzas, viz. 107 'There once were Lanes &c' & 108 'O England, boasted Land of Liberty'—Are these to be omitted also?—If so, others will be offensive next, & your Poem will be like the Man who had 2 Wives. —for I shall pluck out all the white hairs.[3]

It comes as no surprise that Clare's political elegies were Radstock's continuing target. Taylor's equivocation in response presents greater problems. On the one hand we can only applaud his anger at being asked to weaken the force of Clare's poetry, and his taste for Clare's forthright political verse. On the other hand, his hand-wringing and general timidity irritates now as it did then. Clare had suggested the addition of a row of asterisks in place of the 'offending passage' precisely because the poem *would* be marred by Radstock's imposition, and the result would be a public 'reproach' for such interference. Clare's response to Taylor's cautious approach in his letter of January 9 1821 is in sharp contrast:

> —put in *despotic* & in the 5th Edit. alter it agen to 'cursed'   never mind Lord R[adstock]'s pencelings in the 'Peasant Boy'   what he dont like he must lump as the dog did his dumplings   I would not have 'There once were lanes' &c left out for all the Lord Rs in Europe   d——n it do as you like   I tell you if you like to print 'cursed' too print it—'& a fig for the sultan & sophy'[4]

Clare's angry response focused on Radstock, but his frustration with Taylor sounds throughout the passage. He had after all reminded Taylor in his letter of 20 December 1820 that he had foolishly made the inter- ference of Radstock and Emmerson possible by 'giving those lady-birds liberty to peruse M.S.S.'[5]

Displeasure with Taylor had already emerged from another source. Clare's provisional victory in preserving the inherent politics of the poems was tempered by defeat on another front. When the third edition appeared, Taylor had given in to pressure of another kind and excised 'Dolly's Mistake' and 'My Mary' because of their presumed vulgarity. The sexual frankness of the poems offended a certain segment of the reading public, perhaps best represented by the fastidious Mrs Emmerson. Writing to Hessey, Clare blamed Taylor directly, and ridiculed his bowing to social pressure: 'I often picture him in the midst of a circle of "blue stockings" offering this & that opinion for emprove- ment or omission'.[6] This unflattering portrait, the nervous publisher swayed by superficial opinion, indicates the intensity of Clare's bitterness. He took the attack on Dolly to be an attack on him, and on rural folk generally. Inveighing against the hypocrisy of 'false delicasy', he defended Dolly precisely because of her social vulnerability: 'what in the name of delicasy doth poor Dolly say to incur such malice as to have her artless lamentations shut out—they blush to read what they go nightly to balls for & love to practice'. According to Clare, Dolly's recognition of her sexual nature and 'artless' refusal to act the fallen woman offended a middle-class audience by unsettling their repressed sexuality. Clare's refusal to moralise about Dolly's state, pregnant and abandoned, could only be interpreted as an immoral tale. Wordsworth had the decency to drive Martha Ray mad, whereas Dolly faced her ruin as a commonplace of village life. Indeed, the issue for Clare was how this incident, cutting 'Dolly's Mistake' and 'My Mary', reflected a weakness of judgement on Taylor's part. His trusted editor had failed to defend Dolly as a real member of the labouring poor, and in so doing had failed to defend Clare's poetic principles. Instead he had allowed his judgement to be 'tainted by medlars *false delicasy*'. Clare reacted with withering sarcasm: 'I think to please all & offend all we should put out 215 pages of blank leaves & call it "Clare in fashion"', and he recognised that to succumb to 'polite' taste was to abandon his readers among his own class. The very frankness and realism of portraying the everyday problems and concerns of village life had struck a chord with many readers, and Clare defended their taste: '"Dollys mistake" & "my Mary" is by the multitude reckoned the two best in the book'. His outrage at Taylor's presumption even included an idle threat to leave Taylor & Hessey as soon as he was able to serve as his 'own editor'. By writing to Hessey with his complaint he avoided a direct confrontation with Taylor, and the possible consequences of such a scene, while still making his displeasure and disappointment known in the most forceful terms. Indeed, Clare continued to press Taylor to restore the poems in subsequent editions: 'I forgot to remind you about putting in "My Mary" & "Ways of the Wake" in this 4th Edit also the "Country Girl" the omission of the 2 first cut my muses wings cursedly'.[7] The explicit message of his insistence—efforts at censoring his poetry on these 'false' grounds threatened his very ability to write.

'Meddling' did not always take literary forms. Radstock, as his correspondence with Sherwill indicates, was more than capable of interfering in Clare's day-to-day existence. A close examination of one such incident, however, reveals a surprising and complex relationship between poet and patron. During April 1820 Radstock had taken it upon himself to write to Lord Milton to lobby to have a cottage built for Clare, thus putting into motion his and Sherwill's plan for his maintenance. Mrs Emmerson wrote Clare to report on Radstock's efforts and complain that his exhortations had been met by stony silence. Clare wrote to Sherwill on 3 May 1820 to try to calm the feelings of the Radstock camp:

> I understand from Mrs E[mmerson] he [Radstock] has written twice to Lord [Milton] & received no answer I did not feel easy for such neglect he could have been as careless with me he had a right to have it answered—I therefore took up my pen independantly & wrote to him my self stating the kindness Lord R[adstock] had done towards me & that all done was without proposal what ever & that if such things troubld his Lordship I was independant & did not wish it

therefore when you see Lord R. again tell his Lordship not to write any more about requesting a cottage as it seems not agreeable to Lord M[ilton]s intentions I have no doubt he will do somthing but I believe he is one that must have time to consider he is not so open hearted as Lord R.[8]

Clare handles Radstock, via Sherwill's mediation, with great skill. He at once sympathises with Radstock's hurt feelings, yet takes care to suggest that Lord Milton may simply be a 'careless' correspondent, and thus cautions against reading too much into the perceived 'neglect'. Clare further demonstrates his concern by writing directly to Milton on Radstock's behalf, extolling his Lordship's generosity and disinterestedness. At the same time, he achieves a more crucial goal, intervening so that Radstock will stop pestering Lord Milton and cease his meddling. Clare makes it possible for Radstock to believe that the fault in the dispute lies with Milton, without making any negative judgement against the Fitzwilliams in whose patronage he has the utmost faith.

Given Clare's diplomatic skill in this affair, Taylor's response to Clare writing an 'independant' letter to Lord Milton takes on new significance. Taylor wrote on 16 May, fearing the worst: 'If you have said anything which can offend Lord Milton I shall be sorry...In my Opinion, you have no better friends than Lord Milton and Earl Fitzwilliam'.[9] Clare's anger at Taylor's presumption manifests itself in his marginal comment on the letter: 'I know that—who said I had.' He makes it clear to Taylor in his response of 20 May that he believes such concern to be misplaced: 'dont be under aprehensions of an offence to Lord M[ilton] I know my friends too well to offend em so cheaply I know very well the Milton family is my best patrons & I am in no fear but of them continuing to be so.'[10] The evidence of the letter to Sherwill justifies Clare's confidence in being able to mediate in this dispute between patrons, and Taylor's letter comes across as absurdly alarmist in tone, and condescending in its assumption that Clare could not, and indeed should not, attempt to speak for himself. Clare's autonomy is the subject of these exchanges, and he shows himself to be 'independant' and unwilling to accede to Taylor's view of the deference required in his relationships with patrons. Earlier in his letter Taylor had outlined the safe course: 'Whatever your Patrons, as they are accustomed to style themselves, may do, be as quiet & indifferent as possible yourself, & mingle with no one's Quarrel.' Clare chafed at this suggestion in large part because he conceived of his relationship to these men as true friendship between equals, and saw his role in mending the strained feelings as a part of his natural role as a friend. The dispute had to do entirely with his future, so who else could be qualified to mediate between parties. From this perspective, Taylor's concerns can only be understood as unfounded class anxieties, unfounded and unfair to those involved in the dispute. Not even Radstock, in his paternalistic fantasies, objected to Clare writing to him directly on the matter, nor to his intervening on his behalf with Milton. The ultimate irony of the incident lies in the fact that while two powerful men haggled over the material terms of Clare's patronage, and his editor fretted over the possible outcome, Clare, the object of patronage, took the initiative and led the various parties to resolve their differences. His resistance to the deference that Taylor advised not only proved astute, but also demonstrated active participation in defining the terms of his patronage.[11]

Lord Radstock's most potentially serious 'meddling' took the form of efforts to alienate Clare from Taylor and Hessey in an effort to gain complete control over publication of the poems. On 16 December Taylor wrote to Clare in a state of agitation over recent correspondence with Radstock. Without having consulted Clare Radstock presumed to challenge Taylor's legal relationship to the poet, and the terms by which the poems were published. Taken aback, Taylor appealed to Clare for support and demanded clarification of their relationship. He quoted from his response to Radstock: 'I will write to Clare to know whether we are to treat with him or your Lordship for the Copyright of his next Volume.'[12] This response called Radstock's bluff (he had no authority in the matter whatever), and also brought the seriousness of the situation home to Clare. In Taylor's view, Radstock intended to force him out of the game and assume control of Clare's future. Given Radstock's pattern of mindless meddling, and reprehensible attitude toward members of Clare's class, such a possibility must have sent a chill. While understanding his debt to Radstock, Clare had few illusions about his Lordship's motives and interests. Taylor reported Radstock's puffing verbatim: 'had Clare's poems appeared without an Introduction, and no Lord Radstock had stepped forth in support of the Work, my own private Opinion is that a second Edition wod not have shewn itself.'[13] Taylor's strategy of letting Radstock damn himself by quoting from his letters proved effective, and provided Clare with the necessary rationale for the proposition that they draft a formal agreement codifying their hitherto informal arrangements.[14] Taylor made it clear that he believed such an agreement to be unnecessary except as a means of to 'keep off Meddlers like him [Radstock]'. He assured Clare that such an agreement would not affect their working relationship by adding a tone of formality and distance: 'We [Taylor & Hessey] can still act towards you with as much goodwill as if no document existed.' Taylor made it unmistakably clear that he had reached his limit with this latest interference, and that his relationship with Radstock was at an end. The burden of dealing with such an obtuse and somewhat absurd individual could be happily relinquished: 'I am quite happy to be free from Lord R's distressing Civility and the overwhelming Honour of his Correspondence.' However, he ended the letter with a proviso: 'But I would not have you quarrel with him on the present occasion: perhaps he means you well, and would call you ungrateful.' The term 'ungrateful' had already been applied in the case of the contested passage from 'Helpstone', and despite his personal reservations Taylor could not avoid the element of truth in Radstock's exaggerated opinion of his role in Clare's success.

Clare's letter in response, 18 December 1820, conceded Radstock's past kindness and continuing influence while expressing outrage and frustration at his Lordship's presumption. Clare put his debt plainly: 'Lord [Radstock] I own as a friend & one in the first order.'[15] Furthermore, he reminded Taylor that while Radstock may be a 'strutting mountebank', he was a strutting mountebank with impeccable connections to the Tory ministry. Clare included Radstock's promise that Lord Liverpool, the Prime Minister, would himself take an interest in Clare's next volume owing to his Lordship's influence. So despite his grave reservations about Radstock's character and motives, and conceding the justification for Taylor's curt response to Radstock's interfering letters, he nonetheless felt compelled to remind Taylor of the possible consequences of his action: 'but your note to Lord R tho perfectly appropriate on your part will not pass in its progress without (I fear) taring a hole in my next subscription list.' Nevertheless, the general purport of the letter declared his solidarity with Taylor, and shared his outrage at the lamentable display of vanity on Radstock's part. To the proposition that no second edition would have appeared without Radstock's efforts, Clare declared:

> —this urges me to give it readily the lie which (when my merits is put aside for puffing to come strutting in & say I am the mountebank that got Clare a name with the public) I would contradict in the face of any man let his titles be what they may—

Clearly, Clare had the measure of Radstock and was under no illusions about his Lordship's true motives for patronage, the creation of a cultural stage on which to strut. Radstock's machinations had the immediate goal of taking a proprietary interest in Clare's career. Clare, accordingly, encouraged Taylor to have their mutual friend Richard Woodhouse draw up an agreement formalising and securing his relationship to Taylor and Hessey and thus, hopefully, bring Radstock's meddling to an end.[16]

Clare believed that Radstock could be managed and took the initiative with Taylor in developing a pragmatic strategy. Throughout the last part of 1820 and early 1821, Clare performed the difficult task of remaining loyal to Taylor & Hessey, often at the most personal level of comforting Taylor in the face of Radstock's mischief, while taking care not to alienate his Lordship before the appearance of *The Village Minstrel*. Damage to the subscription list could put his career at risk, so the need to remove Radstock from any editorial influence had to be balanced against the short-term need to ensure he felt respected. Again, such inversions of our common understanding of the power dynamics of patronage were part of everyday life for Clare as he waited for the publication of his new volume. Not only did he need to offer reassurance to Taylor, who threatened to withdraw because he was unappreciated, he had to deal with Radstock to whom he was grateful, yet toward whom he harboured few illusions. Radstock was best understood as a petulant child whose moods could be managed, and whose short attention span cut both ways. On the one hand, his capacity for interference could be overcome by taking the long view (short-term amelioration while ignoring his demands in subsequent editions publications), on the other hand, the same childish lack of attention meant that his commitment to Clare might prove equally transitory. Clare tried to convince Taylor of the soundness of his strategy towards Radstock by offering a withering character sketch of his Lordship:

> I must keep his Lordship yet & with all his weaknesses I cannot help but feel grafull for what what he has done me tho I may feel more at liberty when the next vol is come out & you have mentioned him in the introduction he will then I conjecture have his lookd-for-reward & gradually withdraw himself from me to seek another novelty[17]

At this juncture, late December 1820, Taylor was at the end of his rope and fearful that Radstock had some unknown influence over Clare. Clare took the extraordinary step of offering to provide documentary evidence to prove his faithfulness in the form of Radstock's recent letters, which he characterised as absurd instances of his Lordship's capacity for 'flummery'. Radstock's comically portentous tone in those letters, rather than their content, provided Clare with the evidence he hoped would convince Taylor that they were dealing with a delusional child and he had nothing to fear from such a superficial and silly man – whatever his political connections. Clare called attention to a specific phrase in Radstock's previous letter that made his point. Radstock characterised Clare's debt to him for having sent Mrs Emmerson to Fleet Street to interfere in hyperbolic terms: 'kindness in so doing demands more than you will ever be able to repay.' The utter silliness of the proposition that Radstock had set out to save Clare through his emissary Mrs Emmerson doubtless elicited at least a smile if not laughter from Taylor, and doubtless that was Clare's intention, given the psychological portrait he deduced from the letter for Taylor's benefit: 'a man that has weakness to talk so is to be forgiven in all he talks of for I believe vanity is his ruling passion & that I can forgive.' Clare can forgive Radstock because his vanity makes it impossible to take him seriously, and he counselled Taylor to do the same. The several purposes of the 18 December letter, to calm Taylor while ensuring that no premature break with Radstock and his precious subscribers list occurred, make it a fascinating document for understanding the subtle skill Clare required in charting his career. He ended the section of the letter dealing with editorial interference by declaring his unconditional loyalty to Taylor & Hessey and assuring Taylor that if relations continued to deteriorate between him and Radstock, he, Clare, would unequivocally choose his publishers over his erstwhile friend: 'yet when it [Radstock's interference] can no longer be endur I shall be happy to confess I prefer T. & H. to the multitude—but when vanity even if it was on a sign post sees her name & tittle tattle generosity recorded [in the introduction to *The Village Minstrel* and the inclusion of the sonnet 'To Lord Radstock'] good bye patronage & with a welcome I say.' The bravado of this declaration of their future independence from meddlers, however, followed a concise restatement of the practical necessity of keeping his Lordship happy until the success of the next volume released them from the admittedly onerous task of bearing Radstock's machinations and moods. Clare was as forceful as possible in making this clear to Taylor, whose patience was at an end:

> I wish to keep peace & to keep all the friends I have met with in fact those that are worth keeping therefore whatever may be your dislike always as my friend I know you will never dislike to do any thing that is for my benefit in the end & I have the same confidence that you will even be polite to those whom you may find impossible to please rather then make me the looser

While the tone of the letter remained informal, Clare nonetheless intended these statements as explicit authorial instructions for his publisher to follow. He insisted that despite their personal distaste, preserving Radstock as a 'friend' of Clare's career was imperative at that stage. While delivered in a friendly tone, Clare's stated understanding that Taylor would not betray his interests out of personal pique stood as an implicit warning and reminder of his responsibilities as a publisher and 'friend'.

Clare elaborated his shrewd analysis of Radstock's vanity and motives in the letter to Taylor of 21 December 1820, and expanded it to include Mrs Emmerson. His psychological perceptiveness served him well. While he recognised that they were his 'friends' inasmuch as they had worked tirelessly to make his work known to the other members of their social circle, Clare nonetheless detected underlying selfish motives. By offering an arch portrait of these motives to Taylor, Clare further set his publisher's mind at ease about the intertwined issues of editorial interference and control, reconfirming his loyalty. This rhetorical motive, comforting Taylor by telling him what he wanted to hear, does not diminish the insightfulness of the passage:

> If E[liza] L[ouisa] E[mmerson] & L[ord] [Radstock] had found me out first & Edited my poems what monsters they woud have made can it be possible to judge I think praises of self & selfs noble friend & selfs incomparable poems undoubtedly shovd into the bargain woud have left little room for me & mine to grow up in the esteem of the public but shoulderd into a dark corner they woud have servd as a foundation for their own buildings & dwindled away like a tree surrounded with Ivy while the names & praises of patron & poetess flourishd in every page[18]

Clearly, Clare had the measure of his influential friends, and was able to take their professed friendship for what it was without confusing their interest in him with altruism. Their individual searches for self-confirmation led them to Clare, he recognised the fact (even if they did not), and such awareness allowed him to measure the need for subscribers against the prior need for artistic independence.

Despite Clare's tone of comic dismissal, the threat to Taylor was real. He and Clare had no formal agreement, and Radstock clearly had the means to secure a new publisher. A letter to Taylor the following March mentioned Radstock's connections in passing while offering typically frank views on London publishers and printers. Clare lamented the pŕactice of publishers puffing themselves on their title pages instead of their authors. He singled out John Murray and mentioned his connection to Radstock:

> —what conscieted title pages Murray puts out—in this book I have now its called a new Edition so it may in the title page—& at the end its 'London John Murray'   the fellows consiets unbearable   this is Lord R[adstock]'s fine publisher—peoples to be noticed but little that praises one so much & then finds out another that deserves surpassing praises if any one woud be rulable & suffer to be led by the hand of such like they might be dragd from 93 Fleet St Albemarle[19] &c &c &c till they found themselves at last with Mr Pitts at Seven Dials or Evans in Smithfield singing their pennoths of pennyancs on the suppressors of vice in brown & blue paper with the benevolent & enlightening Authors of 'Cottagers Friend' & 'Black Giles'[20]

Radstock appears to have tried to tempt Clare away from Taylor & Hessey with the idea of publishing with Murray. Clare's trenchant indictment of Murray's vanity yet again offered Taylor reassurance. We cannot know what intentions, if any, Murray had towards Clare, but it is not outside the realm of possibility that the prospect of poaching one of the competition's most successful poets might appeal. Clare, however, doubted not Murray's intentions, but Radstock's. He feared that a break with Taylor would make him 'rulable' and thus vulnerable to being 'led'. The prospect that chilled him was ending up losing his autonomy in the service Radstock's reactionary didacticism, as a producer of the poetic equivalent of the Cheap Repository Tracts. That Clare knew the stakes becomes clear with the titles he named. Lord Radstock had sent him various copies of Hannah More's publications, but more importantly he named Radstock's absurdly prescriptive Cottager's Friend'. Clare's ongoing analysis of Radstock's covert motives, reflected in his correspondence with Taylor, showed not only a keen awareness to the possible weakening of editorial autonomy under a less sympathetic publisher, but also that he held his Lordship's hysterical Tory evangelical politics beneath contempt. To find oneself 'in brown & blue paper' at the service of 'the suppressors of vice' meant the end of art. Any critical illusions that Clare considered Radstock to be simply 'benevolent' towards him or any other member of his class should not survive careful consideration of the sarcasm of this letter, and cannot survive an examination of *The Cottager's Friend*, which Clare had obviously read.[21]

Radstock's appetite for meddling persisted despite Clare's hope that he might move on to some 'new novelty'. February 1822 finds Mrs Emmerson writing on Radstock's behalf exhorting Clare that his 'future productions should be brought out through another & a higher channel'.[22] The letter made it clear that the issue was personal antipathy between Taylor and Radstock, and that Clare risked his Lordship's patronage should he refuse to change publishers:

> ...the <u>conduct</u> of certain persons [Taylor], has so thoroughly displeased Lord R. that he cannot take one step to serve you, without feeling he is at the same time serving those who have acted most unbecomingly to him—this reflection necessarily abates the ardour of his Lordships exertions—though very much against the desire of his kind and liberal heart—particularly as far as your welfare is concerned

One of the great virtues of Mrs Emmerson as an historical source is her habit of saying more than she intends. In this encomium to Radstock's 'liberal heart' she let slip a rather 'unbecoming' sullenness, and the letter suggested subtle menace should Clare not consent to value Radstock's displeasure with Taylor above his career. The following year provided an incident for Radstock and Emmerson that, to their minds, justified another attempt to unsettle Clare relationship with his publishers.

In mid-March 1823 Mrs Emmerson wrote to Clare to report a new slight by Taylor against her and Radstock. She recounted how Radstock had met a 'Mr Allen at a country house' and given him the poems. Allen subsequently wrote an effusive 'Critique', which Radstock attempted to place in Taylor's *London Magazine*. Taylor declined, to Mrs Emmerson's obvious outrage:

> After keeping the Article <u>several days</u>, & my writing a 2nd letter to Mr T. the papers were returned to me, with a <u>polite</u> letter explaining Mr T's admiration of the Critique, as to its fine taste, judgements— but regretting that, it could <u>not</u> be <u>advantageously published</u> in the "London", as it would there only be seen by persons, who had already had your Poems—and recommending its publication thro' some other channel.[23] (emphasis hers)

Mrs Emmerson's rush to personalise Taylor's letter and take offence betrayed her, by now, habitual response to anything and everything Clare's publishers had to say. That she could not take Taylor's point that the piece could serve no purpose coming from the *London Magazine* seems odd, yet makes sense if seen as an opportunity to take offence and perhaps finally convince Clare of the unworthiness of Taylor & Hessey. Her letter continued with a bitter rhetorical question concerning both Taylor's judgement and his capacity to act in Clare's best interests:

> Now what pray tell me <u>what</u> <u>you</u> <u>think</u> of your publisher <u>refusing</u> to <u>insert</u> this truly elegant, and in its way Liberal Review of your Poems? (emphasis hers)

Whatever her intent, her letter had no effect on Clare other than to confirm her lack of common sense, her almost comical self-regard, and her absurdly hyperbolic view of Clare's debt to Radstock:

> I hope you will be induced to write a <u>kind</u> letter to the good Lord Radstock—for what does this kindhearted excellent man not deserve from you—I need not say <u>how</u> much, but I will say, all that gratitude & affection can give to him: his generous noble heart overflows with actions good for your welfare. (emphasis hers)

Underlining 'kind' signalled a complaint about the tone of Clare's recent correspondence, and suggests that she and Radstock were concerned that they were losing the battle over control of his career. She characterised Radstock's persistent interference as 'actions good for your welfare', sprung spontaneously from his disinterested 'noble heart'. The over-insistent emotional, interjection, 'but I will say', signalled near panic from the Radstock camp in their ongoing struggle to wrest control from Taylor. However, if her angry emotionalism was strategic, it had little effect. Clare wrote to Hessey with the same concerns Taylor had expressed in his 'polite' letter to Mrs Emmerson, but without the necessity of remaining polite. While sympathetic to the doubtless good intentions motivating his friends, he nonetheless offered a trenchant critique of the proposed purpose of publishing the Reverend Allen's essay and its likely effect:

> Do you know anything of a somthing publishing upon me (a Critique or Essay for I know not the title) by Murray   I can give no opinion on things I have not seen I can only surmise   I believe Lord R[adstock] & Mrs E[mmerson] 2 of my best & very best friends but I have consciet enough in me to think they cannot read the world so well as myself & I must prophecy thus much on its futurity

if its one as to please his Lordship it abounds in praises on my poems which my enemeys will readily conjure up into flatterys: Criticisms overflowing with milk & honey are as vain as those of the reptile uttering nothing but venom of gall & bitterness[24]

He would have been further alarmed had he known the title as it would have confirmed his worst fears, that whatever the essay's merits it could only be received as a partisan piece of flattery meant to further inflate Radstock's sense of his cultural importance. By 1823 Clare had a clear picture of how the reviewing game worked, and easily understood the folly of publishing 'flatterys' after his poetic value had already been established. Such repetition could only create negative responses, and cause Clare embarrassment. That Radstock and Emmerson could not foresee the likely effects of their actions caused Clare to consider them the tolerance one would extend to a wilful child. To publish Allen's essay was foolish and vain; to suggest that it should be published in the *London Magazine* bordering on self-destructive. Clare found himself in the unenviable position of dealing with two friends who had extended personal and public kindnesses to him, yet had difficulty separating their own needs from his and whose actions continually threatened to become counter-productive (harassing the Fitzwilliams, interfering with Taylor, naïvely establishing their status as poetasters, forwarding Radstock's reactionary political agenda). Radstock's work on his behalf came burdened with half-conscious vanity and occasional stupidity.

Clare's worst fears did not materialise. The review in the 28 August 1823 *Sunday Times* used the occasion of Allen's publication to score political points while generally praising Clare's genius. He characterised the review as 'a hardnaturd puff', and conceded that: 'setting politics aside its not amiss'.[25] Radstock's interference continued unabated until his sudden death following an apoplectic fit on 20 August 1825. Clare recorded the news in his journal with typical generosity and candour:

Lord Radstock dyed yesterday he was the best friend I have met with—tho he possessed too much of that simple heartedness to be a fashionable friend or hypocrite yet it often led him to take hypocrites for honest friends & to take an honest man for a hypocrite—[26]

Clare had the grace to convert Radstock's 'simple' nature into a positive characteristic, yet honesty enough to admit his Lordship's intellectual limitations.[27] Radstock's capacity for misjudgement would have been endearing had it not created so much ill will among the range of Clare's 'friends'. Clare would count Taylor among the 'honest men' Radstock had misjudged, and his Lordship himself was guilty of playing the 'honest friend' while acting the 'hypocrite'. In the end, their relationship was unequal not so much in the enormous difference in their social power (patron to peasant), but in Clare's extraordinary dexterity in managing to keep his Lordship as his 'friend'. As Radstock blundered forward through a predictable series of self-aggrandising actions in the self-deluded guise of acting in Clare's best interests, Clare constantly acknowledged the actual good Radstock had done through the organisation of subscription lists and personal promotion of his work. This kernel of good moved Clare to mend fences between this impossible man and his other many 'friends'. It would have been far easier to drop Radstock after the publication of *The Village Minstrel*, but Clare's sense of loyalty to those who helped him caused him to 'put up with distress and be content', at least so far as personal friendship went.

Weighing friends

Lord Radstock presented the most difficult case in Clare's struggle to keep 'all the friends' he had met with, and the demands of such an endeavour forced him to become a shrewd judge of human motives (Radstock's vanity) and of the varieties of human friendship. He experienced both the surprises that evolving friendships provide and the disappointment of discovering the limited scope of static friendships. Radstock offered a constant, if conflicted, set of conditions for friendship. These conditions all came down the same basic demand: that Clare reconfirm Radstock's predetermined ideas of himself as a cultural and political figure. From the demand to 'expunge ungrateful sentiments', to the plan to provide Clare with just enough income to keep him comfortable but hungry, to relishing his status as an arbiter of literary taste by sponsoring the subscription list, Radstock required Clare to reflect a specific image. To Clare's great credit, he was able to extract the 'good' out of the narcissistic enterprise while still recognising that the goodness was a by-product and not the purpose of the enterprise. Until Radstock's death, Mrs Emmerson functioned as an instrument of his Lordship's acts of self-creation (patron, political commentator, moralist), and her friendship with Clare survived and developed following Radstock's death. Her role as Radstock's amanuensis prevented her from becoming Clare's friend despite her ongoing literary advice and passionate need for a kind of literary intimacy. Her effusions of sensibility evolved and became subtler once she wrote for herself and not in the service of his

Lordship. Clare recognised and valued such emotional development, and understood the vast range of human connection possible within the human relationships denoted by the word 'friendship'. Radstock could not be that kind of friend; it is difficult to imagine him performing a disinterested action, and thus for him 'friend' was an honorific. Mrs Emmerson was saved from a similar fate by Radstock's demise.[28]

Clare had long shown the ability to discern the details of the friendship offered by his various patrons. The Marquis of Exeter was his greatest patron if money served as the sole determinant, and Clare's poignant description of their first meeting at Burghley Park says much about the daunting gulf between the two men. As Clare reported in his autobiographical sketch of the meeting, social awkwardness made the meeting almost painful for each party. Clare's obsessive worry about the mud on his hobnailed boots punctuates the entire account. When the Marquis finally noticed his guest's unease he released Clare from his discomfort by sending him to receive his supper with the servants. That action contained equal parts kindness and condescension, but Clare's retelling claims our interest because it displays a reciprocal awkwardness on the part of Exeter as he equally struggled to see his way across the social abyss between them. When Clare reported he had become lost in the enormousness of the great house, the Marquis himself accompanied him into the hall to direct him to the kitchens. That highly informal moment generated the offer of patronage in the form of a slightly embarrassed apology:

> He [the Marquis] sudde[n]ly made a stop in one of the long passages and told me that he had no room in his gardens for work at present but that he would allow me 15 gineas a year for life which would enabale me to pursue my favourite studys at least two days a week (this bye the bye was far better) I was quite astonishd and could hardly believe he had said it[29]

The surprise of this account lies in its description of Exeter's personal quirks. He appears shy and diffident, despite his power and its obvious effect on Clare. Clare's genius obliged him to act, but also destabilised the social hierarchy he dominated. An offer of labour would have been the typical outcome of a cottager's meeting with representatives of the great house, but Clare was not a typical cottager and few cottagers spoke directly to the Marquis. The sudden offer of an income for life takes the place of an offer of employment, and acknowledges Clare's genius. That genius inverted the power relations of the meeting by removing the topic of conversation from the material concerns of employment and into the undefined realm of acknowledging Clare's 'natural' superiority. Clare's poetic gift, and his unlikely story, separated him from others and Exeter appeared sensitive to that difference. At first glance the scene looks like an instance of lordly condescension, a personal response to a sense of *noblesse oblige*, but subsequent accounts of Clare's relationship to Exeter reveal similar moments of awkward mutual respect.

Clare described the specific contradictions of this friendship with Exeter in a letter to Taylor on 15 February 1821. He acknowledged the crass basis of the friendship: 'he's bin my greatest friend yet if money has any conscern for friendship', but went on to personalise their relationship as one based on genuine respect:

> what I value his Lordships generosity was not sought for a soul   he saw the book & the honourabl Mr Pierpoint came over to introduce me to his Lordship   before he was an utter stranger to me & knew no more of me or the Village then yourself did till circumstances occurd[30]

The circumstances of course were the accidental discovery of Clare's poetic genius, and just as Taylor acts to serve and honour that genius, the Marquis has been drawn out of his habitual isolation (he is unfamiliar with both Clare and the village despite their proximity to Burghley Park) to pay his respects to that same genius. To better illustrate the mutual respect that underwrote the friendship, Clare compared the willingness to search out Clare to Radstock's remote self-interest: '—you now see more light on my Patron   what a contrast between Lord R[adstock] & this gentle nobleman'. He had been particularly moved by Exeter's willingness to seek him out: 'twas uncommon kind of his Lordship to come over to helpstone', and confessed that the visit was all the more impressive given his failure to recognise the Marquis in Drury's book-shop in Stamford the previous September. Clare felt embarrassment at having been abrupt to the point of rudeness towards one of his greatest benefactors. That his Lordship could put that incident behind him and seek out Clare in person in his home village to enquire after the status of the forthcoming volume, spoke to the genuineness of the Marquis's admiration for the poetry and its author. The stiff formality of their friendship periodically gave way to moments of genuine respect and concern despite the fact that Exeter's powerful public persona made such connections difficult. As Clare offered by way of psychological explanation for his unintentional rudeness at the chance meeting in Stamford, 'my senses always leave me when I get before these great men'. Significantly, the same can be said for the Marquis in the presence of Clare's genius.

Despite Clare's universal statement concerning the awe created by the presence of 'great men', his experience of his other chief benefactors could hardly be more different. Clare's relations with Milton House and the Fitzwilliams evolved over a few years into an easy intimacy. Through his friendship with the Fitzwilliam retainers Joseph Henderson and Edmund Tyrell Artis, Clare became a part of the household and came and went, used the extensive library, and generally acted as a member of the household. He was included in plans and invited to family events and was treated with intellectual respect as a person of real consequence. Exeter's admirable sense of regard for Clare was always complicated a self-conscious awareness of their difference in social status. Earl Fitzwilliam and his son Lord Milton, as progressive Whigs, honoured Clare because he confirmed for them the 'natural' justice of their political and social goals, support for reform and support for the Greek cause being two conspicuous examples. In a letter to Clare of 12 July 1823, Henderson invited Clare to travel to London to attend the founding meeting of a new British society in support of Greek independence led by Earl Fitzwilliam.[31] For all his genuine kindness, Exeter's friendship never approached this level of respect and inclusiveness, and his Tory politics doubtless served as an inhibiting factor just as the radical Whig cause worked in the opposite direction of deliberately levelling class differences. Needless to say, any glib reference to Clare's relationship to his patrons, as if such a thing were consistent or stable, will not bear scrutiny. Clare and his 'friends', as 'friends', established different degrees of intimacy and different senses of mutuality. Even Radstock's absurd condescension was subject to the ironic inversions necessitated by Clare needing to care for his Lordship as if he were a petulant child. Thus, even if Radstock was oblivious to the nature of his relationship to Clare, Clare most decidedly was not. The unintended irony of *The Cottagers Friend* could not have been lost on Clare, and the politics of 'contentment' (a well established political trope) and the power struggles implicit in determining the terms of patronage were equally clear in his mind. Perhaps Clare's greatest achievement in this regard was to reformulate this overheated social terrain in the terms of 'friendship' without reducing the complexities of such a fundamental human concern.[32] As I have demonstrated, Clare came into a set of already established social and political structures and had to struggle to locate himself in them in such a way that he maintained his own artistic and personal autonomy without sacrificing the personally and professionally sustaining potential of 'friendship'.

6
The Marketplace

In late September 1825 Clare received a letter dated the 22nd from the publisher and music seller James Power requesting permission to publish one of Clare's songs, 'The Banks of Broomsgrove', set to music by John Barnett. Clare quickly replied giving his permission on the condition that he be paid 'a trifle' for the privilege. He offered a brief rationale for such 'remuneration', arguing that he needed to protect his copyright: 'I cannot give them away for nothing lest I forfiet by such permissions any benefits that may arise in future from such publications.'[1] He also acknowledged that having one of his songs set to music could 'go a great way to make a book popular', and he left the amount of 'remuneration' to Power's discretion. Given the mutual benefits of the arrangement, the two parties quickly came to terms. On 29 September Power completed the transaction by agreeing to Clare's terms and promising future trade between them: 'I fully agree & trust you will not find the enclosed (£2—) too small a remuneration for the permission to publish with Music the Words mentioned in my former letter and of which I now send you a proof—With a hope that I may have occasion to apply to you again on a similar subject.'[2] Clare's lack of aggression in the brief negotiation shows an admirable fair-mindedness, yet also again betrays his independence of mind. His advisers had encouraged him to take advantage of Power's situation (Barnett had already set at least two pieces) and demand an extravagant sum. Hessey alerted Clare to Power's interest in advance and told him to 'ask for 5 guineas, even 10'.[3] Mrs Emmerson suggested that two guineas be his future asking price per song. Both Hessey and Emmerson were alert to a new business opportunity as was Clare, but he wanted to establish it on equitable terms. The promise of future trade on these terms justified a cautious approach. After all, Clare did not have to compose songs to be remunerated, but rather release songs already in print. As the poems became more popular, more songs would be set. And, as the songs became popular, more people would buy the poems. This must have looked like a wonderful and near effortless source of supplementary income. Clare soon received further encouragement in this regard when he received a letter from a man named Charles Hodgson requesting permission to publish one of Clare's songs, 'My love thou art a nosegay sweet'. Hodgson set the poem for a friend 'at whose house I frequently peruse your charming poems'[4] confirming the reciprocal nature of the economics of song publication in relation to the continued circulation of the poems. When he replied to Hodgson's request, he apparently applied the rate Power had established because the following letter contained £2, and a remarkable change of tone. Hodgson no longer sounds like an enthusiast caught up in the intimacies of a literary friendship, but rather an entrepreneur who recognises the potential of setting Clare's songs. He, in fact, goes so far as to suggest Clare compose new material to what he perceives to be the current taste:

> Should much like to have another of your songs; one calculated for ladies to sing, and not about <u>love</u>, yet a subject that can be readily felt—if I am <u>intelligible</u>, shall esteem it a favor if you will draw upon the <u>Bank</u> of your <u>imagination</u> for one, about two or three verses long, I have no fear of its <u>stopping payment</u>. Have the kindness to acknowledge the receipt of this, and if agreeable you can take that opportunity of sending me one of your little <u>gems</u> for perusal.[5] (underlining his)

In early 1826 Clare had every right to expect that he had a future both as a song writer, if he so chose, and as his own agent in securing remuneration for setting his extant songs.

This must not have seemed such a surprise to Clare as he had had earlier dealings with Power following the publication of *Poems Descriptive*. In 1820, Clare had been the only one in his circle who had seen the potential in song writing. Despite Power's extraordinary success as the publisher of Thomas Moore's *Irish Melodies*, Clare had been discouraged by Taylor & Hessey in pursuing a project initiated by Power and encouraged by Drury in which Clare would produce a collection of one hundred songs. In the end, some songs were published but the project was not completed. Clare may simply have been too busy. As he wrote to Hessey in July 1820: 'you know by now I have been writing for 'Powers'   he wanted 100 Songs but am worn out'.[6] In retrospect, the loss of such a volume becomes significant. Working on the model of

Moore's celebrated collection, Clare could have produced a volume that established his debt and ongoing connection to the living folk tradition. A letter to Sherwill of the same week makes his intentions clear: 'I have this 7 weeks been weaving up a quantity of Song & Ballad stuff for a celebrated composer in London which I understand will come out in a vol after the form of the 'Irish Melodies'.[7] The reasons for Taylor's reservations about the project were complex. He worried that the copyright would be muddied, and that he would lose his role as copy editor, which, from his perspective, ensured a measure of quality control over the work as it appeared in print. Presumably Power or one of his designees would assume that role. Taylor's reservations made sense, especially in light of the fact that the second volume of Clare's poems had yet to be completed, but his reservations also betray a certain amount of anxiety about Clare's potential independence and ability to deal with several publishers and pursue multiple projects.[8] Despite the fact that Taylor & Hessey's concerns, and those of Mrs Emmerson, were primarily professional and economic, they also betrayed an aesthetic assumption that the songs were less worthy of serious consideration than his poems. Such an assumption shows a misapprehension of at least one of Clare's poetic goals – the recording of the rural society of which he was a part. Mrs Emmerson's distinction between the 'high' and 'low' forms of poem and song would have not made sense to Clare who viewed them as indistinguishable parts of a single compositional process.[9]

Clare's history of interest in composing songs for publication on their own, and to be set to music becomes significant when understood as part of his image of himself as a professional writer. The traditional view has been that Clare was inordinately dependent on Taylor for his professional survival, and while the principal role of Taylor & Hessey in his professional and personal life cannot be questioned, neither can the fact that as early as 1820 he conceived of himself as his own agent in furthering other creative projects outside his primary publication plans. In short, Clare saw himself increasingly as a professional writer capable of making decisions on projects or permission rates as the opportunity or need arose. Changes in the literary marketplace during the 1820s made his judgement in such matters crucial to his creative and financial well being, and his exercise of that judgement was not limited to selling songs.

The annuals and the *London Magazine*

The other new publishing opportunity for verse that emerged in the 1820s was the literary annual. These yearly publications actively solicited manuscripts and poetic contributions, and their quality varied widely. Based on the artistic and publishing successes of *Poems Descriptive* and *The Village Minstrel*, Clare became an obvious target of ambitious editors as they set out stake their claim to a share of the market. The proposal for a new annual for 1826, *The Amulet*, provides a typical instance of how the game was played. The anonymous editor[10] wrote on behalf of the publishers, Baynes & Son, admiring Clare's poetry as 'among the highest literary rank' and alluding to the fine literary company he would be in were he to consent to be 'included among his list of contributers'. The list proves to be impressive in stating that they would be drawing 'among others from Mr Montgomery, Mr Barton, Mrs Hofl [MS torn], Mr Hogg, Mr Conder, Mrs Sherwood, Mr [Miffen?], Mrs Opie, Rev. Mr Marks, Mrs Hemans, Rev. Mr Cunningham, Professor Wilson, Rev. W B Clarke, Rev. I Thornton, Rev. Thomas Wood, Mr Edwin Atherstone, Miss Mitford, Mrs M Leadbetter, Mrs Grant of Saggan &c. &c.'.[11] Doubtless being included in such company played to Clare's vanity as part of the attempt to obtain a contribution, but equally doubtless, inclusion in such a list indicated that Clare was considered a major writer – someone to be courted in the hopes of ensuring a successful enterprise. The editor's appeal proved effective; for example, Clare greatly admired Josiah Conder, both as a poet and as the editor and chief reviewer of the *Eclectic Review*, and he had a similarly high regard for another polymath listed, James Montgomery the poet, essayist, antiquarian and publisher of the influential radical newspaper the *Sheffield Iris*.[12] The plans for the publication were lavish, with the editor emphasising both the network of publication outlets in England, Ireland and Scotland, but also the high quality of paper and engravings to be used in the physical production. Lest his appeals to illustrious company, lavish production, and sophisticated distribution prove insufficient, the editor ended his letter with a skilful offer of financial reward:

> The remuneration will be liberal and just as circumstances will permit, but as there is every prospect of an extensive circulation of the work, the remuneration will of course proportionately increase— and a preference will be always given to those by whose exertions its prosperity may have been established.

Clare succumbed to these entreaties and contributed two poems to *The Amulet* for 1826. The editor responded by paying Clare £2, a pound for each poem. Their subsequent relationship was disrupted because of a mistake at the publishers in which the letter containing the payment and the complimentary copy of the annual were misplaced. A mortified Samuel Carter Hall, the unnamed editor, wrote an abject apology once he discovered the letter among some papers. Despite the lateness of the date, 15 June 1826, and the advanced stage of production, Hall pleaded for forgiveness and hoped that Clare would still send him a contribution 'within a few days'.[13] After being prompted by a second letter on 6 July, Clare obliged and managed to have one poem included in the 1827 edition. Hall sent him £1, and repeated his apologies. The mix-up had meant that there was no time to send back the poems for revision, or the volume would probably have included an additional two poems. Hall, identifying himself for the first time, acted on his own initiative and sent one of the submitted poems to another annual with which he was involved, *Friendship's Offering*.[14] Over the succeeding decade Hall provided Clare with a steady source of supplementary income, and even when Clare later became discouraged with the unpredictability of such publications, he continued to send material to Hall.[15]

The 'liberal remuneration' offered by Hall had obvious appeal as Clare established himself as a professional writer, but there were other rationales besides direct monetary gain for publishing in the annuals and other magazines and newspapers. For one thing, such activity provided at least some independence from Taylor & Hessey, but other complex factors – personal connections, local dissemination of his work, his new social standing as a public man, and the desire to experiment in different poetic voices – played significant roles in deciding whether to contribute to specific publications. An example that appears eccentric on the surface, his participation in the *Scientific Receptacle*, proves a fascinating case in point. Writing in his journal for 4 November 1824, Clare noted receipt of a letter requesting submission of something for a new local venture[16] to be edited by J. Savage. The unusual title of the proposed magazine drew Clare's attention for the wrong reasons:

> Received a letter and prospectus from a Schoolmaster of Surfleet wishing me to become a correspondent to a periodical publications calld 'The Scientific Receptacle'   what a crabbed name for poesy to enlist with.[17]

Clare was not predisposed to poetical schoolmasters, as he noted elsewhere in his journal: 'a rhyming school master is the greatest bore in literature'.[18] Despite his reservations, something in Savage's letter must have appealed. The letter was respectful, but promised no monetary benefit:

> Sir,
>
> I take the liberty of sending you the prospectus of a work, and of saying that the Editors would be highly gratified in having the Honour of your Correspondence. Any thing from your muse would be read with pleasure, and a few Sonnets or short pieces of Poetry would at any time be thankfully received.—The Editors will gladly pay the postage of your Letters.—A good article will be [included? MS torn] in an early number, where your poetical Talents will be noticed in the most flattering manner, and certainly not more so than they deserve.—Your letters addressed to me at Surfleet, will give me the greatest Satisfaction.[19]

Savage could offer postage, generous advertisement of Clare's talents, and literary respect and friendship. Approaching Clare made sense for a new periodical to be produced in Spalding; Clare was the best known and best respected poet in the immediate neighbourhood, and the proximity of the venture put it in good stead. Clare submitted two poems, 'On the Memory of a Lady' and 'Fame—A Sonnet', with an accompanying letter emphasising his admiration for the high moral purpose of the venture and his willingness to assist a 'neighbour'. Somewhat disingenuously, he claimed that he would not normally submit anything, but made an exception in this case: 'I am not in the habit of Writing for Pereodical Publications of any sort—yet as a neighbour I will gladly do anything that may serve to further the Literary Interests of your forthcoming miscellany'.[20] Clare deliberately underplayed the significance of his contributions, characterised as 'trifles', and focused instead on the convivial aspect of the venture. And while the pretence of assisting a 'neighbour' may seem a convenient excuse to send a contribution, part of the gesture must be genuine—how else to explain sending something at all. The promise in Savage's letter of 'a good article' about Clare's talents regardless of whether Clare contributed, and the offer to correspond (also free of conditions), placed the relationship on the basis of friendship rather than business. Clare responded in kind, signifying at least two things: first, that bonds of local filiations and community were important to Clare, and, second, that Clare recognised the potential of developing a local audience. Taylor, Radstock and Mrs Emmerson had carefully developed a sophisticated London readership, but much more could still be done in expanding his readership, especially in the

Midlands and northward, and among the emergent literate middle classes. Savage presented himself as a 'neighbour' who recognised a mutually beneficial relationship. Clare agreed, and was able to expand his audience while securing his new status in his general 'neighbourhood'. Publication of the first issue of the periodical confirmed his analysis of the situation. Savage included both poems and an edited version of Clare's letter of support, and as Clare noted in his Journal entry for 23 March 1825, they 'inserted my poems and have been lavish with branding every corner with "J. Clares"'.[21] As Savage noted in his accompanying letter, this new source of dissemination paid immediate dividends: 'several subscribers to the receptacle have purchased your works on reading your two pieces inserted'.[22] For both participants this established the quid pro quo of the arrangement, and confirmed the advantages of occasional publishing for Clare. This modest success may have influenced his decision to consent to Powers and Hodgson's requests to republish some of his poems set to music.

Clare's desire to create literary friendships through strategic contributions becomes clearer still with the example of James Montgomery. Montgomery was himself a successful poet and editor of the most influential radical newspaper in the West Riding of Yorkshire, the *Sheffield Iris*. Clare's heartfelt admiration of Montgomery's work provided reason enough for him to send a poem for consideration. In the event, he did so behind the mask of having discovered a lost work of one of the 'old poets'. His submission to the *Iris* was the first that he 'fathered on' one of the 'old poets',[23] a practice he soon expanded in his submissions to Hone's *Every-day Book*. Writing in the assumed style of another was not new to Clare. His earlier career at the *London Magazine*, as 'Percy Green', indicates that he wanted to experiment in other poetic voices, and his 'discovery' of lost works, submitted under false names made such experiments possible. J. W. Tibble conjectures that Clare wrote under pseudonyms in order to free himself from the imposed identity of the 'peasant poet', and to receive responses from his readers free from such associations.[24] While the obvious appeal of such a hypothesis – Clare's struggle for artistic autonomy – cannot be denied, there are other considerations that render it too pat a formulation. In a recent persuasive and provocative essay, Mina Gorji argues that Clare's imitation of the 'old poets' marks not an effort at anonymity, but at sociability. She reads Clare's adoption of these poets as an interest in a group of writers already championed by his brother writers at the *London Magazine*, especially Charles Lamb who took them up precisely because they were themselves the representatives of a poetics of sociability and conviviality, a movement against the grain of the rhetoric of the isolated genius.[25] Tibble argues that Clare hoped to gain the 'true' feelings of his fellow writers by hiding behind a mask, but the correspondence with Hessey that forms the basis of Tibble's conjecture shows that the 'deception' was more important to Hessey who felt the delicious thrill of the insider, and presented the idea that unvarnished opinion was to be highly valued:

> We dined at Mr Cary's about a week ago, and among other enquiries Mr C. asked with much Interest who Mr Green was, and expressed himself as being much pleased with the Sonnet in the last number. He had no idea of it being yours, and on that account his testimony was the more valuable.[26]

Clare had been careless in submitting the first Percy Green poem, and the postmark had given the game away. He seemed unconcerned by this, and always viewed it as a literary lark.[27]

In the case of Montgomery, Clare's submission bore all the hallmarks of a literary hoax. He invented an obscure collection of poetry by 'Sir Walter Raleigh, Sir John Suckling, Sir Henery Wooten, Harrington, &c.',[28] and claimed to have found an MS on the flyleaf. The volume, 'The World's best Wealth a collection of choice counsils in Verse & prose',[29] he purported to have been published in 1720, the presumed date of the composition of the submitted poem, 'The Vanitys of Life'. Montgomery was doubtless familiar with the vogue for literary forgery, and, in any event, it appears that the attempt at deception was unsuccessful. In a letter dated 2 March 1825, Clare's friend Joseph Henderson, the head gardener at Milton House, included a copy of the *Sheffield Iris* in which Clare's poem appeared. Henderson congratulated Clare and expressed gratification that Montgomery, in particular, had taken notice of Clare's talent:

> I am greatly pleased at the opportunity that it has offered Mr Montgomery of noticing you in terms so flattering as you will find in his prefatory remarks. I should guess, from the manner in which he notices your Historical sketch that he did not swallow your Red Lyon, but the praise bestowed upon it is equally valuable in either case.[30]

Henderson's pleasure may, in part, derive from his role in Clare submitting work to the *Iris*. A Sheffield newspaper seems an odd choice, and Mrs Emmerson, for one, thought that newspaper publication in general was a waste of Clare's time and talent, an objection noted by Henderson in his letter. However, Henderson's possible participation expands our notion of sociability through his personal connection to Montgomery. The *Sheffield Iris* was the leading voice of radical reform in southern Yorkshire, and the newspaper that best expressed the political views of the Fitzwilliams. Sheffield's proximity to Wentworth Woodhouse, the great northern Fitzwilliam estate, made Montgomery perhaps the key local intellectual in propounding the political ideals for which the family and their Whig faction stood. Montgomery and the *Iris* were to Wentworth Woodhouse what John Drakard and the *Stamford News* were to Milton House. Indeed, the two newspapers occasionally reprinted one another's items.[31] The entire Fitzwilliam household, including Henderson circulated seasonally between these two locales. Mrs Emmerson's dim view of Clare's chosen publication venue may reflect her distaste with Montgomery's politics as much as her view that newspapers were beneath consideration for serious literary work. By corresponding with Montgomery, and participating in the wider cultural activities of the Fitzwilliams, Clare joined a rich intellectual milieu, and the value of such participation cannot be calculated in narrow economic terms. While it seems obvious that cordial relations with his chief patrons was an economic necessity, such a glib explanation cannot account for Clare's genuine excitement in being acknowledged by Montgomery. What particularly pleased him, was not Montgomery's political cachet, but his status as a poet. He recorded receipt of the newspaper in his journal on 19 February 1825, and emphasised his gratification at being recognised by such a man: 'praise from such a man as Montgomery is heart stirring and its the only one from a poet that I have met with.'[32] As Storey notes, Clare admired Montgomery's poetry, especially 'Prison Amusements' written while he was imprisoned in York Castle for political libel.[33] The combination of poetic and political sympathy, and the sociability offered through the extended intellectual family of the Fitzwilliams invested the utmost value on Montgomery's friendship, even if that value did not include monetary gain. During the course of their correspondence, Clare discovered that Montgomery was the author of the poem 'Common Lot', and, as he enthusiastically reported, the poem had been one of his favourites ever since he first came to purchase it 'in a hawkers penny paper'.[34] Clare shared his delight in discovering that one of his earliest enthusiasms for 'modern' poems had been created by his admired brother-poet and friend.

Montgomery forced the issue of authorship the following year. He wanted to include 'The Vanitys of Life' in a collection he was editing,

The Christian Poet: or Selections in Verse on Sacred Subjects. This caused Clare to confess to what Montgomery had already surmised – his authorship. Montgomery's admiration of the poem meant he had to confirm authorship so that he would avoid misleading readers.[35] Clare's confession included an appreciation of the 'old poets' and told the story of his discovery of them in reading 'Ritson's "English Songs", Ellis's "Specimens", and Walton's "Angler"'.[36] Ritson's collection had long been associated with radical politics, and the taste for these writers represented a democratic aesthetic predicated on brotherhood and the free exchange of ideas, a set of poetic values already promulgated by Lamb in his 'Elia' essays in the pages of the *London Magazine.*[37] Clare ended the letter by thanking Montgomery for encouraging him with his praise of the poem, and further confessing that he had 'fathered' other poems on these writers including one called 'On Death' on Marvell in Hone's *Every-day Book.* In addition he had placed several in the *European Magazine,* 'fathered' on Wooton, Harrington and Davies. In the spirit of his full disclosure, he offered Montgomery the poem, 'To John Milton, from his honoured friend, William Davenant'. The poem appeared in that guise in the *Iris* of 6 May 1826, signifying Montgomery's appreciation not only of the verse, but of the intellectual play surrounding it. Indeed that spirit reflected the sociability that Lamb had isolated as a primary value of the poetry they were championing and imitating.

William Hone represented an obvious publisher for Clare's new secondary career as an 'old poet'. Clare probably met Hone in 1823 during one of his trips to London; they knew many of the same writers in Taylor's circle.[38] Clare sent a presentation copy of his poems to Hone in that year in an effort to cement their friendship which Clare feared would fade with their geographical distance from one another. Montgomery was no stranger to Hone either, as they shared the same radical politics and network of political contacts. Hone was a hero to the cause, successfully defending himself against the charge of blasphemous libel three times in 1817, and author of the most trenchant political satire of the age, *The Political House that Jack Built.* He also employed George Cruikshank as his engraver for the *Every-day Book,* and Cruikshank's engravings of the satire formed part of the basis for his fame.[39] However, progressive politics were not the only thing to recommend Hone as a publisher. The *Every-day Book* was a lavish publication, and the most successful annual of the time. Hone produced it as a weekly, and then bounded complete single volumes at the end of the year, creating two markets for a single publication. Hone paid his contributors and they could be assured the additional benefit of a wide circulation of their work. Expansion of his audience, clearly a rationale for participating in this kind of publishing activity, seems somewhat defeated by the subterfuge of 'fathering' the poems on others. Perhaps, as in the case of Montgomery or the earlier speculation about the identity of 'Percy Green', Clare believed that the true authorship would eventually be discovered increasing the cachet of the work as an instance of authorial wit, a gesture valorised by Lamb and numerous others.

The specific details of the frauds perpetrated on Hone fascinate for several reasons. In the first instance, the 'lost' work belonged to Andrew Marvel, following the taste for the 'old poets' already established at the *London Magazine* and elsewhere, and to which Clare contributed via Montgomery's *Iris* and previously as 'Percy Green'. The obscure source claimed for the Marvel poem, 'a Vol of Miscellanys published by the Spalding Society of Literature',[40] appears fanciful, but actually marks Clare as the centre of a self-created network of literary relations. The allegedly defunct society bears a striking similarity to the Spalding Gentleman's Society, a reading and social club founded in 1719 in the spirit of Addison and Steele.[41] Clare's 'neighbour' and sometimes publisher, John Savage, was a member, and the society housed a large collection of old books. Indeed, membership was by invitation and the new member donated a book upon joining. When Clare finally confessed his fraud to Hone in 1828, he recollected the fictional name of the source as the Spalding Society of Antiquarians, and the fictional correspondent as 'James Gilderoy of Surfleet Lincolnshire', Savage's address. Combining the local, the readership of the *Scientific Receptacle*, with the cosmopolitan, Hone's subscribers, allowed Clare to create a plausible story, and to imagine a broad pattern of literary sociabilty throughout the breadth of Britain. His choice of author for this letter, James Gilderoy, extended the pattern further by evoking the Scottish highwayman of that name, a name Clare had first discovered in a ballad dedicated to him in Percy's *Reliques*.[42] When Clare followed up his success in having 'fathered' the poem, 'Death', on Marvel, he chose a new imaginary correspondent, but not one so whimsical as James Gilderoy. He wrote two letters to Hone as Frederic Roberts, giving his address as Milton. Roberts was an acquaintance and one of the Fitzwilliam retainers. Clare's imaginary 'circle' now included his friends at Milton House (and by extension, Montgomery), his 'neighbour' Savage, and Hone's London milieu. Furthermore, his contributions to the *Every-day Book* were just that – contributions. He did not submit his own work, but rather contributed 'lost' or neglected works recovered by his intellectual pursuits and scholarly interests. Clare invented the obscure volume 'Court of the muses',[43] as a pretext to send 'A Farewell & Defiance to Love' 'fathered' on Sir John Harrington. The choice of the 'obscure volume' spoke directly to the excitement surrounding the recovery of these convivial Elizabethan poets. Clare/Roberts expressed excitement that the book was so 'scarce' that it had been overlooked by Ellis in his *Specimens*. Lost manuscripts provided the other potential 'source' of poems, and a second draft of the letter from 'Roberts' to Hone written on the same day announces the discovery of the manuscript of 'Farewell and Defiance of Love', now attributed to sir Henry Wooton, 'on the flye leaves' of an 'old copy of the "Reliquiae Wottonianae"'.[44] Clare completed his self-created network of taste by including his rationale for sending the manuscript to Hone: 'I see by your insertion of a Poem of Andrew Marvels that you give room to such 'Reliques'—I myself am very fond of these old votarys of the muses'. The appearance of a Marvel poem, by Clare, justified the submission of 'lost' Elizabethean poems, also by Clare. This is a very witty game; it not only creates an imaginary network founded on literary sociality, but also constitutes that network through its playfulness. The complexity of the game became even more delicious when Clare also sent a submission as 'John Clare'. Significantly, he submitted not an imitation of an 'old poem', but verses describing a 'popular custom', an early instance in his sense of himself as a folklorist.[45] Clare erased a prose account of country customs from the letter indicating that he toyed with the idea of chronicling in prose the local sources of the poems. This interest in recording and preserving local customs, many of which were under threat from changes in the agricultural system, was of a piece with his developing interest in the local natural history, another interest he shared with Henderson.[46] The structure of the *Every-day Book* lent itself to records of the cycles of local customs and the natural year. Clare, writing as Roberts, suggested as much to Hone when he declared that he often read the *Every-day Book* in conjunction with *Moore's Almanack*. The *Almanack* for 1826 is item 311 among Clare's surviving books in the collection of the Northampton Public Library, and contains numerous notes on the flyleaves, many of which detail cultural and natural events from that year. These interests seem at odds with the witty acculturated taste for the 'old poets', yet seen from a political point of view both interests further a progressive agenda shared by the Fitzwilliams, including Henderson, Roberts and Edmund Tyrell Artis (the antiquarian and archeologist), Montgomery at the *Sheffield Iris*, the *London Magazine* as represented by 'Elia', and epitomised by the life and career of William Hone.

It is difficult to know whether Hone was deceived. Clare eventually confessed his 'offence & blasphemy'[47] in 1828, but correspondence with Mrs Emmerson in September 1825 suggests that Hone knew the submission to be Clare's. She reported that she could not determine if Hone would insert his 'lost' Wooton poem, and suggested that he send it to Harry Stoe Van Dyke for insertion in the *European Magazine*. Van Dyke, she hastened to point out, would pay.[48] Mrs Emmerson's limited sense of the value of publication, based on financial gain and prestige, had been evidenced earlier in relation to Montgomery's *Iris* and indicated that she did not share the sense of play and consequently found herself outside the conviviality of Clare's poetic activity. The democratic taste Lamb championed in the pages of the *London Magazine* did not find a ready audience in the social conservatism of the Emmerson/Radstock circle. Even the decision to submit the poems to the *European* occurred in consultation with the members of his expanding literary circle rather than his ostensible advisers, Emmerson and Radstock or, alternately, Taylor and Hessey. Clare wrote to Joseph Henderson at Milton House about all of the literary magazines of the day, and often followed his publication advice. Henderson was an excellent reader, and Clare respected his taste. Clare's use of the *European* as a place to publish took two different forms. He sent poems there that Hone had declined to publish, providing another outlet for his Elizabethan muse, and some additional income. He also published his 'Essay on Popularity' in Van Dyke's magazine, using it as a venue to try out his poetic ideas and prose. Henderson greatly admired Clare's essay, and, in another example of the convivialty (imagined and real) that Clare and he so valued, wrote to ask Clare for a copy so that he might share it with the real Frederic Roberts who, on hearing Henderson describe it, was anxious to read it.[49] Roberts thus existed in both Clare's literary circles, the imaginary and the real.

Clare concurred with Henderson's view that the *European* had declined in quality by 1826. As Henderson put it upon returning Clare's most recent copy: 'I think it a very poor production indeed. I have seen many newspaper attempts to push it into notice lately, by Puff, and certes it will take a good deal of puffing to keep it afloat, for it is a very heavy laden matter from beginning to end.'[50] In writing to Hessey in December 1825, Clare stated his disappointment with the *European* in particular, and with periodical publication more generally: 'I dont think I shall trouble the 'European Magazine' much more with my contributions as the pay is but poor & the insertion very uncertain as to the Poetical Almanacks they may all go to Hell next year for me for I can get nothing by them & my contributions are so mutilated that I do not know them again'.[51] This outburst appeared in the context of his growing frustration with Taylor and his stalled manuscript, but nonetheless shows that these new avenues for publication were far from ideal for all there other pleasures. In the end, Clare maintained his relationships with Hall, for the simple reason that he paid well and promptly, and with Hone and Montgomery because of the value he placed on literary sociability. Van Dyke and Hessey both argued against such publications, and in favour of the financial rewards of the *European*. But the shoddy quality of Van Dyke's magazine made it unworthy, as did the meagre nature of its monetary rewards.

It has been a commonplace of Clare studies to note that the annuals, newspapers, magazines and other periodical publications that sprang up in the 1820s marked a general shift away from the publication of single-authored volumes of poetry and towards the new taste for novels. For Clare this shift proved most significant because of his vulnerability, both financial and cultural, and because of the interminable delay in publication of *The Shepherd's Calendar*. Clare alluded to this shift himself in a letter to Taylor, but hoped it might prove temporary and a sign of the fickleness of the public taste: 'the Poems [the much anticipated *Shepherd's Calendar*] may turn the tide & sell better for Novels & such rubbish were in as bad repute once as Poetry now & may be again.'[52] Nevertheless, the portrait of Clare attempting unsuccessfully to cobble together a living from such publications during the delay in publication of his third volume cannot be taken at face value. Clare involved himself with these publications for many reasons, among them the narrow goal of payment. He spent more time engaged in activities that had neither a direct monetary benefit nor the possibility of furthering his fame. The value of sociability cannot be overstated. It allowed him to expand his connections beyond the narrow focus of Taylor & Hessey, and the interference of Radstock, and confirmed in his own mind the value of his poetry. His frauds allowed him to write in styles unavailable to the 'peasant poet', and make connections between his local interests and the broader literary world. In this regard Henderson acts as a perfect representative, interested in the minutiae of the local scene as a botanist and connected to the sophisticated world of the Fitzwilliams and radical Whig politics. Even Savage, his 'neighbour', combines the intimacy of local conviviality and the larger world of scholarly enquiry, represented by the title of his publication, the *Scientific Receptacle*. While he waited for the *The Shepherd's Calendar* to make its way through the press, Clare involved himself in creating systems of reciprocity and exchange that offered him an expanded outlook on the possibilities for his own work ('old poems', critical prose, folklore, natural history, and so on.), and connected him to a sophisticated network of writers, publishers and political activists.

Clare actively developed this conviviality, and even led the way in the expansion and shaping of literary taste. Lamb's 'Elia' theorised the taste for the democratic poetics of the Elizabethans, but Clare had contributed to that taste early on through the work of the popular 'Percy Green'. While the poems he published in the *London Magazine* as Percy Green in 1822–23 were not imitations of Elizabethan verse, they nonetheless developed a 'high & refined style'[53] that anticipated the new taste. The first submission, simply titled 'Ballad', took as its subject the transitory nature of human affection:

> O throw aside those careless ways
> My conscious heart to move
> Affected anger but betrays
> Suspicious doubts of love
>
> That face were frowns at will can dwell
> Were cold deciet beguiles
> May just as easy and as well
> Dissemble while it smiles
>
> Tis cruel when false smiles betrays
> The heart into a snare
> But crueler when slighting ways
> Turns pleasures to despair
>
> Thy face is fair let that suffice
> And scorn a meaner power
> Truth adds to beautys fading price
> Like fragrance in the flower
>
> Yet tho you frown or smile in jest
> My folly must declare
> A weakness burning in my breast
> Feels all in earnest there[54]

Writing about the vagaries of love and friendship constituted an ethos of conviviality, the necessity of unaffected 'affection'. Clare made it clear in his postscript to the accompanying introductory letter that he realised that such poetic subjects represented a new poetic direction for the *London*, but he was willing to take his chances:

> I have heard it affirmed that your predilection for the Northamptonshire Peasants poetry has made you blind to the more high & refined style be as it will I have made the attempt wether it be attended with success or not[55]

Clare's self-created intertextuality, developed throughout the 1820s in his 'frauds', here displays considerable wit. 'Percy Green' was free to write in his own style and challenge the taste for the 'peasant poet' that dominated the magazine. The letter, whether or not it intended to actually deceive Taylor, represented a challenge to the poetic definition, in part created by Taylor's Introductions to the volumes, that confined Clare. Taylor appears to have taken the submission as deliberate subterfuge, occasioning a pained response from Clare in a letter to Hessey: 'my letter of P. Green was merely a joke for a christmass puzzle which was quickly unriddled by the parcel as I did not recollect the seal would betray me.'[56] Having given the game away with his postmark, Clare underplayed the seriousness of his intent. However, earlier responses from Taylor & Hessey to his efforts to write in different styles suggest that he may have had good reason to employ a mask in developing his range in the pages of Taylor's magazine. As early as the summer of 1821, Clare had sent a comic poem on the taste for peasant poetry for Taylor's consideration under the name Stephen Timms. In response, Hessey, on Taylor's behalf, wrote: we do not think it one of your happiest efforts—The best thing you can do is write in your own natural Style, in which no one can excell you.'[57] In pursuing new styles and submitting them for consideration, Clare asserted that his 'own natural Style' was a critical contrivance. Thus he positioned Green's work directly against that style. Such early self-consciousness of poetic style complicates the common portrait of Clare as the unaffected producer of 'natural' verse, and calls attention to the fictionality of the Gilchrist/Taylor construction of John Clare, the peasant poet. Reception largely followed that lead (whether in positive or negative terms), and Clare's use of pseudonyms suggests that he realised the constraining power of his literary identity almost from the outset.

Despite their reservations Taylor & Hessey soon came around once the publication of Percy Green's poems proved a great success. In fact, the immediate circle of writers at the *London* were among the most enthusiastic admirers of their new colleague. Hessey took special pleasure in writing to Clare to describe a dinner at Cary's house in which the host expatiated in praise of a recently published sonnet:

> We dined at Mr Cary's about a week ago, and among other enquiries Mr C. asked with much Interest who Mr Green was, and expressed himself as being much pleased with the Sonnet in the last number. He had no idea of it being yours, and on that account his testimony was the more valuable I know you will be pleased to hear this as your friend Cary's Judgement is not to be despised on matters of this kind.[58]

Hessey had come full circle; from abhorring Clare distracting himself from his 'natural' talents in 1821, he now took pleasure in the game. Furthermore, he confirmed Clare's broader point – that his poetic talent had many potential forms.

Cary's admiration represented a fulfilment of the desire for a form of poetic sociability. The subject matter of the Green poems indicates the primacy of that poetic value, and the use of a pseudonym allowed Clare participation in the intellectual life to the *London Magazine* circle. This latter aspect must have been doubly significant for Clare given that he could rarely afford to be physically present in that company. News of his much admired friends speculating about the identity of the brilliant new writer, Percy Green, must have created feelings of pride, amusement and intellectual satisfaction. Clare created a convivial circle of writers in his own mind, and made the connections real through publication. He ultimately expanded the membership of the circle, as he became two of the most important poetic contributors to the magazine, John Clare and Percy Green.

Clare contributed to the success of Taylor's editorial leadership at the *London Magazine*. Along with Lamb, De Quincey and others, Clare provided a steady supply of high quality work that contributed to the variety and stylistic texture of the magazine. During this period, Clare began to conceive of himself as a professional writer in the company of professional writers, and the magazine as their joint enterprise under Taylor's leadership. His journal recorded his frank reviews of each number, and he was quick to communicate his views through Hessey as he submitted new work.[59] Feeling a part of a collective enterprise, Clare increasingly thought about his writing as his means of making a living while contributing to the public taste. He began to refer to both his annuities from his patrons and the monies he received from Taylor & Hessey as his 'salary'. The word choice is significant. He was rewarded, not because of feelings of kindness towards an unaffected 'natural genius', but as a result of intellectual and imaginative labour. The fact that Taylor & Hessey held the purse strings in administering payments from the patrons as well as determining any profits from sales inevitably led to bad feelings, and it often fell to Hessey to send the actual funds, apologise for delays, berate Clare for his lack of thrift, and so on. Clare wrote a memorandum on one of Hessey's letters[60] showing that he had begun to keep his own parallel accounts and that he knew his professional value to the firm:

> Mem: My Sallaries from Lord Spencer & the Funds have not been separately mentioned this year from the other monies I asked for & it has puzzled me which to account for those sums but I have had not a single farthing more than is here mentioned in these letters from which my salaries must be deducted ... Mem: Never had anything for the writing for the Magazine as yet accounted for tho a year & half & to prevent mistake I have set down the money sent for independant of the fund money & salary as "Credit" from which the Magazine money must be deducted.[61]

Clare clearly expected to be paid like the other contributors to the magazine, but until he could impress this fact on his publishers he had to ensure that he was fairly compensated. Taylor & Hessey sent Clare money for his expenses, but did not directly tie such payments to his literary contributions. Such lamentable paternalism (one can hardly imagine Lamb or De Quincey accepting payment as an act of the publisher's largesse) was not lost on Clare, and his use of the word 'salary' in the correspondence may reflect an effort to correct Taylor & Hessey's mistaken view of their professional relationship.

Clare worked hard in these years to develop the range of his literary gifts. The first Percy Green letter, for example, included the prospectus for an entire volume to be written around the long dramatic poem, 'Edmund & Helen'. Taylor & Hessey simply ignored that manuscript, and Hessey, much to Clare's annoyance, also ignored the manuscript of his long social satire, 'The Parish': 'if you will give an opinion of my poetry you shall have the 'Parish' but if you will not I am determined I will send no more for your Criticism at present.'[62] Clare supplied Hessey with samples of the verse and a description of the scope and rationale for such a work: I have just finished my 'Parish a Satire' & this is its motto 'I have injurd no one as a nameless character can never be found

out but by its truth & likness' from Pope—here is a specimen—an over-
seer [he included a 28-line sample recording the tyrannical cruelty of
the overseer]'.[63] It was not so much that Hessey told him they were
uninterested in publishing satirical works; he was met with silence. Clare
responded in a way quite unlike the common picture of him bearing
the weight of long-suffering neglect. He sent both the Percy Green
manuscript, 'Edmund & Helen', and 'The Parish' to his friend Joseph
Henderson at Milton House. If Hessey was unable to respond to new
work, Clare needed a new reader. Henderson proved a good choice—
sympathetic to Clare's genius and an extremely careful reader, he nonetheless responded honestly. Bob Heyes evaluates Henderson's editorial
contributions in his essay, 'Writing Clare's Poems: "The Myth of Solitary
Genius"'.[64] As Heyes makes clear, Henderson participated extensively in
these two literary projects. After becoming frustrated with Hessey in the
spring, he sent the manuscripts on to Henderson, not just for comment,
but for editorial assistance. Like all of Clare's editors, Henderson struggled
with the handwriting and lack of punctuation, but, unlike Hessey, he
proved very attentive to the goal of moving the projects forward:

> I have been so busy that I have been hardly able to look at the
> "Parish" & to tell you the truth there is a good deal of it that I cannot
> make out, I shall be unengaged this evening & shall have another try
> at it. I will return it in a day or two with any remarks that I may be
> able to make.[65]

Heyes argues that Clare had required secrecy from those to whom he
sent his manuscripts, and shows that Frank Simpson had read 'The Parish'
before it reached Henderson. However, in commenting on Henderson's
role, he suggests that it consisted primarily of 'general observation',[66]
and presents that role as similar to that played by Simpson or other
friends who may have seen or heard unpublished works in progress. In
citing an early letter to Taylor from 1820, Heyes equates Henderson's
contribution to Clare's practice of testing his poems on family members
and neighbours: 'it is undergone the Criticism of my father & mother &
several rustic Neighbours of the town & all approve it.'[67] However, that
early practice of seeking confirmation of the accuracy of his descriptions
and expressions through the actual inhabitants of the rural scene he
wished to represent cannot be easily compared to Henderson's detailed
comments. The very nature of 'The Parish' made discretion necessary – it
was not a poem that would universally please the neighbours – and
Clare elicited both general comment on the subject matter and style

(trenchant social satire), and strategies for revision. Heyes's broader point, that 'Clare tells us nothing about his writing and revising processes',[68] is well taken, but, as he has shown, we can nonetheless deduce certain practices from the evidence we do have. Henderson broadly approved of the satire, but nonetheless offered specific advice about possible revisions:

> No one possesses in a greater degree the natural simplicity of language fited for such a subject & few are better acquainted with the general details of the subject, your general plan, & the characters you have marked out, are in my opinion just what should be, & you have already succeeded in making the poem sufficiently interesting to deserve your attention in removing its triffling defects. I will now tell you what in my humble opinion is objectionable in it, & you must treat it as a humble opinion only. It is rather too severe—too pointed, & perhaps too personal—not that I think you have overdrawn any character or thrown his delinquencies into broader light then they deserve,—but that I think the poem would be equally effectual, gain more readers, & more admirers, if it were less pointed & less severe.[69]

Henderson's general point that the humor inherent in the satire could provide some balance for the trenchant nature of many of the portraits, which he admits are not 'overdrawn', seems well taken. The general purpose of the satire could only be served if making it 'less pointed & less severe' had the effect of gaining 'more readers & more admirers' without making it any less effectual. Nor did Henderson stop with this subtle general observation. He went on to offer specific advice about transitions in the narrative:

> In passing from one character to another in some instances it is rather too abrupt, it would be better if the extension of the last couplet were framed so as to forworn the reader that he was about to enter upon a new character, because in a rapid transition from one character to the other one is apt to confound one with the other.

In fact, his suggestions ranged from gentle complaints about repetitive diction to ideas for expanding the work by inserting episodes into the narrative: 'What would you think of a little episode here & there throughout the poem? such as an interesting sketch of faithless love & deep distress recited by a young & interesting girl before the Revd Magistrate.'

The subject matter of 'The Parish' did not shock Henderson who approved of its artistic and social aims, so the need for secrecy as the manuscript circulated between Clare, Simpson and Henderson remains somewhat of a puzzle. In part, as Henderson noted, 'you must feel anxious about it as everyone would about an unpublished manuscript'. Fear of the manuscript coming to light before it was ready, anxiety about its physical location (Clare did not seem to have a copy), and any number of other minor concerns contributed to his desire to be circumspect. However, even though we can never know Clare's specific plans for the manuscript, a not unreasonable conjecture presents itself. Clare had determined that Taylor & Hessey were not possible publishers for 'The Parish'; he set out to edit and revise it by other less formal means. Henderson made sense because of his sympathetic politics, and perhaps because his extensive social connections might assist in the search for an alternative publisher. Clearly, Clare could not send the manuscript to Radstock for offer to Murray or some other of his Lordship's literary outlets. Apoplexy might well have proved the result, and Clare would have been risking the loss of Radstock's patronage. Such complex social considerations make the entire project fascinating. Had 'The Parish' appeared under Clare's name, many of his key backers would have taken offence. Discretion made sense, but not enough to inhibit the prior need to record the destruction of the rural social fabric. Clare felt compelled to write the poem and to publish it as a record of the social hypocrisy and disintegration of his community he had observed firsthand.

*

The period when the early promise of Clare's career collapsed, between the publication of the second edition of *The Village Minstrel* and belated appearance of *The Shepherd's Calendar*, paradoxically coincided with a complex expansion of his literary and intellectual pursuits. Participation in the many manifestations of magazine culture (from the *London Magazine* to the *Scientific Receptacle*), rather than indicating financial desperation, showed Clare as the active centre in an expanding set of literary relations. He self-consciously set out to cultivate local connections, the Fitzwilliam household proving the most significant, and built on such connections through a variety of means. His invention of Percy Green allowed him to deepen his artistic relations with the contributors of the *London Magazine* by sharing poetry with them in two distinct voices. He actively participated in the rediscovery and recreation of the taste for the 'old poets' by writing poems that participated in the revival, and by arguing for the cultural and artistic importance of such works in the provenance stories that accompanied his submissions. He took up the conviviality and sociability inherent in the 'old poets' and championed by Lamb and others as features of a democratic muse, and applied them directly to his own life. He submitted 'old poems' to the radical *Sheffield Iris* thereby establishing a connection with its publisher James Montgomery, a connection which both built on the long association of the Earl Fitzwilliam and Lord Milton with Montgomery. Reciprocally, this further cemented his connections with Milton House, the Stamford brother-editor John Drakard, and the champions of the radical Whig cause generally. It cannot be coincidence that his other preferred outlet for such poems was Hone's *Every-day Book*, given that Hone not only shared his taste, but equally understood and promoted the cultural and political value of conviviality. Consequently, such poetic activity allowed Clare to constitute a convivial literary brotherhood, both real and imagined, as he participated in the ongoing cultural project of the *London Magazine*, and in his expanding networks of local and national connections. He became a national figure, a poet sought out by publishers of new periodicals of all kinds and relied upon as a key contributor of poems to the brilliant intellectual flowering that was the *London Magazine* between 1822 and 1824. The creation of new sources of income to supplement his 'salaries' from the houses Exeter, Fitzwilliam and Spencer and from his work for the *London Magazine* provided a happy corollary to the intellectual stimulation his many and varied pursuits afforded, and doubtless led to a growing confidence in his abilities as a professional writer. His physical isolation dubtless necessiated some of this activity as a means of creating a community in his mind in response to the marked lack of any actual community in Helpstone. However, this explanation fails to acknowledge the richness of his intellectual relationships in his immediate neighbourhood, from his friendly mentoring of Frank Simpson's aspirations as a painter to his complex collaborations, literary and scientific, with Joseph Henderson to his archeological explorations with Edmund Tyrell Artis. The common view of Clare in this period, isolated and victimised by Taylor's editorial neglect, cannot be sustained once the wide range of his activities becomes clear. Clare *was* a victim of editiorial neglect, but not just in the delay in publication of the *The Shepherd's Calendar* and its clumsy insensitive editing. Taylor's fixation on Clare's status as the 'peasant poet' rendered him unable to recognise the merits of expanding the range of Clare's poetic styles, let alone efforts to write indifferent genres altogether. The success of Percy Green at the *London* came despite Taylor's advice to abandon all parallel projects in favour of writing under the exclusive influence of the rural muse, perhaps with an occasional moment of quasi-Wordsworthian reflection (even though Clare consistently referred to such moments in Wordsworth with contempt). Clare could not find a sympathetic editorial ear at Taylor & Hessey for a Green volume built around 'Edmund & Helen' nor for a long satire like 'The Parish', a work that has garnered him extensive posthumous critical fame. Even earlier, his negotiations with Power to produce a collection of one hundred songs on the model of Power's phenomenonally successful volume of Thomas Moore's *Irish Ballads* met with obstruction and disdain from Taylor. We can only speculate on how successful and popular that volume might have been.[70] Clare's other great interest of this period, and indeed throughout his lifetime, natural history, met with a similar fate at his publishers. The desire to catalogue and describe the natural world, and to represent it by various means (he took up watercolours) followed directly from Clare's central poetic concerns – the creation of the aesthetic value inherent in the object. He shared this enthusiasm for nature and its sustaining power with James Hessey, and through Hessey commenced work on an array of natural history projects. Those projects died with the dissolution of Taylor & Hessey, and Taylor's personal collapse. The publishing house literally failed, and in that historical accident we as readers lost any finished works of natural history, either by Clare or by Clare and one of his natural history collaborators: Hessey, Elizabeth Kent, or, most importantly, Henderson.

7
The Natural Histories of Helpstone

Margaret Grainger collected, transcribed and edited much of Clare's writing on natural history as *The Natural History Prose Writing of John Clare*. Only one fault mars her otherwise wonderful volume – an over-emphasis on the 'natural history letters' Clare produced in correspondence with Hessey as the foundation of any coherent prose project. Otherwise, she edited the various notes and fragments scattered through the Clare manuscripts as a series of beautifully delineated moments of perception and description – what we might call poetic field notes. Following the model of Gilbert White's *Natural History of Selborne*, the natural history letters look like a literary conceit constituting the substance of the work. White's own treatise evolved from his 'Garden Kalendar' which he commenced in 1751 to his more expansive 'Naturalist's Journal' to his final 'Natural History' written in epistolary form. Following Hessey's lead Clare created the series of letters and clearly intended them to be published on the model of White. For his part, Hessey followed his own enthusiasm for White's natural history, and his own deeply held faith in the spiritual power of the natural world in pursuing the project. While the project did not begin to take shape until late summer and early autumn 1824, its impetus was Hessey's desire to imagine himself free of the confines of London and to live vicariously in the minute beauties of Clare's landscape: '—what lovely May weather for you this is! I long to be among the Hawthorn blossoms & the Cowslips, and to run away from the noise & dust of London.'[1] Hessey's letters often contained a sense of physical longing, and served as a declaration of his natural sensibility. His ardour connected him to Clare, grounding their friendship in the spiritual void he felt in lacking what Clare had so close at hand:

> The season seems now to be setting in very pleasantly, and I long to see the face of nature again, for I have left my house at Brixton & taken up my abode in Fleet Street—the only bit of green I can see, without walking some miles for it, is the Temple Garden, and there after a short time the grass gets burnt up by exposure to the southern sun, and the flowers soon droop & wither—My own little plants will I fear feel the want of country air more than I do, but they are all pretty well at present.

The sympathetic quality of the landscape, the vulnerability it suffers by urban exposure, and Hessey's equating of his own condition to the suffocation his 'own little plants' feel for 'want of country air' combine to express his sensibility as suffering. Doubtless Clare felt moved by his friend's plight and by the intimacy implicit in declaring his analogous vulnerability. Sensibility provided the foundation of their friendship and coloured the terms of their professional relationship. The natural history project grew from the intimacy of shared enthusiasms.

The possibility that their correspondence could be transformed into a book arose in a letter from Hessey in September 1824. Clare recorded their intention to create such a work in his journal: '"A Natural History of Helpstone" in a Series of Letters to Hessey who will publish it when finished.'[2] His journal entry followed an excited letter from Hessey relating his particular enthusiasm for Clare's speculations about the migration of swallows. Clare's ideas had evoked the famous passage from White's *Natural History of Selborne* on the possibility that swallows remained in hiding throughout the winter and the old folk tradition that they sank into lakes at the end of the season. Characteristically, Hessey shared his love of White with Clare, and explicitly connected this taste with the hidden capacities of his inner life. In advising Clare about how he might relate his minute natural history observations, Hessey emphasised their potential moral purpose – their power to improve the reader as instances of meditative reflection:

> thank you for the information you have given me about the Swallows—the observations you have made agree in the main with my favorite White of Selborne who was a very minute observer of the various branches of the Swallow tribe. Your Devil Martin is what we called the Swift—what a beautiful provision is that which you

mention & which I have not seen elsewhere noted, the tuft of feathers for the protection of the eye of this rapid bird. There is Poetry & Philosophy and Religion too to be found in the works of nature as we call them, but it is not every one who can discover them. The supposed sinking of the Swallow in the water at the approach of Winter would make a pretty subject for a Fable, or an Episode in your Calendar for September—the leave takings and the mutual encouragements & condolences of the members of a family of Swallows about to sink to another term of existence beneath the dark waters—the fears, & doubts, & anxieties which arise in their minds as they feel the osiers bending under their weight, the clinging to a life that is known & understood in preference to that which is untried, through the changes of the climate & the experience & admonitions of the elders [warning?] them of the impossibility of a much longer stay—all this and more in the way of scenic description might be wrought up I think into an interesting Poem.[3]

The letter reveals that Clare's new idea for his natural history probably arose from Hessey's recognition of his 'favorite White' as a model. However, from the outset the correspondence imagined various other projects that would proceed concurrently. Hessey recognised that such observations could provide moments of beauty and philosophical depth in the ongoing revision of *The Shepherd's Calendar*, a title that in this context appears to emerge from the tradition of keeping a calendar of field observations, the activity that had served as necessary prelude to White's final work. As he allowed his imagination to run, Hessey began to flesh out the narrative of a poetic fable. His suggestion served two separate functions: professionally, it spurred Clare to create new poems in a somewhat different vein (and one for which there was a ready audience), and, personally, it demonstrated once again his imaginative effusiveness (and his worthiness as a literary correspondent). How this material would fit into the proposed 'Natural History of Helpstone' is not clear. Perhaps the completed fable of the swallows would be interpolated into the passage on swallows in the corresponding natural history letter. If so, the project would follow White only in the broadest outline. Clare's would be a new genre, the poetic natural history, and the subsequent natural history letters bear this out as they vacillate between passages that read like entries for such a work and others that read like general plans for that work. Hessey closed his letter of 7 September with a selection of passages from Chaucer describing various birds, and his effusions on each passage. The intention appears to have been to have

Clare include apposite poetic descriptions within the text of the natural history notes, and his poems would take pride of place. 'The Natural History of Helpstone' would entail composing natural history field observations as letters to Hessey, choosing selections from his own published and manuscript poems, composing occasional poems specifically for the work, and incorporating the works of other poets as appropriate. 'Natural History Letter III'[4] followed directly out of Hessey's letter. Clare integrated a passage from Chaucer as per Hessey's direct request, and then expanded his observations of the nightingale and other birds. The opening of the letter looks like a demonstration of what specific entries in the work would look like, but then turns to a discussion of how they might proceed in the project. The success of the Chaucer selection prompted Clare to suggest that Hessey collaborate by reading and selecting passages from various works that he, Clare, would suggest: 'you have a better opportunity of consulting books then I have therefore I will set down a list of favourite Poems & Poets who went to nature for their images so that you may consult them.'[5] Clare's letter thus provided Hessey with a specimen of the work, and with a detailed plan of how to proceed; Hessey would provide research to Clare's specifications and on his own initiative (as the Chaucer example shows), while Clare engaged in the actual fieldwork and wrote poems out of the aesthetic perceptions arising from that fieldwork.

We cannot know why 'The Natural History of Helpstone' did not proceed as planned. However, several factors conspired against it. Hessey's intentions were always divided by the concurrent need to organise *The Shepherd's Calendar* into a finished work. Almost a year previous, Hessey had taken up the task of responding to an early version of that manuscript and had made general suggestions about how it might be organised. Unlike a natural history, he felt the poems needed 'a human interest', narratives interspersed throughout the natural descriptions. One of his main concerns was that Clare would be accused of repeating himself, and that the new volume must therefore reflect poetic growth. He took care to explain that he still appreciated the poems, but that he was an ideal and, thus, untypical reader:

> Those that please me most are the Day Dream in Summer, Morning in the last of Summer—Spring—& the little Tale of the Grasshopper. I do not mean to say that several of the others are not good, but they are all so very like what you have written before that they would not do to publish. I can read them myself with great pleasure—my knowledge of the author, & my former familiarity with

such scenes & objects give a charm to the descriptions that is not felt by all.[6]

As usual, Hessey took the opportunity to assert the quality of his sensibility by arguing that such capacity for feeling was sadly not universal. This perceived lack in the general reading public governed his response and led to his suggested outline for revisions:

> The Shepherd's Calendar should consist of delineations of the face of Nature, the operations of the husbandman, the amusements, festivals, superstitions, customs & of the Country, and little stories introduced to illustrate these more accurately and to fix an Interest on them.

Hessey's initial response to the manuscript, as such, can hardly be faulted. He provided editorial guidance and good suggestions about how the work might be shaped. Even the most prescriptive of his suggestions responded directly to the book as a work in progress. Clare took the letter as constructive advice, and marked the margin of Hessey's proposed outline with his own ideas about organisation. Hessey had written out a list of months with possible subjects next to them. For example, next to the heading 'April', Hessey wrote '—The Poem of Spring already written, with the addition of some little Story'. In response to this suggestion, Clare wrote in the margin, 'Jockey & Jenny', as a possible 'little Story'. Given the unhappy future of Clare's manuscript at the hands of Taylor & Hessey, the congenial mood of these early exchanges with Hessey stand out as evidence of wasted potential and opportunity. Hessey foresaw different kinds of literary work from Clare, and Taylor's failure to follow up his partner's initiatives doomed *The Shepherd's Calendar* to its interminable delays and unsatisfactory final form. The other potential Clare books from the same period simply disappeared through neglect.

Hessey cannot entirely be blamed for the loss of momentum after September 1824. Their plan was interrupted by Clare's illness, which had begun the previous autumn and persisted for most of a year. Hessey played a central role in treating Clare's ailment by serving as the contact between him and Dr Darling, the London physician favoured by the Clare's city friends. On the evidence of Hessey's letters over the course of 1824,[7] Clare seems to have been suffering from an intestinal or bowel disorder, perhaps colitis, and Darling prescribed a strict diet and his own specially produced pills. While Clare described symptoms in the spring of 1824 as headache and feverish chills, his physical indisposition became the focus of treatment over the course of the year. Hessey complained most frequently about Clare's failure to stay on the diet, a sore point between them, but Clare dutifully took the pills and consulted other physicians, including one in Peterborough recommended by his friends at Milton House. Henderson also brought medical advice from Dr Darling back with him after a trip to London. The critical consensus has long been that Clare's illness was psychosomatic, but this notion originates with the most dubious of sources, Mrs Emmerson. The Tibbles followed her diagnosis: 'It is the mind's disease, and the body only suffers in sympathy',[8] and subsequent critics have simply followed theirs. The obvious objection to such an assumption would be to point out that even a cursory examination of the letters of Mrs Emmerson reveal her to be extraordinarily neurotic. All illness was psychosomatic for her, and provided evidence of her fragile artistic sensibiltiy. Regardless of the cause of Clare's illness, the result was a lack of vitality and stamina that made it difficult to write, yet he still managed to send letters to Hessey containing natural history observations, and dutifully recorded similar observations in his journal when he felt well enough to walk.

Another of Clare's symptoms was spiritual. Throughout 1824 both Hessey and Radstock sent him religious material in the hopes of offering spiritual consolation in the face of his physical, emotional and psychological suffering. Radstock sent a copy of Thomas Erskine's *Remarks on the Internal Evidence for the Truth of Revealed Religion* in early October, and Clare responded to the methodical air of certainty in the volume: '... find in it [Erskine] some of the best reasoning in favour of its object I have ever read   I think a doubting christian may be set right at a first perusal and a reasoning Deist loose doubts sufficient to be half a christian in some arguments and a whole one ere he get to the end.'[9] The more interesting manifestation of this symptom occurred the previous spring at one of the heights of the illness. Clare briefly joined a congregation of Ranters who met in the local open fields. His friends reacted with guarded optimism that suggests that Clare had rarely evidenced any deep religious feeling despite his keen appreciation of religious ideas. Taylor stated it boldly in commenting that he was pleased that Clare was getting 'practical religion',[10] but Hessey expressed more caution, noting that while such religious enthusiasm provided short-term emotional relief, its powerful effects were often fleeting. Once having been 'wrought up', adherents often experienced emotional letdowns.[11] Hessey stated his reservations and doubts about Clare's religious practices in more forceful terms the following October:

You must not scoff at these matters [of religious belief] my good Johnny. The time is not far distant when both you and I shall have the opportunity of convincing ourselves, and if (as is most likely) we should find what is written in the scriptures to be true it will be no slight consolation to us not to have added insult to disobedience, not to have been willfully unbelieving if our faith has been weak. How do you go on in respect to this important affair? Do you visit your methodist friends, or go to hear Mr Mossop, or walk in the fields instead and set a *good* example to your neighbours & children? (emphasis his)[12]

This letter indicates that, as he had predicted, Clare's fervour had waned. Hessey was concerned that a lapse into irreligion might put Clare in moral danger, but the list of possible Sunday activities that he included provide an excellent example of the limited choices open to Clare in a search for such solace. Mr Mossop, the local Anglican vicar, was a good man and one of the proposed executors of Clare's will, but he had little to offer Clare as a spiritual guide. The freedom of the Ranters, 'his methodist friends', from the doctrinal confines (and the physical confines of a church) that limited Mossop had provided Clare with but a short respite from his sense of spiritual isolation. Ironically, the Sunday activity that Hessey attacked, walking in the fields, provided the best hope for Clare. Not only was the exercise and fresh air beneficial in combating his illness, the meditative calm he achieved in his detailed field studies provided him with more solace that he could have hoped to experience through either conventional or unconventional religious means. Despite Hessey's ongoing declarations of his faith in the restorative power of the natural world, he nonetheless scolded Clare for participating in this power on the Sabbath. The moralistic tone created by the sarcastic underlining of the word 'good' shows Hessey to be limited in his spiritual scope, and raises the interesting question of whether or not he knew that Radstock was a strict Sabbatarian, and thus certain to have been appalled had he heard reports of Clare walking the fields on a Sunday.

The medical problems that created a more serious impediment to the project afflicted not Clare, but Taylor. Beginning in the spring of 1823, Hessey increasingly began to make medical excuses for Taylor's tardiness in writing, in producing the second edition of the *Village Minstrel*, and in responding to the *Shepherd's Calendar* manuscript. On the subject of the *Village Minstrel* delay, he wrote: 'Taylor has been confined to his house with a severe cold for some time past, & has been really very poorly or he would have written to you before now.'[13] The phrase 'really very poorly' suggests that Taylor suffered from something more serious than the 'severe cold' that had kept him housebound recently. The chronic nature of his ailments became clearer in letters that autumn. In October, Hessey wrote that Taylor's annual retreat to the country had been delayed by business and ill health, and that he hoped the country would have the restorative effect on Taylor that it had on him: 'his journey will I hope quite set him up again.'[14] The following letter confirmed Hessey's faith in the power of nature in two contradictory modes: Taylor had indeed recovered and wrote 'in good Spirits from the country', but Hessey himself had recently felt a darker power: 'Without pretending to any poetical inspiration or a more than ordinary nervous irritability, I find a rainy day or a November Fog deranges my whole System exceedingly.'[15] The letter also ominously let slip the pressure that Taylor's absences put on him. He apologised for not having had time to look at a prose manuscript (probably a version of the 'Essay on Popularity') because: 'I have been so much occupied with my own Business & with Taylor's also.'

The reoccurrence of Taylor's bouts with illness, and their impact on Hessey's ability to meet the obligations of the firm, conspired against the 'Natural History of Helpstone'. In September of 1824, Clare recorded the title and scheme for the book in his journal.[16] Just three weeks later, Hessey wrote to make a further apology for their slow pace on the *Shepherd's Calendar* manuscript: 'Taylor is but poorly—he has had another attack of his old Complaint but is getting better.'[17] This letter introduced the euphemism, 'his old complaint' to refer to Taylor's illness, and the precise nature of the 'complaint' remains obscure. However, whether it referred to a chronic physical condition or a history of depression becomes neither here nor there given the contemporary confusion of physical cause and psychological effect witnessed in the correspondence surrounding Clare's concurrent illness. The fact remains that ill health hampered Taylor's editorial effectiveness and the day-to-day running of both Taylor & Hessey and the *London Magazine*. The first manifestation of Taylor's problems, as far as Clare was concerned, arrived in a letter from Hessey less than a month later. The letter began with a condescending scolding for not following Dr Darling's instructions, especially the prohibition on alcohol, and quickly moved on to a report of his and Taylor's initial response to the *Shepherd's Calendar* manuscript. The letter reads in sharp contrast to Hessey's letter from the previous autumn. Whereas in the earlier letter he had gone out of his way to suggest how the manuscript might be expanded and revised, a plan to which Clare responded, the November 1824 letter attacked the poetics on which the manuscript depended. Their demands repeated Hessey's earlier appeal for more narrative episodes, arguing that the poems contained too much 'mere description' and were 'deficient in Sentiment and Feeling and human Interest'.[18] But their criticism went well beyond the creation of narrative interest to demand a fundamental change in Clare's poetry from his first two volumes: 'A man who has travelled & mixed in society, and read, as you have, should give us some of the fruits of his experience & the result of his reflections.'[19] Nothing had prepared Clare for this change, and he noted his perception of something amiss at the press in his journal: 'Received a packet from London with the Mag. and some copies of M.S.S. that come very slowly and a letter very friendly worded but I have found that saying and doing is a wide difference too far very often to be neighbours much less friends.'[20] His trenchant entry indicated that he had difficulty taking Taylor and Hessey seriously. The 'friendly' words masked something else, and hardly excused the slow pace of progress of the manuscript. He may have been responding to the unusual situation of Taylor and Hessey working together on the manuscript. The established pattern had relied on Taylor reading, correcting and punctuating, and part of Clare's faithfulness to the press in the midst of Radstock's constant efforts to unsettle him was his belief that Taylor was necessary to the project. Hessey had responded the previous year in lieu of Taylor who was otherwise occupied by the magazine and his illness, and Clare already perceived some sort of evasion in this editorial change. Unfortunately, this was perceptive indeed.

Clare ignored the letter and its artistic demands, and, perhaps as a result, the following letter arrived bearing a more conciliatory tone. The letter reported that they had liked the subsequent section of the manuscript much better than the first section, and believed it would require many fewer revisions. Hessey added that once Clare became re-involved the project would quickly forward: 'No exertion shall be spared on our part you may rely on it.'[21] The embedded accusation in the phrase, 'on our part', was all that remained of the hectoring tone of the previous letter, but nonetheless Clare perceptively heard the assurance, 'you may rely on it' in ironic terms. His journal entry expressed disappointment and growing disdain:

I have not answerd his last [letter] and know not when I shall   the worlds friendships are counterfits and forgerys on that principal   I have provd it and my affections are sickend unto death and my memorys are broken while my confidence is grown a shadow—in the bringing out of the second Edit of the Minstrel they was a twelv-month in printing a title page[22]

Clare's lack of 'confidence' had its origins in the history of delays since Taylor assumed control of the *London Magazine*, in the tactlessness of the previous letter, and doubtless also in evidence that Hessey, perhaps under Taylor's influence, had lost track of the plans for the 'Natural History of Helpstone'. In the final lines of the letter, Hessey responded to Clare's most recent natural history notes by suggesting that they might make 'pretty episodes' in the revised poems for *The Shepherd's Calendar*. Clearly, under Taylor's direction, no other projects would proceed.

The situation with the publishers continued to deteriorate. In late January, Hessey wrote to apologise for the delay, blaming Taylor's work-load. They had done nothing since November, yet Hessey expected Clare to accept new assurances: 'it is I assure you a fact that Taylor has been so occupied by his various editorial duties that he has not been able to go regularly through the MS. & make the requisite selection for the press.'[23] Asserting that this was 'a fact' rather alerted Clare to the possibility that it was a lie, and Clare could be forgiven for thinking that his manuscript should fall inside the purview of Taylor's 'various editorial duties', especially given the amount of time it had simply sat at the press unattended. February brought another unwelcome surprise, the absurd effort by Taylor to delegate the editing of Clare's manuscript to Harry Stoe Van Dyke. Clare's journal entry clearly indicates that he was not consulted on the matter despite his concern about the progress of the manuscript through the press: 'they chuse who they please [as editor] this time but my choice comes next and I think I shall feel able to do it myself.'[24] Van Dyke may have been an able editor, but Taylor had to know that he would not be able to make headway in the admit-tedly chaotic manuscript, even by Clare's standards. Taylor had the most experience deciphering Clare's hand, and Clare worked on the assumption that he would be the reader. Hessey had complained about the effort required to get through the manuscript when he read it in autumn 1823, declaring he would appreciate: 'a little more pains on the writing, the mechanical operation of writing I mean.'[25] Taylor and Hessey had repeated the refrain on their initial reading, which they claimed to have accomplished only with 'great difficulty'. Introducing a new editor at this stage in the process struck Clare as the latest in a series of excuses and evasions, and his journal entry indicated both that he was eager to remove himself from the capriciousness of editors and that he deliberately submitted poems without revising them. In stating that he would serve as editor on the next volume, he assumed that after the creative act of composition there would be an interval followed by a critical reassessment of the material, including grammatical and spelling corrections and broader issues of organisation and arrangement.

Clare suspected that Taylor was simply stalling, and voiced his suspicion in an angry letter to Hessey: 'Wrote to Hessey in a manner I am always very loath to write but I could keep my patience no longer.'[26] Clare's loss of 'patience' could not have come as much of a surprise. Taylor & Hessey had offered assurances for several months that the proofs of the volume would soon begin to arrive for his consideration. A letter from Van Dyke confirmed his view that little or nothing was actually being done: 'Received a letter from Vandyk which proves all my suspicions well founded   I suspected that he had not seen those M.S.S. which I considerd my best poems and he says in his letter that he has not.'[27] Affronted by the discovery that 'VanDyk [was] going out of town for a while'[28] at the very moment when the production of proofs was to have been at its height, Clare's frustration and suspicions burst out in the letter to Hessey. He accused his publishers of misleading him about Van Dyke's role, and about the anticipated pace of their work: 'Vandyk said I should have a proof in three days it is now 3 weeks & none has yet come.'[29] Clare brought the matter to a head by threatening to demand the return of the manuscript so that he could be 'left to do them [the proofs]' himself, and more seriously that he might consider the more drastic step (long advised by Radstock and Emmerson) of changing publishers:

> my friends have been long busy with advice & cautions &c. but I did not heed it then tho I find at the wrong end of the story that it would have been much better as a preventive to an often uneasy mind of restless anxietys had I taken an earlier heed of what they told me as to the determined neglect & mysterious manners of the profession [of publishers] in general

Such a move would obviously have pleased Lord Radstock who most likely would have attempted to convince Murray to publish the book. Cooler heads among Clare's friends counselled caution. Henderson expressed hope that the current difficulties with Taylor could be resolved, and reminded Clare that Taylor and Hessey had provided friendship and excellent service in the production of the first two volumes:

I am sorry to hear that you are likely to [break?] with Taylor & Hessey, for I still think that if you could come to a spoken understanding, all might yet go on well, can you not, through the medium of some mutual friend in London find some method of adjusting your differences, could you not prevail on Lamb, or Cary, or some of those friends whom I have heard you mention, to act as a mediator between you, it would at least show that you were willing to meet them half way, & when a mutual explanation takes place you may perhaps find things altogether not so bad as you expected, I own I am surprised that they should not have sent the proofs, after having promised them so long ago, but I would have you not drive things to the extreme if you possibly can avoid it. I would try some milder means first, for you can always depend upon the friendly offices of Lord Radstock in seeing you finally righted.[30]

Henderson's letter showed that Clare had not been pacified by Taylor's initial response, hardly surprising given that it amounted to veiled threats that no other publisher would be capable of editing or willing to publish his work: 'If you or any of your correspondents think you can put your Poems into the Hands of any one who is more likely to do you Justice, I will part with them willingly.'[31] Taylor ended his discussion of the publication delays with, to put it bluntly, a series of lies: 'I never intended to delegate all Control to Vandyk, & cannot make it [the manuscript] such as I think will be creditable to you. With all my Corrections which are very numerous, it will still be unsatisfactory to me—and it is this Feeling, more than anything else which has occasioned the Suspension of Work.' He came close to admitting that Van Dyke's contribution was a subterfuge, and blamed the delay on the state of the manuscript. His assertion that this difficulty caused 'Suspension of the Work' seems particularly laughable considering he offered no evidence that he even begun to 'work'. The letter, after all, came only in response to Clare's pointed letter to Hessey, not as a report of editorial progress.

Henderson's well-considered advice on this vexing situation coincided with another letter from Hessey, this time excusing Taylor's lack of 'exertion' on medical grounds: 'Taylor has had one or two attacks of his old complaint lately.'[32] This news proved ominous. Despite receiving some small satisfaction with the belated delivery of the proofs for 'January', even that event was tempered by Hessey's equivocating assurances: 'this [the editing of 'The Sorrows of Love'] I hope will go on tolerably quickly though Taylor has not been able to do much of it of late.'[33] Things had not gone 'tolerably' for some time, and Clare soon discovered that the state of his volume was symptomatic of something larger. Hessey wrote at the end of June to announce the dissolution of Taylor & Hessey:

> You have doubtless heard from Taylor that a change is about to take place in our relation to each other, & that in future he is to publish & I to sell books. This will however make no difference in our ancient friendship nor in any of our Connections I trust—I shall hope therefore to still reckon you my friend as well as his, though I may not hereafter so often have occasion to communicate with you on matters of Business.[34]

Given the absolutely pivotal role Hessey had performed at the press, the news could not have been worse. Hessey had provided a buffer between Clare and Taylor, had proved a more thoughtful reader of the manuscript, and had run the firm and the *London Magazine* during Taylor's increasingly frequent bouts with 'his old complaint'. The other shoe dropped less than two weeks later with another letter from Hessey, this time informing Clare that he and Taylor had agreed to sell the *London Magazine*, the production of which had 'almost wore [them] out'.[35]

Significantly for Clare, these changes brought with them a new distinction between his 'friendship' with Hessey and their former business relationship. What effect this change would have on the 'Natural History of Helpstone' was not immediately clear, but Clare had continued to work on the project throughout this difficult period. In March he had noted in his journal: 'Intend to call my Natural History of Helpstone "Biography of Birds and Flowers" with an Appendix on Animals and Insects.'[36] And the day after he sent his letter to Hessey registering the end of his 'patience' with the pace of *The Shepherd's Calendar*, he wrote in his journal: 'Resumed my letters on Natural History in good earnest and intend to get them finished with this year if I can get out into the fields for I will insert nothing but what comes or has come under my notice.'[37] True to his word, the journal soon recorded meticulous observations from nature: 'I observed a Snail on his journey at full speed and I markd by my watch that he went 13 Inches in 3 minutes which was the utmost he could do without stopping to wind or rest   it was the large Garden snail.'[38] This entry captured two of the key principles Clare followed—the detailed observation of the botanist, and reliance on specific experiences. The formal end of Taylor & Hessey left this work in limbo. From the beginning, natural history had been a shared enthusiasm with Hessey, and the compositional conceit, following Gilbert White, involved a series of letters addressed to Hessey. Once Hessey ceased to be a publisher, and became a mere bookseller, this project, and indeed all natural history projects at Taylor & Hessey,[39] were in the unsteady hands of John Taylor. Taylor was not an enthusiast like Hessey, and in no position to assume new editorial duties.

Clare continued to struggle with Taylor over his manuscript. In June, recovered from his most recent attack of his 'old complaint' and in the midst of dissolving his partnership with Hessey, Taylor wrote with a new gambit—the manuscript was now judged to be too long: 'I have been reckoning the number of Lines and Pages which the present Plan of our next Volume gives us and I find that we shall have about twice as much Matter as we require.'[40] Clare registered his disappointment in his journal, but had little choice but to proceed under Taylor's renewed editorship:

> Recieved a Letter from Taylor in which he says that there is twice as much more as he wants for the Shepherds Calender and a few months back one of his causes for delay was that there was not enough to begin with   nothing has made a wide difference here but time and left a puzzling Paradox behind it which tells he is a very dillatary chap[41]

The problem at the press had appeared to be Taylor's lack of involvement in the project, but now things appeared more serious yet. Henderson's advice to stay with Taylor & Hessey had been based on their past performance with the first two volumes, but perhaps he would have been more supportive of looking for another publisher had he known that the delays in sending proofs were not the sum total of the problems. Clare lost faith in Taylor, and with good reason. His behaviour had been erratic, his editorial decisions arbitrary, his tone hectoring. This new 'puzzling Paradox' of too little material changing overnight into too much material suggested that Taylor was not familiar with the manuscript, confirming Clare's worst fear – the poems had sat unattended to for over four years, but for Hessey's occasional perusal and van Dyk's ludicrous and brief involvement. Taylor's editing proved to be a disappointment. His decisions of what material to include, and of the shape of the volume, displeased Clare, but Clare continued to try to bring the project to some conclusion. He noted that: 'the plan is again altered and he [Taylor] now intends to print the Months only and leave out the Tales', and despite his belief that this scheme would 'put the worst first' and, furthermore, omit 'the best for a future opportunity,'[42] he still worked to Taylor's specifications as best possible. Given the new conditions under which he had to revise, Clare made hard editorial decisions. For example, his perception that the 'April' section of the manuscript was weak led him to rethink his 'poem on Spring' as a replacement – a change meant to strengthen the volume as much as possible within the confines of Taylor's continuing blunders and inconsistencies. The entire process became stalled indefinitely early in the autumn with the news from Hessey of Taylor's collapse into what can only be described as a severe nervous breakdown. The symptoms were described in physical terms, but their psychological source was made equally, if delicately, clear: 'A bilious attack with inflammation in the bowels was the first form of the disease, but when the bowels were better his head was affected & for ten days he was in a high state of delirium.'[43] The seriousness of Taylor's condition cannot be doubted; he was unable to work for many months and never really recovered his former stature. Whether the stress of reorganising Taylor & Hessey and the loss of the *London Magazine* led to his collapse, or vice versa, cannot be determined with any certainty, but so far as the effect on Clare's career goes the damage was clear. Following a disastrous and embarrassing delay in publication, the volume that finally appeared was clumsily edited, poorly selected, and promoted by a failing publisher. A full year after the onset of his debilitating attack of his 'old complaint', Taylor entrusted Hessey with the task of writing to Clare to request that he write a brief Preface for the volume, 'chiefly to account for the long delay in the coming out of the volume on the score of ill health'.[44] That Taylor would ask Clare to lie, and pretend that his own illness caused the delay in publication must have rankled but we do not have a record of his response. Clare's illness had left him incapacitated for most of 1824, but Taylor was ill throughout the same year, and subsequently with increasing frequency until his final collapse. Taylor's illnesses, his misjudged decision to remain Clare's editor despite being completely overwhelmed by his dual roles at Taylor & Hessey and as publisher of the *London Magazine*, and simple professional negligence, all contributed to the delay. To ask Clare to falsify the public record in order to protect his professional reputation may represent the nadir of Taylor's behaviour in this sorry affair.

Clearly, any chance of 'The Natural History of Helpstone' being produced through Taylor was lost by 1826, but Clare had other ongoing natural history projects that showed promise and could potentially allow him to salvage the field notes that he had intended to incorporate into the 'natural history letters' addressed to Hessey – the initial publication plan.

Botanizing

Even as Taylor & Hessey dissolved, Clare continued to walk and collect field notes with Joseph Henderson. These activities formed the foundation of their friendship: 'went a Botanizing after Ferns & Orchises'.[45] Indeed ferns and orchises were only two of their common interests, interests that carried them continually into the fields. Their walks began as a natural consequence of their acquaintance. Henderson had an interest in expanding the botanical knowledge of the surrounding countryside, and integrating it into the expanding subject of British natural history. Clare had better local knowledge of northern Northamptonshire and southern Lincolnshire than perhaps anyone else. Based on meticulously detailed observation, Clare's natural history grew directly out of his poetics. By striving to locate poetic value in the natural objects he observed, Clare developed an intense interest in their variety and in their well-being – such objects were the centre of his art and universe, and from the beginning their preservation occupied his thoughts. The elegiac tone of his earliest poems mourned their loss. Henderson's interests were equally fervent, but couched in the language of science. He wanted to establish as complete a set of lists of species as possible, and Clare could not have been a better resource. For his part, Clare received from Henderson a sense of excitement for an activity that he, Clare, had prized in solitude for most of his life. Henderson's companionship cannot be overvalued, especially in light of Clare's expanding emphasis on sociability as a central personal and aesthetic value. Henderson also provided access to the extensive natural history library at Milton House, and both men shared the friendship of Edmund Tyrell Artis, whose archaeological and geological explorations in the neighbourhood overlapped with their activities.

Henderson's admiration for Clare's poetic flowers initiated their shared activity. In July 1823, Henderson wrote to Clare suggesting a project:

> I think of making a list of the wild flowers mentioned in your poems as soon as I can get time to read the vol. through, & some time or other I should like to make an excursion among the commons with you for the purpose of identifying them.[46]

The letter combines three important things: the aesthetic appreciation of the accuracy of Clare's representations, the scientific urge to classify, and the necessity of field observation. From the outset, each man understood his role in the relationship and the value of their relative contribution. Poetry may have been the impetus, but Henderson expressed confidence in the sensibleness of his scheme. The combination of interests and reciprocity of value provided them with a rich foundation on which to build.

A clear example of how the relationship developed emerges with a careful consideration of their growing interest in ferns during 1824 and 1825. In November 1824, Henderson wrote to say: 'I have sent by John [a servant a Milton House who served as their delivery boy] the Ferns & Lichmidea & I would have sent them sooner but that I have been so busy. I do not recollect if there was any other plant that I promised to send you but if there was pray let me know, or what will be better come & tell me'.[47] Henderson sent the plants from his garden collection to be included in Clare's collection, an activity that extended to their field collecting. They would carefully remove a specimen of any new find and transplant it at home, creating a living list. Henderson's gift implied pleasure, the expansion of Clare's garden, and knowledge, the expansion of his store of local botanical specimens. Enthusiasm for ferns had grown throughout the month. Clare had gone walking 'to lolam brigs to hunt for species of fern that usd to grow on some willow tree heads' in the hope of discovering a rare species he remembered from when he 'was a boy'.[48] Such walks were part of his newly instituted plan to produce the 'Natural History of Helpstone', but the focus on ferns and interest in discovering hitherto unknown ones had to have originated in his discussions with Henderson. Clare spent part of the following day setting 'box edging round a border' intended to enclose his 'collection of ferns'.[49] And his enthusiasm dominated his journal entry for the following day as well:

> went into hilly wood & found a beautiful species of fern on a sallow stoven in a pit which I have not seen before—there are five sorts growing about the woods here   the common brake   the fox fern   the harts tongue   & the polopdy   two sorts the tall & the dwarf[50]

Henderson paid a visit two weeks later, and they spent the day discussing ferns (Henderson informed him that there were '24 different species or more natives in England & Scotland'[51]), and celebrating Henderson's discovery of a new species in one of the local bogs. The gift of the ferns at the end of the month may have included this new discovery and came as part of the ongoing exchange of both specimens and information.

Like Henderson, Clare was excited by the search for and discovery of new species, and his extensive local knowledge ensured success in his new pursuit. He returned to hilly wood, the site of an earlier search, and was rewarded with the discovery of 'a very small fern' 'scarcly larger then some species of moss & a little resembling curld parsley'. He 'namd it the Dwarf Maiden hair' and pronounced it 'very scarce'.[52] Naming the discovery was part of the pleasure, as was its rarity. A December visit to Milton House for a few days cemented his interest, and expanded it through the perusal of the extensive collection of botanical volumes in the Fitzwilliam library.[53] During the visit Clare consulted various books, identifying one of his discoveries as 'the thorn pointed fern',[54] and discussing insects with Henderson and 'fossil plants & Roman Antiquitys' with Artis. The visit culminated with Henderson showing him his collection of ferns. Clare responded with a mixture of scientific distance and aesthetic pleasure (the combination that defined their relationship): 'Saw Hendersons collection of Ferns which is far from compleat tho some of them are beautiful'.[55]

The fern collecting expeditions continued into the spring of 1825, and by March their interesting confusion of the categories of amateur and academic, poetic and scientific, became a more focused project. Henderson proposed:

> With respect to the Flora of this neighbourhood I cannot satisfy myself as to my plan, except the old one of Notes on the plants mentioned in your verses, a mere catalogue of the plants found in the neighbourhood might easily be made out, but that would neither meet your needs nor mine. I have been thinking that if you were to take on the subject & title of a poem <u>The Poets Flower Garden</u> you would lay the best foundation for the scheme. The woods & the fields, where Nature is gardener, would furnish your materials & in it you might embody all the local names you are acquainted with & when we make our long talked of excursion I shall perhaps be able to help you to others, I would even go so far as to coin a few for there are many of our most beautiful wild flowers that have no familiar English name. In these & the plants mentioned in your works generally, I would write notes giving the Botanical name & any other remark that might be thought interesting, which with your own observations might follow as an appendix to your works.[56]

Henderson clearly wanted to move beyond his original scheme of providing an appendix to Clare's flower poems, and to develop a mutually beneficial project. Henderson could further his career as a botanist, while Clare could fulfil his ambition to create an English botany of wild flowers. While the collecting and research began as part of his activities toward producing 'The Natural History of Helpstone', it now had the momentum of a distinct project. Unfortunately, Clare appears to have concentrated his natural history activity on his project with Hessey, and the Henderson project never came to fruition. A collected volume of Clare's flower poems, taken from those already published, in manuscript and written especially, with an extensive apparatus consisting of his and Henderson's field notes and the double set of names (common and botanical), would have been timely. Natural history books were popular; it was a new area of popular enthusiasm; and it might well have been a great success. Its potential literary value cannot be doubted. Clare had first considered a wild flower book the previous autumn when he read Elizabeth Kent's *Flora Domestica*. He recognised the potential market for a similar book based on his particular expertise and combination of gifts:

> I will write one on the same plan [as *Flora Domestica*] & call it a garden of wild Flowers as it shall contain nothing else with quotations from poets & others   an English Botany on this plan woud be very interesting & serve to make Botany popular while the hard nicknaming system of unuterable words now in vogue only overloads it in mystery till it makes darkness visible[57]

Clare and Henderson shared the immediate goal of producing a work of popular botany based on Clare's wild flower poems, and the broader goal of popularising natural history. Curiously, their views on the merits of Linnaean nomenclature could not have been more different. On the one hand, Clare held it in contempt as a form of obfuscation, while Henderson was an elected Associate of the Linnaean Society.[58] Indeed, one of the books Clare consulted during his December visit was Linnaeus's, but their differences can best be seen in a later project, collecting information about local orchids. Earl Fitzwilliam was an important cultivator of orchids,[59] and Henderson's botanical interest fitted nicely with his patron's. For his part, Clare assisted Henderson in locating various species, an activity in which he had no equal, as attested by Henderson's response to one of his finds: 'where the Devil did you find the fly orchis for the [fly?] it certainly is & I have never seen it before in this neighbourhood'.[60] The same letter contained their cumulative list of located and identified species, but this final work of scientific classification and exhaustive thoroughness was not where Clare found pleasure in his role. On the flyleaf of a book on the cultivation of various kinds of flowers,[61] Clare made his own kind of list with the title, 'Orchis counted from Privet hedge'. The list contains 22 individual flowers, each identified by common name:

1–Tway blade	13–Male or Wood
2–Pyrimidial Spotted	14–Birds Nest ['Tway blade' has been
3–Lily Leaved	crossed out]
4–Ditto	15–Red Man
5–Red Man	16–Green Man
6–Aromatic	17–Spider
7–Lily Leaved	18–Military
8–Pyrimidial Plain	19–Green Man
9–Butterflye	20–Ditto
10–Tway blade	21–Bee
11–Female or Meadow	22–Green Man
12–Butterflye	

The most striking thing about this list, apart from the extraordinary variety of specimens on offer in a single hedge, is its lack of interest in scientific classification. There are fourteen species listed, but twenty-two individual flowers. True to his poetics, and ethics in general, Clare ensured that each flower was recorded – their primary value lay in their individual beauty, not in their status as specimens. Henderson appreciated the beauty of each flower and Clare's poetic representations of them, but his focus was on their scientific value as part of the sum total of English botanical knowledge. Clare willingly engaged in this grand scientific enterprise, but continued to focus on his wider life-project, the establishment of the inherent value of the natural inhabitants of his neighbourhood.

*

Clare's journal recorded one of the inevitable by-products of his collecting expeditions, elegiac responses to the loss of some of the natural inhabitants of the countryside. Consistent with his analysis from the beginning, Clare associated these losses with the enclosure of common lands and the crass economics of profit and gain. Among the most beautiful entries in the journal, these descriptions recorded Clare's mourning and expressed his continuing anger at the upheaval of the traditional rural economy. Many of these entries concerned trees because they had once seemed to be outside the scope of human time, and now were particularly under threat from enclosure. The specificity and depth of feeling of his prose 'elegies' make them unique:

> Took a walk in the fields saw an old woodstile taken away from a favourite spot which it had occupied all my life the posts were overgrown with Ivy & it seemd so akin to nature & the spot were it stood as tho it had taken on a lease for an undisturbd existance it hurt me to see it was gone for my affections claims a friendship with such things but nothing is lasting in this world last year Langley bush was destroyed an old white thorn that had stood for more then a century full of fame the Gipseys Shepherds & Herd men all had their tales of its history & it will be long ere its memory is forgotten[62]

Clare's entry memorialised both his beloved stile and the 'old white thorn'. His diction told much of the tale. The phrase, 'as tho it had taken on lease', made reference to the relationships of property. The stile, like most of Clare's 'friends' was a tenant, and the liberty of tenants was at stake. Human inhabitants were also elegized. 'Coz. Day the Mole Catcher' received an entry when he died, and Clare referred to him in similar terms: he was 'a tennant of the Meadows & fields for half a Century.'[63] Day's ability to remain a 'tennant of the fields' had been compromised by enclosure.[64] He required a large physical territory in order to eke out his existence killing moles for a meagre bounty, collecting mushrooms in season and whatever other opportunities presented themselves in season. As with the destruction of Langley bush, the physical disruption of the countryside made it difficult to circulate freely and had direct consequences on rural inhabitants – especially the most vulnerable. Clare mourned the loss to those inhabitants in elegizing the loss of the 'old white hawthorn'. The 'century full of fame' that the tree had garnered originated with the humblest of local inhabitants, 'the Gipseys Shepherds and Herd men'. Gypsies appear throughout Clare's poems, and his close associations with the local Smith family, in particular, make it clear that he valued their friendship. In addition to being an invited guest to two Smith weddings in 1824–5, a prized guest for his fiddle playing, Clare also relied on Wisdom Smith as an authority on folk tunes, and a source of new tunes.[65] 'Herd men' refers, at least in part, to another stigmatised group, the Scottish drovers who habitually travelled through the county and sought shelter among the ancient trees that punctuated their route. Clare could count himself among the

final group in his list. Shepherd had been one of his many rural occupations as a child. His ability to identify intimately with the plight of the
countryside and its inhabitants differentiates Clare's elegiac voice from
what might be called the standard Romantic elegy. Unlike Wordsworth,
whose elegies most often construct his poetic sensibility as their
ultimate product, Clare does not have the luxury of distanced sympathy.
Rather, he finds himself among the natural objects under threat. His
poems often make this clear, as in the famous parenthetical phrase,
'wretches such as me', in 'Helpstone'. Clare's elegiac voice records his
participation in social upheaval and deliberately resists the temptations
of quasi-Wordsworthian self-aggrandisement – the creation of 'the poet'
(see Chapter 2, n. 10). Clare circulates among his neighbours, and his
elegiac power serves to honour and preserve to the memory their value
and the value of the landscape they inhabit.

The oral tradition, as a living force, created the 'fame' of the tree, and,
in valuing the 'history' spoken by these most stigmatised members of his
community, Clare continued that historical tradition while transforming
it through his prose into a written memorial. Keeping a journal allowed
Clare to preserve for memory both the value of the landscape and the
agony of its loss. He recorded similar losses, both of the rural inhabitants
and the landscape and history represented by the neighbourhood trees.
During a walk he wandered upon the funeral of John Cue of Ufford,
drawn by the village bells. Clare memorialised Cue's 'fame' for 'turnip
hoeing', and in so doing transvalued a common act of rural labour. In
addition to his physical prowess, John Cue 'was once head Gardener for
Lord Manners' and left behind a small natural history library including
Parkinson's Herbal.[66] By combining John Cue's village 'fame' and his
intellectual sophistication as natural parts of his identity, Clare invites
us to rethink assumptions about rural labourers. To be 'famous' for
'hoeing turnips' sounds a modest achievement, but such men could not
be underestimated, and their cultural value was unquestionably great.
Even individuals of less 'fame' gained value by Clare's record of their
passing:

> Old Shepherd Newman dyd this Morning an old tenant of the fields
> & the last of the old shepherds   the fields are now left desolate &
> his old haunts look like houses disinhabited   the fading woods
> seem mourning in the autumn wind   how often hath he seen the
> blue skye the green fields & woods & the seasons changes & now he
> sleeps unconscious of all   what a desolate mystery doth it leave
> round the living mind[67]

The landscape mourned the loss of 'old shepherd Newman' along with Clare. As a 'tenant of the fields' he had worked in a natural reciprocity with the countryside, and the neighbourhood cannot but experience his passing. As 'the last of the old shepherds', Newman represented the final loss of a way of life. Enclosure put an end to open pasture, and a 'desolate' emptiness overtook the landscape. The double sense of 'the fields left desolate', their physical emptiness and their emotional grief, continued in the simile describing the emptiness as 'like houses disinhabited'. The passing of the shepherd, 'like' the passing of a cottager, left behind a world forever changed, and the 'fading woods seem[ed] [in] mourning' for the loss. Typical of Clare's poetics, the emotional intensity of the experience remained unassimilated – no psychological self-expansion ensued and Clare remained, like the scene, 'desolate', unable to overcome the 'mystery' that the death of the shepherd and its mirroring in the condition of the landscape had on the 'living mind'. The profound undifferentiated condition of mourning Clare described constituted a complex form of elegy in which the healing capacity of memorialising cannot, indeed must not, recuperate the moment. A Wordsworthian aesthetic performance in such a moment,[68] considered a staple of the dominant stream of Romantic aesthetics, must for Clare have represented a heartless exploitation of who and what was lost, and a pointless evasion of his vulnerability.

The 'botanizing' excursions provided material for scientific and poetic projects, and further deepened his sense of the cultural and poetic magnitude of his loss. Out of that condition, he attempted to memorialise not himself, but the neighbourhood, and that focus presented its own potential project: 'I have been thinking to-day of all the large trees about our neighbour hood & those that have curious historys about them'.[69] The example of 'a Walnutt tree (now cut down)' served as a sample of a possible method. He would include local oral history, the spoken record of 'old Will Tyers' in the case of the walnut, with the clear assumption that some trees held such significance that many individual histories would be required to create the complex, and necessarily incomplete, history of its life and presence. An experience of the previous week put the seed into his mind, and his journal entry stands as an exemplary instance of the pathos, beauty and cultural insight such a 'history' might have yielded:

Went to see if the old hazel nut tree in lea close was cut down & found it still standing   it is the largest hazel tree I ever saw being thicker then ones thigh in the trunk & the height of a moderate

Ash—I once got a half peck of nutts when in the leams [green in their shells] off its branches when a boy—the Inclosure has left it desolate its companions of oak & ash being gone[70]

The physical and emotional 'desolation' of the tree, stripped of all companions, matched Clare's, and he made the cause of the 'desolation' clear. Together, Clare and the landscape *felt* the enclosure. All of the natural history projects he conceived served to value what was at stake. Recording all of the extant varieties of ferns in northern Northamptonshire with Henderson served to proclaim the intrinsic value of each, and the expansion of scientific knowledge may well have seemed like a means to make the case for the preservation of open field land.[71]

Miss Kent's 'History of Birds'

The other relationship that shaped Clare's thinking about natural history in this period was with his fellow Taylor & Hessey author, Elizabeth Kent. Hessey sent Clare Kent's volumes as they appeared, and encouraged a correspondence between them. Hessey's goals in so doing appear, in retrospect, to be somewhat confused, and that confusion did not help matters as Clare struggled to define his own project. Hessey's initial letter concerning Kent's *Flora Domestica* directed Clare to consider the book on its merits, but also wanted to alert him to the fact that his poems appeared throughout as poetic illustrations. Presumably, Taylor had approved Kent's use of the poems, and had not bothered to consult with their author. Hessey made sure to frame the news as an opportunity to make the work known in new circles, with the possibility of perhaps even more Clare poems in future editions:

I have waited till to day that I might send you a Copy of a pretty volume just published, (on a subject that will be interesting to you) in which your name is honourably mentioned—You must add it to your collection for our sakes if it is not worthy of a place on your shelves for its own. You have done as much as most poets towards the investing of Flowers with Interest and Sentiment & Imagination, and our friend has endeavoured to bring into one view the pleasant labours of your poetical [muse?] and to raise the flowers of the field to a rank which they deserve to hold. Should a second edition of it ever be required many additions might be made with advantage, and I dare say you could help us to many—If you should find any little beautiful passages in the course of your poetical reading you may as well mark them for us.[72]

Hessey emphasised the collegial nature of the project – Clare contributed poems, and collected poems from his reading to use as illustrations. Elizabeth Kent, their 'friend', synthesised the 'interest and sentiment' with which Clare invested his representations of common flowers with her own knowledge of cultivation and botany to form a book that raised 'the flowers of the field to a rank' they deserved. A worthy project with a worthy goal, Clare responded with enthusiasm. More than anything, the book fired his imagination and began the process of conceiving his new hybrid form, 'the poetic natural history', combining poetry and botany. By the following autumn he realised that he could 'write one on the same plan'[73] focusing on wild flowers – relying on his extensive knowledge of indigenous wild flowers, his already existent fund of flower poems, his ongoing production of occasional poems on the subject, and flower poems discovered in his exploration of other poets. *Flora Domestica* served as the original model and inspiration for his proposed 'Natural History of Helpstone', and coupled with Gilbert White's *Natural History of Selborne*, introduced to Clare by Hessey in the autumn of 1824,[74] held out the promise of an expanding market for natural history books.

Clare's initial response, while positive, was tempered somewhat by Kent's condescension in her preface. She referred to Clare directly: 'None better understood the language of flowers than the simple-minded peasant-poet, Clare, whose volumes are like a beautiful country, diversified with woods, meadows, heaths, and flower-gardens.'[75] The fulsome praise compensated for the insult, but Clare nonetheless took an authoritative tone in reply. He wrote to Hessey to correct some of the author's mistakes, especially her low opinion of the cowslip, which he insisted was 'a very favoured flower, and no cottager's garden...without it.'[76] This turned out to be a public criticism when Hessey decided to publish it in the August *London Magazine*. In writing to Kent, Clare took a very formal tone, and rather than appearing 'simple-minded', presented himself as an authority offering advice. He suggested she expand her project and produce a general Botany, and his arguments in favour of such a book expressed the desire to combine science and art (the project he subsequently pursued with Henderson), and restated Kent's own views on the power of nature as an ameliorating force. Clare reminded her of the democratic potential of making nature available to as many people as possible – the entire rationale for a book on cultivating flowers in pots. His emphasis was on the effect such a study would have 'in the minds' of such individuals:

> I do not mean the mere science for of that I know but little but the reflections it creates to see the various colours of field flowers & the eternal variety of shapes & different tintings of the leaves of herbs & trees & when we notice these things we feel a desire to know their names as of so many friends & acquaintance & the easiest way to become acquainted with these is by the assistance of Botany which is so far a very useful system & every one who attempts to render a useful system popular deserves the thanks of those interested in it for his labours & you deserve them in many instances & if I might put in a plea for the future shepherds & ploughmen of my country (as intelect is the heritage or birth right of every sphere of life) I think your abilitys might render Botany popular enough to win their attention by making them acquainted with the flowers of their own country[77]

The gentle but firm assertion in the parenthesis, reminding Kent that intellect was not a matter of class, answered the condescension of the comments in her preface, but it also established common cause with the wider purpose of the book. Kent, Leigh Hunt's sister-in-law, had clear political goals for the work. Active participation in nature served to improve our moral beings, and a keen interest in a garden reflected the moral fitness of the gardener: 'Was a cruel, unfeeling, or selfish man ever known to take pleasure in working his own garden? Surely not. This love of nature in detail (if the expression may be allowed) is an union of affection, good taste, and natural piety.'[78] This subtle piece of agitation worked on several important fronts. Sensibility was presented as 'naturally' progressive; the rhetorical question performed a negative construction of a wealthy landowner, alienated from his 'own garden'; the invention of the 'expression', 'love of nature in detail' removed the necessity of substantial property for the creation of natural beauty. Landscape aesthetics were no longer the exclusive province of the gentry, as Kent moved them, in miniature, to a suburban site. Moreover, the emphasis on 'detail' suggested that an even finer aesthetic achievement was possible in this intimate scale. The analogy to Clare's poems was obvious – the detailed representation of the most common plants and flowers provided the reader with abundant scope for self-improvement, just as the suburban gardener refined the mind through attention to the 'detail' of natural beauty. Her radical aims became clear enough when she turned to an example of an individual improved by such contemplation:

In our own time, we may instance the late Mr Shelley. Of a strong and powerful intellect, his manners were as gentle as a summer's evening: his tastes were pure and simple: it was his delight to ramble out into the fields and woods, where he would take his book, or sometimes his pen, and having employed some hours in study, and in speculations on his favourite theme—the advancement of human happiness, would return home with his hat wreathed with briony, of wild convolvulus; his hand filled with bunches of wild-flowers plucked from the hedges as he passed, and his eyes, indeed in every feature, beaming with the benevolence of his heart.[79]

Her elegy for Shelley, the natural man, announced her partisanship, and Clare's comment must be read, in part, as an affirmation of democratic goals and faith in human amelioration, Shelley's 'favourite theme'.[80] Clare's faith in the possibility of human amelioration through 'detailed' attention to nature caused him to want to expand its influence to include the 'future shepherds & ploughmen'.

Clare responded favourably to Kent's second book, *Sylvan Sketches*, impressed by her professional skill as 'a thorough book maker'.[81] Hessey extravagantly praised the book in an accompanying letter, and made Clare a significant proposition:

The volume is a new one by the author of the Book of Flowers which you liked so much and I think it is even a pleasanter book than its predecessor. The author is now at a loss for a further subject. I mentioned to her the one we were talking of, "The Birds," under a Promise that she should not mention it nor take advantage of it so long as you entertain any Idea of doing it yourself. I told her that you had thought of it and that I should immediately write to you on the subject. I think she would make a very pretty volume if she knows any thing about it already. [But?] the poets have not been quite so familiar with the Birds as with Trees & Flowers. Let me hear from you soon to say whether you think you have materials enough at your command to make up such a work, or if not, whether you would like to furnish your stock of Information to the lady author, and tell me how you like her Book of Trees.[82]

Hessey's suggested collaboration with Kent on 'The Birds' had an immediate effect. In a journal entry the following week, Clare retitled his project, 'Biographys of Birds and Flowers',[83] so the letter served as a catalyst in the reorganisation process. The exact shape of 'The Natural History of Helpstone' had yet to be decided. Hessey's letter seemed to suggest that Clare might focus on wild flowers, and provide his 'stock of Information' on birds for Kent's use, but in the short term he decided to hold on to the most comprehensive version of the work. Henderson also wrote on 11 March suggesting his 'The Poet's Flower Garden' project. At this stage, Clare had simply too many potential books in mind. The Hessey letter also showed that he had lost his focus on 'The Natural History of Helpstone', and wanted to employ Clare as an expert contributor to the works of their most successful natural history author.[84] Clare's poems already had a significant place in the two published volumes, and now his store of general knowledge and gift for observation could be used to provide Kent with material for a new project – material she did not have. Unfortunately, it did not occur to Hessey or Kent that a formal collaboration might work, and Hessey's divided attention amounted to wavering support at Taylor & Hessey for Clare's proposed volume. In the end, Clare had second thoughts about his ability to muster a sufficient 'store of Information' to make a success of a book on birds.

Clare wrote to Taylor offering to share his information with Kent, and collaborate on the book. Whether the book would be formally co-authored, or what his exact role would be was left open, but his recent activities with Henderson had provided a model for collaboration based on the division of roles according to specific talents:

> I told Hessey that I was ready to join the Young Lady in writing the History of Birds but I have heard nothing about it & I have such a fear of my own inability to do any thing for such a matter that I cannot enter into it with any spirit as I find that I dont know half the Swimmers & Waders that inhabit the fens & I understand that there are many of them strangers to the Natural History bookmakers themselves that have hitherto written about it[85]

His inability to enter into the project 'with any spirit' was not surprising given that two paragraphs earlier he had threatened a change of publishers over the rate of progress on *The Shepherd's Calendar*. His professed anxiety over his limited knowledge was based on the physical limits of his world. Clare did not walk the fens in the way he walked the fields, woods and heaths around him, and he had no firsthand knowledge of the birds of that nearby, but nonetheless alien, environment. His anxiety originated in his friendship with Henderson. Clare had been assisting in Henderson's efforts at comprehensive accounts of both British ferns and local snails, and would later contribute to Henderson and Earl Fitzwilliam's researches on British orchids. Clare knew from his studies in the Milton House library that extant natural history books could not provide the information he lacked. A year earlier, this might not have made any difference. After all, the 'Natural History of Helpstone', by definition, would include only those species with which he was familiar. His growing scientific interests may have confused the issue. Whether he still intended to complete the 'Natural History of Helpstone' as 'Biographys of Birds and Flowers' *and* collaborate on a 'Natural History of British Birds', remains unclear.

Whatever the case, Hessey passed Clare's offer on to Kent:

> I told Miss Kent, the author of Flora Domestica, of your willingness to communicate any of your knowledge to her and she has in consequence availed herself of your permission to write to you—I enclose her letter in the Parcel.[86]

Clare's response to the enclosed letter indicated that his offer of collaboration had been misconstrued, most probably by Hessey, as an offer of information on Northamptonshire birds in the service of *her* book. The impression recorded in his journal was curt: 'a note also from Miss Kent accompanied the parcel to request my assistance to give her information for her intended History of Birds but if my assistance is not worth more then 12 lines it is worth nothing & I shall not interfere.'[87] Despite the false start, Kent's subsequent letters proved to be complex requests for detailed information, and showed a keen curiosity and willingness to exchange ideas, scholarly sources and her own discoveries. Unfortunately, Clare's half of the correspondence has not survived (or at least has not been found).[88] Their work was also delayed by a piece of bad luck. A detailed letter that she thought she had sent via Hessey turned up amongst her papers causing considerable consternation and embarrassment:

> I believed until a few days ago, that [he? MS torn] sent it. Judge my vexation in finding it among a number of letters, which had hastily been cleaned out of my desk. If you have had leisure to think of me at all, you must think I make a poor return for your kind offer of assistance. Pray accept my apology.[89]

Kent's 'history' progressed steadily, and Clare assisted by sharing detailed knowledge of his local birds and their habits. Kent incorporated his information, joined him in his disdain of much of the available natural history, and offered her insights in return. 'I thank you for the fact of the Goldcrest gluing its egg in its nest, and building only upon pine trees', she wrote in a long detailed letter. And such specificity was precisely her goal. No one had observed birds with more care than Clare; this gave their correspondence an extraordinary scope. In the same letter, she explained her strategy and also acknowledged Clare as her scholarly equal:

> My reason for troubling you about books, was, that I am more anxious to consult travels, or to gather anecdotes and historical facts connected with the birds than merely to describe their colours, &c. and among the immense variety of travels published, my friend may meet with some that I do not see, and therefore I ask my reading friends, to let me know if they meet with anything of this kind.[90]

She wanted to gather scientific data, anecdotal accounts, field observations and literary illustrations, and had received Clare's natural history letters from Hessey: 'I have read your letters from Mr Hessey, and shall avail myself of them.'[91] Her greatest frustration was at the state of disorganisation at the British Library, and must have been apprised of Clare's reading in the Milton House library as she asked him to recommend the books in the field he found most useful. Despite her sense that the project was very much an ongoing investigation, Kent was under financial pressure that cut her researches short:

> I am afraid *Necessity* will compel me to make an end of my work as quickly as possible, and I hope to have finished it in four or five weeks; But if you should be able to favor me with any interesting information, at a later period, it can be added as the work goes through the press. (emphasis hers)

Invoking 'necessity' indicated that Kent was a professional author, and hoped to live off her work. Clare had been struck by her professionalism, and, in part, it sprang from her middle-class background. The most threatening aspect of the members of the 'Cockney School' for conservative critics like Lockhart at *Blackwoods* and Croker at the *Quarterly Review* was that in reaching beyond their station they might professionalise subjects hitherto the exclusive province of the educated gentry. From *Flora Domestica* onward her aim had been democratise natural history by expanding its audience, a goal that had drawn Clare to her work.

Unfortunately for Kent, the opportunity to publish the book through her regular publishers probably disappeared the previous summer along with Taylor & Hessey. Hessey had always been the partner with an interest in natural history, and by the time Taylor reported receipt of the manuscript in a letter to Clare, his rationale for publication had narrowed to financial considerations:

> I have the MS of her Birds in hand but have not yet formed a judgement of it, though I think from what I have seen it is as interesting as the Flora at least, & much better than the Sylvan Sketches: the last work has not yet paid its Expenses.[92]

Despite recognising the clear merits of the book, Taylor ominously focused on the poor performance of the previous volume. By now Clare was full of enthusiasm for the project and had worked diligently gathering information in advance of Kent's self-imposed deadline. He expressed his excitement to Taylor in April: 'I have been very busy these la[st] few days in watching the habits and coming of spring birds so as to [be] able to give Miss Kent an account of such as are not very well known in books.'[93] Clare was anxious to know Taylor's plans, and requested an 'interleaved' copy so he could 'make remarks' and 'insert' his own knowledge to send to her. His excitement took the form of a collegial exchange of knowledge, and emphasised the sense of the work as ongoing. Presumably, future editions would integrate new information. Clare showed great generosity in his willingness to assist Kent in her research, especially given that it would have been easy to perceive her as a rival. Once he decided her project was worthy, and that he would not proceed with his own book of birds, he offered advice, information, and friendship. The value of the last of these for Clare cannot be overestimated.

In response to Clare's ongoing enquiries about the book, Taylor eventually wrote:

> Miss Kent has sent her work, I think, to some other Publisher. I told her I would take it in the Autumn, but she wanted to sell it immediately, & I suppose has parted with it, as I have heard no more of it.[94]

This response was probably disingenuous. Taylor had made up his mind that the book would not return his investment, and declined to publish it. His claim that Kent could not wait until 'Autumn' confirms the 'necessity' she mentioned to Clare, but Taylor simply lacked enthusiasm for the book, despite admitting it had merit. There can be no question that delays by Taylor in preparing and publishing *The Shepherd's Calendar* compromised Clare's career, and it seems likely that similar neglect had similar consequences for Kent. Taylor's effort to shift responsibility for the book not being published onto Kent soon found a parallel when Hessey wrote on Taylor's behalf to say that all that remained for the publication of *The Shepherd's Calendar* was the Preface 'to account for the long delay in the coming out of the volume on the score of ill health'.[95] The request that Clare write this introduction, which amounted to an absurd lie in an effort to salvage Taylor's professional reputation, repeated the pattern of self-delusion and subterfuge emanating from the press. Taylor's delusions could not mask his professional failure. The poor quality of *The Shepherd's Calendar* aside, his failure to take responsibility for the project and its delays shaped the period from 1824 to 1827. Had Clare had an honest response to his constant inquiries about the progress of the book, he could have used his contacts to secure an alternative publisher. The collapse of Taylor & Hessey came about, in part, because they were simply overextended. In retrospect, Taylor's assumption of the *London Magazine* was professional suicide, and he took Clare and Elizabeth Kent with him. No natural history book by any author was going to be published after the departure of Hessey, and Taylor's negotiations with Kent were almost certainly in bad faith.[96] For all of his work on the subject, Clare ended up with nothing to show. His intentions were clear enough. Another publisher would have encouraged the natural history letters and formalised their production. Hessey's distractedness and then departure prevented this from happening. An edition of the flower poems with a detailed appendix by Henderson would have been easy to produce and probably popular, and Clare and Henderson intended a more complex work, their 'Poetic Natural History'. Clare finally asked a direct question: 'What has become of Miss Kent & her Birds?'[97] Taylor's response served as a sad coda on the fate of the natural histories Taylor & Hessey might have produced:

I felt unwilling to undertake the work in times like these, when so few Books repay the Expense of Publishing.[98]

8
Clare, Cobbett and 'Captain Swing'

John Lucas and P. M. S. Dawson have established the debate over the nature of Clare's political commitments in their two influential essays: 'Clare's Politics' and 'Common Sense or Radicalism'. Lucas argues for an interpretation of Clare's poetry that attends particularly to its radical sentiments, while Dawson questions whether or not those same sentiments are truly radical or are more properly understood in the British tradition of 'common sense'. Dawson pursues his argument by historicising the term 'radical'.[1] Understanding political terms as they were used proves fruitful, and much more research remains to be done before we can be certain of how Clare viewed himself. This ongoing debate has been enhanced by the publication of *John Clare: A Champion of the Poor, Political Verse and Prose* which has made Clare's political prose writing available to a much larger number of scholars. In addition, one of the editors of the volume, Eric Robinson, has joined the debate by asserting that: 'His [Clare's] politics are local, or at most regional, rather than national; conservative rather than radical; monarchical rather than revolutionary or republican.'[2] None of these distinctions bears scrutiny. Robinson's use of the terms conservative and radical confuse the issue. Arguing that Clare was conservative because his position on the reform of church property was not as radical as Cobbett's renders the terms hopelessly relative. As I argue below, Clare's position on tithes was certainly more radical than that of Herbert Marsh, who as Bishop of Peterborough was ordained to defend church property. Neither of these claims illuminates Clare's position, and only a close reading of Clare's correspondence in the overheated atmosphere of the 'Swing Riots'[3] and the run-up to the Reform Bill in 1830–2 reveals his position. Clare's ambitious publication plans from 1824 to 1826 call into question the claim that his focus was 'local'. While careful to cultivate his 'local' neighbours like Savage at the *Scientific Receptacle*, he equally corresponded with national figures such as William Hone and James Montgomery, and he was a member of one of the most sophisticated intellectual circles of the day at the *London Magazine*. Even his 'local friends' had broad 'national' interests, especially those connected to Earl Fitzwilliam and Lord Milton, Joseph Henderson and Edmund Tyrell Artis. While I agree there is no evidence that Clare was a republican, that does not mean he did not favour reform. In support of his claim that Clare was a monarchist, Robinson includes the poem 'On Seeing a Lost Greyhound in Winter Lying Upon the Snow in the Fields' and argues that it contains evidence of a belief in the Great Chain of Being and by extension the divine right of kings: 'He [Clare] also accepts, at least on one occasion, the Great Chain of Being which posited that every part of creation was in that position in which God had placed it, so that the social hierarchy was part of the divine plan, and should be accepted as such.'[4] On closer examination the poem actually interrogates the sanctity of such hierarchies and struggles to free itself from them. His master has abandoned the greyhound after the hunting season, and Clare exploits the obvious analogy to the condition of labourers. The stanza that draws Robinson's attention reminds the reader of the equality of all creatures in God's providence:

> For dogs are equally
> A link in natures chain
> Form'd by the hand that formed me
> Which formeth not in vain
> All life contains as't were by chains
> From him still perfect are
> Nor does he think the meanest link
> Unworthy of his Care[5]

While this stanza certainly makes use of the commonplace figure of all living creatures constituting the Kingdom of God, it does not create a hierarchical structure. Clare's chain is radically horizontal, and insists on the equality of all creatures. It can more easily be read as a levelling image than an endorsement of aristocratic privilege. Those members of society who would place themselves above Clare and the greyhound on the basis of birth and title are the targets of the poem's scorn – the masters who own slaves, exploit the peasantry and abandon their faithful servants once they have exhausted their usefulness. Clare employs the language of levelling when he addresses the dog: 'So rise and gang wi' me'.[6] Clare erases a false and arbitrary hierarchy in elevating the fallen dog. The contention that the poem supports the idea of an immutable social hierarchy ordained by God simply cannot be supported by the poem. I return to the more serious matter of Robinson's argument about Clare's 'local' focus in the final section of this chapter,[7] but first want to turn to the debate over Clare's political commitments during the 'Swing Riots'.

Paul Dawson sets out the terms of the debate over Clare's politics by taking the title for his essay from the question Clare posed in one of the numerous drafts of 'Apology for the Poor': 'is it common sense or radicalism ... when the many express their disapprobation of the tyranny & domineering of the few?'.[8] Dawson pursues this question by asking the further two-part question, what do we mean by 'radicalism'? And what might Clare have meant by it? He urges us to conclude that Clare would identify himself with 'common sense', and in order to make that case he sets out to define 'radicalism' as Clare would have understood it. Dawson divides 'radicalism' into three types: parliamentary radicals or radical Whigs, constitutional radicals like Cobbett or Henry Hunt, and popular radicals in the Spencean tradition of direct action.[9] I want to concentrate on particular events happening around Clare during the height of the 'Swing Riots' in December 1830 and January 1831, and which, in one way or another, involve all of these versions of radicalism. Each of these designations is complex in the specific context of Clare's experiences.

Equivocation

Clare's antipathy to party politics is well known: 'Politics may be said to be the art of money catching—the terms Wig & Tory & Radical are only distinctions between actors in the play—their discourse is of their country but when their parts are done we see they only meant themselves.'[10] Clare had plenty of experience observing this kind of political self-interest. A report in the issue of *The Bee* for 17 December 1830 refers to the petty greed and corruption of local party politics described by Clare. *The Bee* was a conservative Stamford newspaper that Clare contributed poems to in 1830 and 1831. The staunchly Tory editor accuses the local Whigs of nepotism and abuse of privilege in conducting the 'Stamford Lying-In Charity': 'The result of our investigation is, that the majority of Stamford women, who received relief during those months, were wives either of men who voted for Mr Tennyson, or of those who, not having votes, rendered themselves very conspicuous among his friends.'[11] This attack is typical of political discourse at the local level. Clare recognises that playing games of political advantage over the distribution of charity to the poor disgraces all sides. He has no illusions about the local Tories putting an end to the abuses they claimed to have uncovered. In a prose scrap from roughly the same time he despaired: 'I fear these tory radicals these out of place patriots (or parrots) who are so loud in their insults against the present ministry only want to make paddles of the people to sail into their harbours of old sinecures & then to be again themselves they will be silent of suffering people & all such allusions – as an old maid is of her age or an old borough monger of common honesty.'[12] His use of the word 'radical' is contemptuous and implies an absence of good faith. It is not that 'radicalism' is to blame, but rather the cynical destruction of the term's content. 'Tory radicals' was an oxymoron, and a sudden professed concern for reform did not blind Clare to the underlying motive of personal and political power. Clare saw the practice of party politics as shameful self-interest and cynicism, so it is hardly surprising that in a letter to Mrs Emmerson from this time he declared: 'I wish success heartily to my friends wether wigs torys or radicals', but to his enemies he wished none because he could not 'alter their opinions'.[13] From Clare's contempt for party politics, it does not follow necessarily, then, that he was not a 'radical' in questions of reform. Disclaiming party affiliation left him free to judge his 'friends' according to their 'opinions' without being asked to adopt an entire ideological agenda that he saw as corrupt. He could discriminate between individual Whigs, Tories and Radicals, and it is a mistake to conclude that he completely rejected specific policies just because a particular party espoused them. Rather, he examined the actual 'opinions' of various political figures as the grounds on which he judged them. So on the basis of parliamentary politics we cannot say whether Clare considered himself to be a 'radical'. Local political parties were often corrupt and of no value to anyone but their self-interested local operatives. However it does not follow that Clare rejected policies because of suspect party affiliations – if these 'out of place' Tories worked for meaningful change they could count on Clare, and the rural population at large, for support.

Clare's attitude towards 'popular radicalism' is equally difficult to evaluate. He condemns the violence of the 'Swing Riots' and their apparent futility, but that does not mean that he opposes the political goals of the so-called 'incendiaries'. Dismay over the violence that Cobbett referred to as the 'Rural War' was widespread in all political circles. It is difficult, for example, to differentiate the politics in the various newspaper reports of disturbances near where Clare lived. As I indicated earlier, Clare contributed poetry to the conservative newspaper *The Bee*, but he also contributed poems to *Drakard's Stamford Champion*, the leading radical newspaper in the area. This dual publishing programme has been offered as evidence of Clare's political ambivalence, but on the subject of the 'incendiaries' the two newspapers strike very similar notes. *The Bee*, predictably, in reporting a local fire at the farm of a Mr Clark on 19 December 1830, denounced the irrationality of the violence and in particular the cruel destruction of livestock. Clare alluded to this fire in his letter to Frank Simpson (probably written the same week[14]): 'on saturday night that horrid tragedy in deeping fen occured that chills my blood almost into water to think of.' The fact that Clare shared the shock and dismay of *The Bee*, and that he declared this response to his friend Frank Simpson, who was a magistrate,[15] could lead us to conclude that this was a conservative response. Things are not that simple. The more moderate local conservative newspaper, the *Stamford Mercury*, responded in kind: 'What adds greatly to the horror of this calamitous affair is, that 14 beasts, 4 horses, and 2 pigs, were burnt to death.'[16] And, Drakard's other newspaper, the *Stamford News*, also radical in its outlook, repeated the feelings of horror in even stronger terms: 'The cries of the poor inoffensive animals for relief when no relief could be afforded them, were, we understand, painful in the extreme.'[17] Clearly then, outrage at the destruction of property and livestock cannot be used reliably to attribute political views. In fact the mood of the neighbourhood, feeling itself engulfed in violence, was such that it is difficult to establish whether a statement from this brief period is an instance of a deeply held political view, or a momentary response to the growing panic.

The farmers of Northamptonshire and Lincolnshire had seen the violent troubles in the countryside as a distant problem. And as the acts of the 'incendiaries' spread into their region, panic ensued. The panic can be traced through the first few issues of *The Bee*. Initially, the editor's tone was self-congratulatory: 'we feel convinced, not withstanding the lamentable occurences so rife in the neighbouring counties, that the "System" [of insurrection] cannot extend to our own immediate neighbourhood.'[18] This confidence was shortlived. A week later, a fire in the immediate area produced the offer, printed as the first item in *The Bee*, of a reward of £500 and 40 Guineas for information about the blaze. Over the next two weeks, several more fires occurred, and the reward for the original blaze inflated, first to £1000 and then to £1330 plus amnesty for all those involved save the actual 'incendiary'.[19] We can gauge the growing hysteria in this rapid inflation of the reward. In such a climate, it is not surprising that Clare's letter to Simpson was full of typical 'Swing' paranoia (strangers in a gig who mysteriously appeared and disappeared throughout the countryside). Clare's account of events was identical in detail and tone to the accounts published by the Stamford papers of whatever political stripe. It is more interesting to note that Clare later satirised this panic, in his poem 'The Hue & Cry'. He had been caught up in the general mood that saw the monstrous 'crooked old man' everywhere, and associated him with Cobbett, the bones of Tom Paine, or some other scapegoat. Such monsters conveniently shifted the source of the trouble away from local conditions, and into an inexplicable outside force. Given a few weeks to reflect, Clare was able to satirise the panic of which he had been a part.

However, not all responses to acts of violence against property lacked political analysis or were obscured by panic. Cobbett in his notorious 13 November 1830 number of the *Weekly Political Register* had written against the violence, but had also struggled to understand the material conditions in the countryside that led to such desperate acts. The 11 December 1830 number ended with the dangerous piece of analysis that eventually led to Cobbett's trial for sedition: 'Without entering at present into the *motives* of the working people, it is unquestionable that their acts have produced good, and great good too.'[20] The view that smashing machinery and setting hayricks ablaze produced beneficial results for rural labourers was understandably unpopular with the authorities. But such analysis was not limited to Cobbett. Even *The Bee*, in reporting the Clark fire in Deeping Fen, acknowledged that the motives for the attack were clear enough: 'the occupier had been using a threshing machine on Friday, and fearful of the consequences had set a watch.'[21] In fact, the first editorial that appeared in *The Bee*, under the heading 'The Incendiaries', offered advice to the area farmers based on a distinction between incendiaries and machine breakers. The paper conceded that trying to convince local labourers that more labour might be created through the introduction of machinery (a counter-intuitive claim to say the least) was probably hopeless. The editor reluctantly recommended: 'the doing away of these unpopular instruments of husbandry, and thus by yielding on a point, on which you cannot convince men of their mistake, assist in opening their eyes upon those in which you can.'[22] The editor makes a distinction between the irrationality of burning crops and the rationale for machine breaking. He argues that, in the first case, the labourer destroys his share of the crop along with the farmer's share, and, in the second case, that the labourer acts based on his analysis of the effects of machinery on labour conditions. The editor's admission rather proves Cobbett's point: the pressure of the insurrection on farmers could bring about favourable change – the suspension of the use of threshing machines – even if that change were temporary and cynically strategic. Farmer Clark had failed to heed the newspaper's advice, so the fire was not so much an irrational outburst as a predictable result. Hayrick burning sometimes settled local scores and was thus often reactionary, whereas machine breaking had clear short-term economic goals.

Given time to reflect on the unrest of December 1830 and January 1831, Clare could still be horrified by its violence, but also understanding of the causes behind it. In a letter of the following July to Marianne Marsh, Clare said as much:

> I never saw so terrible a threatening of rev[o]lutionary forbodings as there was in the mashine breaking & grain destoying mania of last winter—& I am sorry to say they had too much apology for joining in such disturbances as their wants had been so long neglected as to be forgotten untill it burst out into terrible jepordays[23]

The question that arises then: is this Cobbett's 'radical' line or *The Bee's* cautionary tone? The evidence leans towards Cobbett. Basing political assumptions on Clare's dual publication practice – his political equivocation or ambivalence – does not bear scrutiny. The reasons for publishing in the two newspapers were significantly different. Frank Simpson was involved with *The Bee* and Clare contributed out of friendship. More decisively, he published there as part of his sponsorship of the aspiring poetic career of his long-time patron Mrs Emmerson. She contributed more poems to *The Bee*, under her poetic pseudonym E.L.E., than did Clare, and his participation ensured hers. Mrs Emmerson's letters from this period emphasise the enormous significance she placed on her new career. On the other hand, Clare contributed anonymous political satire to Drakard; it is difficult to imagine two more different rationales for publication. Clare's anonymity allowed him to express his views in a forthright manner. The reason, then, to believe that Clare's analysis of the crisis was of a piece with Cobbett rather than *The Bee* lies in his satiric poem, 'The Hue & Cry'.

Clare published 'The Hue & Cry' anonymously in *Drakard's Stamford Champion* on 11 January 1831, just as the local panic was abating. Several stanzas in the poem indicate Clare's understanding of the riots as a political strategy, and, furthermore, provide evidence of a bitter recognition of the temporary nature of any benefits gained. He satirised the impact of the riots on local political culture:

> Fair speakers got up of real goodness to teach,
> They had said,—and done nothing before,
> And danger, like steam, might force good in the speech,
> Which might fall when the danger was o'er.[24]

He went on to specify the cynical nature of the farmers' changed political views:

> Masters unstrung their purses and said to their men,
> 'Twas all their intentions before
> To give better wages—then nine out of ten,
> Only gave it till danger was o'er.

The poem seems prophetic in light of an item in the *Champion* two weeks later:

> A correspondent mentions that in some parishes within a few miles of Maidstone, the farmers have begun to reduce the wages of their labourers from 15s. to 12s. and 10s. a week. In these places, the farmers had either been intimidated into the payment of the higher rate, or had volunteered to do so in the hope of keeping the incendiary or rioter from their premises. With the return of tranquility they have thought fit to revert to the ordinary scale of wages. We must question the propriety or policy of this course of proceeding. The farmers must be sensible that the cessation of outrage is as much owing to the late increase in wages, as to the terrible examples which justice has singled out in this and neighbouring counties.[25]

The analysis in Clare's poem should be considered in the light of this forthrightly 'radical' analysis. Improved wages, not hanging and transportation were the only long-term solutions to rural insurrection. The cynical response of farmers was destructive of both labourers' livelihoods, and rural peace and prosperity in general.

Clare's letter to Marianne Marsh, seen in this context, reads as a measured reflection on the similar events in Northamptonshire and Lincolnshire. He was genuinely shocked and dismayed by the violence and its likely futility, but had a 'radical' analysis available to him that made a provisional, if unhappy, sense of the situation. Clare's judicious estimation of Cobbett, typical distaste for party politics coupled with general agreement 'that a reform is wanted', is a thoughtful response in an ongoing political discussion. The letter finally reflects the difficulty and isolation implicit in Clare's distaste for both 'the reform of the mob', and 'the reform of partys'.[26] Clare's attitude towards what Paul Dawson terms 'popular radicalism' thus reflects a set of understandably contradictory responses to events, and those responses shift over time. They therefore cannot be used to establish definitively whether he considered himself a 'radical', but it is nevertheless clear that he held the 'radical' view that 'a reform (was) wanted'. I am not arguing that Clare's views on tithes were identical to Cobbett's. He would probably have been appalled by Cobbett's ultimate goal of redistributing church property, but support for a reduction of tithes nonetheless placed him on a continuum of views that must be considered 'radical' if measured against state policy.

This brings us to Dawson's final category, 'constitutional radical'. What can we conclude from Clare's ambivalent attitude towards Cobbett? I have already suggested that there are real similarities between the two men's views concerning the efficacy of the 'Rural War'. But Dawson argues that the real test is whether or not Clare was interested in 'the reform of Parliament . . . the point at issue'. Dawson suggests, on the evidence of the February 1830 letter to John Taylor, that Clare's interests and political goals lay elsewhere, and included 'a reduction in tithes, clerical livings, placemen's pensions and taxes.'[27] But, the reduction of church tithes was at the very centre of 'radical' debate about Parliamentary reform. There was probably no other issue that more defined political debate at this particular historical moment. Cobbett's 'Rural Ride' for 1830 that took him through Northamptonshire and Lincolnshire illustrates the point. In Stamford, he addressed an audience of 'about 200 farmers and others'[28] on 31 March, and again on 1 April he spoke to a crowd that included many farmers from the neighbouring small county of Rutland. The Stamford papers of the following week were in agreement about the subject of Cobbett's lecture if not their attitude towards it. The conservative *Stamford Mercury* sneered at Cobbett and suggested that he did not make any money from his Stamford engagements, but nonetheless considered his lectures worthy of detailed coverage. The editor summarised Cobbett's argument:

> That the distress which pervades the country has been occasioned by the acts of Government. That the taxes make the distress. That the poor ought to be relieved out of their tithes; and that it is their right

by the law of the land to be so relieved. That the church property is mis-applied; and that it is legal, and due to the necessities of the people, to take it from the Clergy. And, lastly, that a great reduction of the public debt can be justly made.[29]

Cobbett's argument was pitched directly to the farmers, and presented an alternative to the current economic state of the country. If church property could be redistributed, then the debt could be tamed and tax pressures eased. He used this argument to address the plight of the poor and the labourers, reminding the farmers in his audience that 'it is the taxes that have brought ruin into the country, not the poor-rates.'[30] Calls for a reduction of tithes, and a redistribution of church property, then, were at the centre of 'constitutional radicalism'. The responses to Cobbett's campaign make this clear.

At the height of the troubles of December 1830, *The Bee* reprinted a long article from *The Times* defending tithes as an integral part of 'a Church which ... since the dawn of Protestantism, has been stamped as the purest, the most holy, and the nearest approaching to perfection, that has yet been instituted on earth.'[31] An open letter from Herbert Marsh, written in his official church capacity as Herbert Peterborough, appeared a week later, and took up the conservative rhetoric of the evolving perfection of national institutions. The Bishop reminded the farmers that: 'Property in tithe is no less sacred than property in land: both kinds of property are under protection of the law.'[32] The target here, and the source of anxiety, was Cobbett. Remember that Cobbett's audience was also the farming community, and the Bishop therefore felt moved to counter the current 'radical slang'.

This anxiety about Cobbett's potential influence on political issues reappeared in *The Bee* in January 1831 with the publication of an anonymous poem called 'Captain Swing'. This accused Cobbett of responsibility for the troubles:

> By him the wicked heart is brought
> To aid the coward hand;
> By him is disaffection taught
> To desolate the land.

The poem concluded that Cobbett's teaching and actions were seditious:

> How can the poor unlettered mind
> Such instruments [his rhetorical skill] withstand?

> On who can wonder that we find
> Sedition in the land?[33]

Cobbett's lecture campaign of 1830 was considered inflammatory and seditious, and reduction of church tithes was at the centre of that campaign. The reaction against Cobbett culminated with his trial for sedition. He was accused of being directly responsible for the incendiarism, the skilful manipulator of 'the poor unlettered mind'. The attack on Cobbett was inevitable given the course of the 'Rural War' over the previous year. For example, under the title 'Labourers' War Against Tithes in Norfolk', Drakard's *Stamford News* reported, again in December 1830, that several Norfolk ministers had been attacked when their annual tithes had come due. One, the 'Rev. Mr. Jack', had foreseen trouble and fled leaving instructions that 'the tithe feast' be distributed to the poor. This measure was unsuccessful. The mob ransacked his house, 'vowed vengeance against him', and 'proceeded to the poor house and pulled down part of it.'[34] The relationships between violent 'popular radicalism' (physical attacks on church property), and Cobbett's 'constitutional radicalism' (rhetorical attacks on church property) were difficult to separate, and the State took advantage of this confusion in bringing its prosecution.[35]

In light of this political ferment, Clare's February 1830 declaration to Taylor that he believed that 'a universal reduction of tythes' was necessary 'to bring salvation to the country' can only be understood as the expression of a 'radical' political goal. The drafts of Clare's 'Apology for the Poor' provide evidence of his commitment to that goal and others, and offer a glimpse of his emotional and intellectual responses to complex events. The polemical mood of the 'Apology' suggests that Clare was angry at being forced to defend himself against the tired charge of 'radicalism'. The term 'radical' had come to be used, as 'jacobin' had before it, as a general term of abuse to denounce the perceived enemies of the State. In his 'Apology', Clare responded with bitterness at this debasement of political speech. His support of the reduction of church tithes was certain to brand him as a 'radical' in the public political discourse,[36] and he must have felt himself confined by the empty, but effective, rhetoric of his critics. His question of whether it was 'common sense or radicalism' to call for meaningful political reform, was a highly rhetorical one. Clare attempted to rehabilitate language by ridiculing the notion that his views were 'radical' in this commonplace pejorative sense. 'Common sense' and 'radicalism' could be understood as synonyms, and had been in 'radical' circles since Tom Paine's famous pamphlet those many years ago. The political beliefs that Clare's critics would dismiss as 'radical' were vindicated by his rhetorical question as simple 'common sense'.[37]

Clare and Mrs Marsh

In the aftermath of the crisis of December and January Clare carried on an intense correspondence with Marianne Marsh, the wife of Herbert Marsh, Bishop of Peterborough, which provides us with a detailed picture of his political and emotional responses to the recent violence.

It has been assumed that the unequal relationship of author to patron governed Clare's exchanges with Mrs Marsh. For example, John Lucas has argued that we should be suspicious of anything Clare had to say to her because she was: 'undoubtedly on the side of...those whose land had been attacked during the Swing Riots.'[38] Such suspicion is unwarranted. The letters reveal a complex exchange of ideas, surprisingly outside the bounds of narrow class interests. While her husband, the Bishop, publicly defended the sanctity of Church property Mrs Marsh was sending Clare copies of William Cobbett's *Two-Penny Trash* in an effort to initiate a detailed and comprehensive discussion of the political and social issues at stake. The apparent contradiction of the Bishop's wife disseminating radical pamphlets demands a re-evaluation of assumptions about the terms of conservative patronage. And a detailed understanding of the relationship between Clare and Marianne Marsh recovers Clare's political analysis of complex and emotionally fraught events. This insight into Clare's political thinking, in turn, deepens our understanding of his sense of class identity and class interest.

*

Marianne Marsh was not a typical Bishop's wife. She met Herbert Marsh while he was in hiding in her family home in Leipzig. Bonaparte had proscribed Marsh for political agitation (pamphleteering) while ostensibly studying in Leipzig. Once Marsh returned to England he sent for Marianne, and married her 'immediately on the lady's landing'.[39] The Pitt ministry rewarded Marsh's political activities with a pension until a suitable church position could be arranged, and he resigned the pension once he gained his bishopric. So, Marianne Marsh found herself in a new country, and married to a brilliant, ambitious and well-connected churchman.[40]

Her early correspondence with Clare is unexceptional, as evidenced by this sentence from her first letter of 1821:

> The Bishop of Peterborough received your letter this morning and has commissioned me to say that he hopes to see you and Mrs Clare soon after the coronation.[41]

This is the respectful tone of official duty, the Bishop's wife thoughtfully including the local genius in the intellectual life of the Cathedral. However, over the next ten years their correspondence becomes more intimate. She sends gifts for the children, a favourite tea for Patty, medicine and medical advice for Clare's rheumatism and depression. The formality of the early letters gives way to a conversation between friends, full of everyday things. This apparently relaxed correspondence still displays a keen sensitivity to the social divide between them, and she takes care not to condescend: 'To show you how much I wish to cheer you, I am trying to make you laugh at sending you cakes as one does to children.'[42] This letter from January 1832 shows concern for the precariousness of Clare's mental state, she wants to 'cheer' him, but also takes pains to make sure her gesture is not misconstrued. Recognising that her concern could be taken as condescension indicates a finely developed sympathy, a subtle understanding of class power, and a determination not to abuse it.

Their correspondence records many of the books they lent one another and discussed, and provides frequent glimpses into their intellectual interests. What Mrs Marsh recommends as suitable reading material depends on specific occasions and events. For example, it would be easy to draw evidence of a conventional poet/patron relationship from her advice to Clare in February 1828 to read the Bible as a means of overcoming one of his bouts of depression:

> I trust you will not think me troublesome if I add, I hope you read your Bible. In a state of depression and for you as a poet I should further say [?] read the book of Job and admire its beauty and compare yourself with that holy man and trust like him that your sufferings are not unheeded by the great ruler of the universe.[43]

On the one hand, this advice sounds like the typical quietism preached by the Tory status quo (not unlike a Radstock letter): you will find your reward in the next life. But, on the other hand, her emphasis on the aesthetic experience of the text, 'admire its beauty', suggests a therapeutic use of the Bible. And Job, in particular, presents an example of the poetic mind overcoming adversity. Furthermore, not only is her suggestion not prescriptive in the religious sense, she is at pains to make it clear that she does not intend to be 'troublesome'.

During a different bout of depression in October 1830 she recommends a very different remedy:

> By degrees you will find power and leisure to read, for what is commonly called amusement, and will do so with advantage. As an intermediate kind of reading, I recommend to you the book which I send by Mrs Clare, and beg that you will read the essays *first*. (emphasis hers)[44]

Mrs Marsh provides an 'intermediate kind of reading' as if it were a medical prescription, yet she is keen that he read the didactic section first and is clearly anxious for his response. Even when she prescribes, the reciprocity of their relationship remains intact. Rather than recommending religious solace, she attempts to spur Clare into intellectual activity, and she, as well as Clare, will be a beneficiary of his renewed vigour. Increasingly this becomes the pattern of their exchanges. One of them suggests a piece of writing to which the other responds, leading to a detailed discussion of a given topic.

Some of the flavour of their reading pattern can be observed in a letter, probably written in January 1832,[45] in which Mrs Marsh promises to send Clare an exciting new find:

> I send you a book which I trust you have not read and which I value highly for its own sake and because it is the gift of a dear friend.... You would hardly have believed that Moore could speak of Christianity as he does in that book.

A subsequent letter identifies the book as *The Epicurean* by the Irish poet and satirist, Thomas Moore. Moore's book was notorious for both its irreligiousness and for its scathing attack on James Mill and the utilitarians. However, the Bishop's wife is not scandalised. She is excited by the intellectual challenge the book presents, and wants to draw Clare into a discussion of its merits. She may not approve of Moore's attack on Christianity, but she values the book 'highly' for its intellectual stimulation.

It was into this established intellectual relationship that the 'Swing Riots' intruded in the winter and spring of 1830–31. The 'Swing Riots' by their very nature inspired panic and confusion. They seemed to spread without warning from county to county, and local panic ensued – reports of strangers loitering suspiciously and asking too many questions, followed soon after by fires and vandalism.

Clare's letter to Frank Simpson reporting the appearance of suspicious men in Helpstone captures the mood:

> I have made a few enquiries respecting those strangers whom the 'Hue & Cry' leads me to suspect are the [?creators] of those horrid mysteries that darkness envelops & daylight discovers—The Gig was very light & apparently small for two men to occupy   one was dressed in a light great coat & the other in a dark one   they came in at the end of the town no strangers ever enters as it is a bye road leading no where but to bye places—they passed my father & another & asked the way for Spalding   when near the public Hous 'Blue Bell' they met another man on horseback . . .—the day after this—Dr Johnsons stacks at spalding was destroyed[46]

Accounts of 'strangers' destroying the contentment of the neighbourhood, and the corollary that the 'local' peasants were perfectly content, are puzzling, given that newspaper accounts clearly acknowledge the causes of unrest. Throughout the two years of rural insurrection, the only proven remedies for the violence were the suspension of the use of the machines and/or increased wages. Clare came to see that he had fallen into the hysteria of the moment, and less than a month later he published his anonymous poem 'The Hue & Cry' in the radical *Stamford Champion*. In the poem, he recognised that lacking any specific enemy to attack, the authorities exploited the confusion by targeting William Cobbett, who was eventually tried for sedition. Clare satirised this policy by ridiculing the hysteria that caused the authorities to see 'the crooked old man' everywhere, and that conveniently associated him with a demonised caricature of Cobbett, the ghoulish keeper of the 'bones of Tom Paine'.[47]

It was Cobbett's writing that provided the focus for Clare's correspondence with Marianne Marsh in the aftermath of the crisis, and their discussion, remarkably free of caricature, attempted to cut through the propaganda of both sides and analyse the political and social meaning of events. Each wrote a letter reflecting on the crisis on 6 July 1831. Clare's begins his with a detailed description of the chaos and danger of the previous winter:

...in the winter it was dangerous for any lone person to go even a journey to Peterbro—such was the feeling among that useful but ignorant class of people our peasantry that mischief became so predominant & daring as to threaten the peacable even in their cottages & I hope for the sake of my own feelings never to see such a threatening winter again—for I fear there is even in our day a class of desperadoes little or no better than the rabble that made up the army of Jack Cade

'a ragged multitude
'Of hinds & peasants rude & merciless
'All scholars lawyers courtiers gentlemen
'They call false caterpillars & intend their death'

the universal wish of such ignorance is 'that henceforth all things shall be in common' & surely when such a desperate flood gathers into strength—the mind must feel terror at its threatning destruction—their passions are not softened by reason or common sense—the mob impulse of the moment kindles their minds into mischivous intentions & reflection never stays their course for a moment[48]

This is an extraordinary passage for several reasons. First, it indicates that Clare both is and is not a member of the class he describes as 'our peasantry'. He admits the ignorance of his neighbours, but he too was caught up in the village hysteria. The very fact that he can quote from *Henry VI* separates him from other cottagers, and, furthermore, he makes it clear that the 'rabble' do not represent the entire peasantry, most of whom are 'peacable' and afraid to venture from their cottages. This is one of the passages that troubles John Lucas, and leads him to want to disclaim all of the letters to Mrs Marsh. Taken at face value, the passage could be presented as evidence of Clare's conservative opinions, and Lucas wishes to guard against such an interpretation by arguing that the letter is disingenuous. Closer examination of the passage, however, reveals that Clare says little about the goals of the mob. In fact, lacking 'reflection,' a 'mob' cannot be said to have goals. This is precisely the problem; it is the irrationality of the mob to which he objects. He makes this clear in the remainder of the letter where he attempts to understand the causes of the violence in the fact that the peasants' 'wants had been so long neglected as to be entirely forgotten untill it burst out in terrible jepordays'.

Clare accepts that the peasantry has legitimate grievances; after all he is still often reliant on his rural occupations, and thus has first-hand knowledge of rural privations. What is needed is 'reflection' on these problems, not violent reaction on both sides. The official response of hanging and transportation was equally irrational in its denial that the peasantry had 'too much apology' in taking such desperate, and in Clare's view futile, actions.

Mrs Marsh's letter also attempts to conceive of a course of action that might defuse the threat of violence in the countryside, and hopes to find such a middle path in Clare's response to the riots:

> I begin to hope that better days are drawing nearer, though the exertions of all good people in all stations, will be wanted to right our nearly foundered Vessel. If it were possible that you could communicate to many your own excellent view of our danger, yours would bestow a real benefit upon your Country.—Try to write something for insertion into one of the periodical publications to which you contribute.[49]

The prose draft from this period that best matches this request is 'Apology for the Poor'[50] which takes a forthright radical position vis-à-vis the causes of the distress in the countryside, a position indistinguishable from Cobbett's.

Clare must have the redistribution of church property in mind when he writes to Mrs Marsh in January 1832 that 'a reform is wanted'. In fact, at the end of her letter of 6 July 1831, Mrs Marsh tells Clare she will be sending him 'a little collection of pamphlets, some of which are very clever'. Subsequent correspondence shows that among these pamphlets were two copies of Cobbett's *Two-Penny Trash* that addressed these precise issues. The December 1830 issue was addressed: 'To the Farmers of Kent; On the measures which they ought, at this time, to adopt and pursue, in order to preserve their property and restore their country to a state of peace and harmony', and the January 1831 issue was addressed: 'To the Labourers of England; On the measures which ought to be adopted with regard to the Tithes, and with regard to other property, commonly called Church-Property'.[51] A note to Clare on 5 December 1831 invited him to call at the Bishop's Palace in Peterborough. During that meeting they discussed Cobbett's ideas. Three weeks later she sent him: 'the tracts of which she spoke, 3 numbers of Cobbett's penny trash which Mr Clare may keep.'[52] Within two weeks, Clare, having reflected on Cobbett's political rhetoric, stated his own view of the current situation:

I look upon Cobbett as one of the most powerful prose writers of the age—with no principles to make those powers commendable to honest praise—the Letters to farmers contain some very sensible arguments & some things that appeared to be too much of party colouring—there is no medium in party matters where there is excess it is always on one side—& that is the worst of it—I am no politician but I think a reform is wanted—not the reform of mobs where the bettering of many is only an apology for injuring the few—nor the reform of partys where the benefits of one is the destruction of the other but a reform that would do good & hurt none—I am sorry to see that the wild notions of public spouters always keep this reform out of sight—& as extreams must be met by extreams—the good is always lost like a plentiful harvest in bad weather[53]

Clare takes a measured view of Cobbett, commending his rhetorical power and perspicuity while decrying his unprincipled use of those gifts for narrow political ends. In Clare's view, Cobbett's arguments often degenerate into 'party' politics, a realm where the political 'good' is usually 'lost'. So Clare can assert with Cobbett that 'a reform is wanted' while disapproving of the means chosen to achieve that end. Clare's disingenuous disclaimer, 'I am no politician'[54] introduces a succinct political analysis of the problem of ideology: despite noble intentions, political ideologues lose sight of the greater principle of the political 'good' in their pursuit of narrow 'party' goals.

Throughout their correspondence, Mrs Marsh shows herself to be of independent mind. She is willing to entertain arguments for the reform of church property, the reduction or elimination of church tithes, in the service of the greater political 'good' of social stability. Dismayed by mob and state violence, she and Clare strive to find a middle path. Cobbett may have been willing to use the riots to pressure for reform, but this strategy repelled Clare as he witnessed the ferocity of the state sanctions imposed on the peasantry.[55] In the midst of this violence Clare and Mrs Marsh reached agreement on the pressing need for reform, and strove to conceive of a legitimate means to achieve it.

Mrs Marsh's struggle with political issues is all the more impressive given that her husband was institutionally wedded to the most extreme conservative position – no reduction in tithes. In his open letter to the farmers of Northamptonshire, published in *The Bee*, the bishop proclaimed: 'Property in tithe is no less sacred than property in land: both kinds of property are under protection of the law, and the law will protect them both alike.'[56] This article was occasioned by local farmers' requests for relief in their payment of tithes in anticipation of financial losses at the hands of the 'incendiaries'. Marsh rebuffed them, pointing out that they had not 'really lost property' and reminding them that the legitimacy of their own 'property in land' was inextricably bound up with the principle of 'property in tithe'. In short, Marsh was attempting to undo some of the rhetorical damage Cobbett had done in his speeches to local farmers the previous spring.[57] The need to shore up public support for tithes indicates that the riots did indeed serve Cobbett's constitutional goals. Violence was a price Cobbett, but not Clare, was willing to pay for the achievement of those goals.[58]

*

Careful reconstruction of the Clare/Marsh correspondence challenges assumptions about the conservative nature of the Marshes' patronage. The assumption that the power imbalance casts the veracity of Clare's statements in doubt, as John Lucas suggests,[59] blinds us to the mutuality of their relationship and to the details of their political discussions. We might as well turn the idea around and be suspicious of Herbert Marsh's official statements, given that his wife held such progressive political views – views that could prove embarrassing if aired in public. What we lose with selective reading strategies is Clare's distinction between political goals and the means of achieving those goals, the very place where he and Mrs Marsh would hope to develop the political 'good', outside the violent impasses of state violence and demagoguery.

How are we to understand the ambiguities of Clare speaking of 'our peasantry' as if he were not a member of the rural labouring class? His ability to reflect on political cause and effect separates him from his fellow villagers, despite being caught up in village hysteria and subject to rural privations. Perhaps Clare and Mrs Marsh corresponded out of feeling isolated, Clare from the panic of his neighbours, and Mrs Marsh from her husband's blind allegiance to church property. Together they hoped to establish a middle path towards meaningful reform free of both mob violence and violent state repression.

'The Hue & Cry'

Once Clare had completed 'The Hue & Cry' he immediately gave it to Drakard to be included as an anonymous contribution for the *Stamford Champion*. Stephen Colclough argues that anonymity gave Clare 'free range to express his radical voice'.[60] And while that is doubtless true, he came to have ambitious plans for the poem. He hoped to interest Cruik-shank in producing a set of caricature illustrations for the poem so that it could be sold as a pamphlet. Clare knew Cruikshank's work from Hone's *Every-Day Book*, and his political work from Hone's famous rad-ical satire *The House That Jack Built*, the work that had brought about Hone's first charge of sedition. Clare had an established connection with Hone, and another contact with Cruikshank through their mutual friend Henry Behnes Burlowe. Clare first wrote to Burlowe at the height of the chaos in the final week of 1830, inquiring about Cruikshank's possible interest in illustrating his earlier satire, 'The Summons', that had been anonymously published to much praise by Drakard, first in the 25 September 1830 *Stamford News* and then again in a revised version in the 30 November 1830 *Stamford Champion*. Clare sent 'The Summons' 'as a sample' of his satiric style in the hope that Cruikshank might con-sider a new poem 'detailing the alarms',[61] 'The Hue & Cry'. The project got as far as Burlowe showing the 'The Summons' to Cruikshank. He reported that the artist 'wishe[d] to see a specimen of your intentions ere he can pronounce upon the applicability of his pencil to them—he has a decided objection now to anything *political*.'[62] Clare had mistaken the Cruikshank of 1818 with the increasingly prosperous book illustrator he had become. If the tone of 'The Summons' alarmed him, then what hope was there for 'The Hue & Cry'. Clare admitted feeling defeated by this response in his letter to Burlowe on 4 January. His disappointment caused him to refer to the poem as 'good for nothing'[63] and upbraids himself for having sent such stuff to Cruikshank. However, exactly a week later it appeared in the 11 January 1831 *Stamford Champion*. The apparent contradiction can be resolved by considering Clare's divided motives in wanting to publish the poem.

In a letter to Samuel Wilson, one of Drakard's partners, probably written the same week, he confessed that part of his motive had been financial: 'circumstances has this year deprived me of a part of my little sallarys or godsends & having another Poem just written in the manner of the Summons I fancied if the trifle could procure me a trifle it would be of service'.[64] The crassness of Clare's stated motive indicated the severity of his financial straits, but also indicated his continuing inter-est in developing new publishing venues and experimenting in different published poetic voices. Had the pamphlet been produced with Cruikshank illustrations, it would have had a national audience and established Clare as a satirist of the contemporary political scene. Robinson admits this fact in pointing out that Clare and Cruikshank might very well have faced prosecution had they published a pamphlet version of 'The Hue & Cry',[65] rather undermining his central claim that Clare was concerned primarily with the 'local'. Clare had 'national' ambitions for 'The Hue & Cry', and they were not purely professional or driven by financial concerns. Clare's satires represented sincere efforts to be 'a champion for the poor', a role he attempted to develop through the auspices and encouragement of Mrs Marsh. She saw Clare as a possible spokesperson for the rural peasantry at a time when the countryside was enveloped in the violence of the 'incendiaries', of excessive state sanctions, and of the threat of the mob. Clare satirised extremists on all sides, offered precise political analyses of the motives of the farmers and the state, and hoped to locate the fugitive 'political good' in a 'common sense' call for constitutional reform.

Epilogue:
Clare's Agency

Clare was a 'discontented' peasant. He began as one as attested by the 'accursed wealth' passage in the first poem of his first volume and remained one as Lubin served as a witness to the local devastation of the countryside in *The Village Minstrel*. If anything, he became more bitter about the loss of his local landscape and its inhabitants. 'The Parish' remained unpublished, but probably because Taylor and Hessey feared its political tone. His journal of 1824–26 recorded a profound sadness at the loss of trees, watercourses and human individuals – all destroyed by enclosure. 'Apology for the Poor' presented a litany of grievances brought about by these changes, and of made them a public declaration. Fortunately for readers, Clare was much more than a 'discontented' peasant; he was a creative genius, and out of his 'discontent' he fashioned a powerful and profound elegiac voice that at once mourned the passing of the things he loved and transvalued them beyond the everyday into the realm of art. To portray Clare as an isolated, conservative villager misconstrues the source and power of his art. Clare's 'discontent' moved him to create poems in defence of the landscape and people he loved. It led him to develop a trenchant satiric voice that he attempted to disseminate as widely as possible, and to put himself forward as a 'champion for the poor' by publishing essays and letters denouncing the destruction of the rural economy and way of life and putting forward ideas for sensible reform.

Clare was not a passive victim of overbearing patrons and insensitive editors. He worked diligently to mediate disputes between erstwhile friends, often in overheated circumstances. His skill in managing the obtuse Lord Radstock, especially as relations between Radstock and Taylor disintegrated, serves as stunning example of his understanding of interpersonal psychology. Undoubtedly Clare's career fell victim to

Taylor's professional neglect and ultimate incompetence, but he did not simply sit by and watch, powerless to intervene. He worked diligently on the manuscript whenever he received editorial suggestions, and even when it became clear that things had gone terribly wrong at Taylor & Hessey he worked to ensure that at least some volume, even if it was the disappointing *Shepherd's Calendar*, appeared. More importantly, during the long delay Clare expanded his publishing interests and began to work on numerous parallel projects. Our view of Clare would be very different had he and Henderson produced a collection of his flower poems with detailed field notes and lists of common and Latin names, or a more ambitious poetic natural history incorporating their extensive study of local plants and Clare's passion to preserve their memory. Similarly, had Taylor & Hessey published 'The Natural History of Help-stone', or helped arrange another publisher for 'The Parish', Clare would have become known as more than the 'peasant poet'. This artistic goal existed from the start. Only Taylor's nervousness about copyright prevented Clare from producing a collection of one hundred songs, on the model of Moore's *Irish Melodies*, for James Powers between publication of *Poems Descriptive* and *The Village Minstrel*. His sense of himself as a professional writer capable of many literary styles and voices led to his 'impersonation' of Percy Green, and numerous 'old poets'. Percy Green's success at the *London Magazine* suggests that a collection organised around 'Edmund & Helen' would have found a ready audience.

The taste for the 'old poets' was more than professional; it connected him to the circle of writers at the *London* and in the so-called 'Cockney School', and to the important editors and radical intellectuals James Montgomery and William Hone. Sociability became a primary value for Clare, both personally and artistically. His various submissions and acts of ventriloquism connected him to a complex and widely scattered group of literary connections, and aligned him with what the wits at the *London*, Leigh Hunt, or Keats, would have recognised as a 'democratic muse'. With better luck, Clare might have used his relationship with Hone to convince Cruikshank to illustrate 'The Hue & Cry', a new satire by the author of 'The Parish'. Sadly that Clare did not appear in print, but he existed.

Clare's life in Helpstone was not isolated. He walked whenever he was able, and moved in the most diverse set of social circles imaginable. In 1824–25, his journal records playing the fiddle and drinking at the wedding of his Gypsy friends Israel and Lettyce Smith, and a letter from Joseph Henderson invites him to a party at Milton House to celebrate the birth of Wentworth, the Fitzwilliam heir. An intimate relation both with one of the most powerful aristocratic Whig dynasties and with members of the most stigmatised group in the country demonstrates an extraordinary range of interaction. His associations with Milton House were especially rich and rewarding. Henderson's enthusiasm for natural history and respect for Clare's genius made him an ideal friend. Their joint projects allowed Clare to define his interests and expand his knowledge, both through conversation with Henderson and use of the Milton House library. William Tyrell Artis provided another source of intellectual stimulation, and another set of destinations for walks – rediscovered Roman pottery works and other places of local archaeological interest. In the early 1830s his relationship with Marianne Marsh and her friend and secretary Miss Morlock provided Clare with another source of intellectual friendship, and encouragement in developing his social and political views. In addition to these physical friendships, Clare developed detailed correspondences with intellectuals like Hone and Montgomery, the *London* circle, and his 'neighbour' Savage in Spalding. Furthermore, his conception of this correspondence, including his playful 'frauds', was such that he imaginatively placed himself at the centre of a complex convivial network working together towards a vision of a new era of democratic art. It makes no sense to believe Lamb or Keats or Hone understood the political stakes in recovering the 'old poets', but that Clare remained innocently unaware. Such condescension remains a legacy of the 'poor Clare' tradition, and the time has come to dispense with that caricature, and celebrate the complex, deeply committed intellectual and literary genius who was John Clare.

Notes

Introduction

1. 'Autobiographical Fragments' in *John Clare's Autobiographical Writings*, ed. Eric Robinson (Oxford: Oxford University Press, 1983), p. 129.
2. The tradition of reading Clare in this way has the best of intentions, and most often begins in a belief that Clare has been victimised and thus needs defending. Paradoxically, such interventions perpetuate the notion of his helplessness in the face of circumstance.
3. Cambridge: Cambridge University Press, 1972.
4. The ongoing critical debate about the merits of Robinson's editorial decision to publish the uncorrected manuscript versions of the poems continues. My study touches on the issues raised by this decision but is not directly concerned with the debate.
5. In order to teach a truly representative selection of Clare's poetry, the instructor must create his or her own reader.
6. The poems have been published in the following order: *The Later Poems of John Clare*, ed. Eric Robinson and David Powell, 2 vols (Oxford: Clarendon Press, 1984), *The Early Poems of John Clare*, ed. Eric Robinson and David Powell 2 vols (Oxford: Clarendon Press, 1989), and *The Poems of the Middle Period*, ed. Eric Robinson and P. M. S. Dawson, 5 vols (Oxford: Clarendon Press, 1996, 1998, 1999).
7. The name manuscript is somewhat misleading. Following their agreed upon method, Clare sent unedited material to the press where it accumulated. Hessey and Clare attempted to begin the process of arranging some of that material into a coherent manuscript, but those efforts were suspended. See Chapter 7 for a more detailed discussion of this process.
8. Eric Robinson and Geoffrey Summerfield, 'John Taylor's Editing of Clare's *The Shepherd's Calendar*', *Review of English Studies*, vol. 14, 1963, p. 365.
9. 'Taylor's Editing', p. 365.
10. 'Taylor's Editing', p. 366.
11. 'Taylor's Editing', p. 366.
12. Letter to Clare, 6 June 1820, *Letters*, p. 69.
13. Letter to Clare, 27 September 1820, *Letters*, p. 98.
14. British Library, Egerton MS 2246, fol. 45–7.
15. Letter to Clare, 28 January 1826, *Letters*, p. 357. See Robinson and Summerfield's discussion of Taylor's resigned recognition of the change in market conditions as expressed in letters to Clare of 30 March and 20 November 1827, 'Taylor's Editing', p. 363. The most thorough discussion of the subject remains Tim Chilcott's chapter, 'No Publisher of Poetry Now', in *A Publisher and His Circle: the Life and Work of John Taylor, Keats's Publisher* (London: Routledge & Kegan Paul, 1972), pp. 183–98.
16. J. W. and Anne Tibble, *John Clare: A Life* (London: Michael Joseph, 1972), p. 240. Correspondence indicates that Taylor had decided from the outset

that Clare should send poems unedited and without selection, and that Taylor should then shape each book in collaboration with Clare. The letter of 12 February 1820 concerning the proposed second volume makes this clear: 'Whenever you have the Poems ready for another volume, I shall be glad to see them <u>all</u> without selection' (emphasis Taylor's). Egerton MS 2245, fol. 37.

17. Robinson and Summerfield draw attention to this 'change of heart' in 'Taylor's Editing', pp. 362–3. Also see Chilcott's chapters: 'No Publisher of Poetry Now' (cited above), and 'The *London Magazine*, 1821–5', pp. 129–60, and Edmund Blunden's chapters on Taylor's shift from literary to educational publishing in *Keats's Publisher: A Memoir of John Taylor* (London: Jonathan Cape, 1936), pp. 180–216.

18. *A Publisher and His Circle*, pp. 108–9.

1   Clare's Minorness

1. It is important to remember that in many of the reviews Clare was the subject, not the poems. Lockhart, for example, admitted that he had not read the poems, and instead offered condescending advice about the wisest course of action for a versifying peasant. His advice that Clare remain a peasant repeated his advice to Keats that he remain an apothecary.

2. *The John Clare Society Journal*, 18, 1999, pp. 70–8.

3. *Clare in Context*, p. 222.

4. This date is, of course, arbitrary. I am dating the debate approximately from the publication of Jerome McGann's *Romantic Ideology* in 1983, but John Barrell's historical reading of Clare predates that by over a decade. I use the McGann date for the simple reason that the general debate about the constitution of the Romantic canon originates around that year.

5. It is impossible to date the poem more precisely. No manuscript version survives. The poem was among those collected in 1841 by Cyrus Redding, the founding editor of the *New Monthly Magazine*, and included in a selection of Clare's poems in the short-lived *English Journal*, 15 May 1841. Redding had visited Clare in the asylum at High Beach, Epping. The published account of Redding's meeting with Clare is reprinted in *Critical Heritage*, pp. 247–56.

6. *Later Poems*, p. 25.

7. *Biographia Literaria*, ch. 22, pp. 119–42.

8. MS torn.

9. *Letters*, pp. 86–7.

10. In a letter to Taylor on 6 December 1821, Clare commented that Wordsworth's recent poems were 'ridiculous' and gave him the 'itch of parody' which he satisfied with the poem beginning 'Reforming men of England', *Letters*, pp. 221–2. Curiously, this poem has no explanatory note in the Clarendon Press edition of *The Early Poems*, and nothing is made of the fact that the original letter version of the poem was signed 'William-----worth'.

11. 'The Journal', 8 September 1824, *By Himself*, p. 171.

12. 'The Journal', 27 September 1824, *By Himself*, p. 178. Significantly, 'The Journal' as a whole is dominated by entries offering detailed descriptions of the local plants and animals. He devotes much of his time to 'botanizing', and collects and identifies types of ferns, for example, or acquires paints so

that he can record the markings of snails and butterflies. Many entries also mention his various plans for a poetic 'natural history' of Helpstone. In the entry for 18 April 1825, Clare proclaims a compositional principle for the proposed book that is an obvious cognate of the poetic principle I am elucidating: 'I will insert nothing but what comes or has come under my notice', p. 223. I will discuss Clare's plans for his 'natural history' in Chapter 7.

13. *By Himself*, p. 347. At the March 2003 inaugural conference of the John Clare Society of North America, Robinson described the scope of the problem. In his research on eighteenth and nineteenth-century dictionaries, he found that many words that he had assumed were specific to Clare and his Northampton-shire dialect were listed as generally accepted usage.

14. The reviewer in the *Literary Gazette* bemoaned the 'frequent use of words radically low and insignificant', which 'marred' the work, and advised Clare to abandon the 'sluggish rivulets of a marshy part of Northamptonshire' for a 'landscape of a more sublime and beautiful order'. It hardly needs comment that such a review missed the entire point of the poetry. Reprinted in *Critical Heritage*, pp. 142–3.

15. Quoted from J. W. and Anne Tibble's *John Clare: A Life*, (London: Michael Joseph, 1972), pp. 159–61.

16. *Early Poems*, p. 413.

17. Quoted in the note on Peterborough MS A58, *A Descriptive Catalogue of the John Clare Collection in the Peterborough Museum and Art Gallery*, by Margaret Grainger (Peterborough: Earl Fitzwilliam, 1973), p. 10.

18. *The Oxford Authors: John Clare*, ed. Eric Robinson and David Powell (Oxford: Oxford University Press, 1984), p. 248.

19. *Oxford Authors*, p. 492.

20. This famous phrase from 'Tintern Abbey' identifies the intellectual com-pensation to be created through the contemplation of the natural world. That compensation is the ultimate goal of Wordsworthian poetics.

21. 1850 'Prelude', Book First, *The Prelude, 1799, 1805, 1850*, ed. Jonathan Wordsworth, M. H. Abrams and Stephen Gill (Norton: New York, 1979), p. 51.

22. Wordsworth was understandably influenced by Coleridge's deep involve-ment in German aesthetics, and the formulation I mention here is Kant's famous one from *The Critique of Judgement*. However, I do not mean to suggest that Wordsworth consciously employed Kantian ideas in the course of his composition. The emphasis on reflection in the Preface to *Lyrical Ballads* could as easily have been influenced by Burke's discourse on the aesthetic value of 'terror' in his *Philosophical Inquiry into the Origin of Our Ideas of the Sublime and the Beautiful*. In either case, the value of the sublime is located in its ability to produce moments of self-aggrandisement, rather than in the natural objects that create the aesthetic effect.

23. *Oxford Authors*, p. 263.

24. This returns us to Clare's critique of Milton's overly formal use of 'the rules of art in the Sonnet just as an architect sets about a building'. Odd as Clare's use of the sonnet may appear in the context of Romantic versification, the development of poetics since Clare provides ample scope to read the poems on their own terms. A notable analogue is with William Carlos Williams's famous poetic dictum: 'No ideas but in things', 'A Sort of Song', *Selected Poems*

(New York: New Directions, 1949), p. 108. Compare, for example, Williams's long perceptual list that begins the first poem in *Spring and All*:

> By the road to the contagious hospital
> under the surge of the blue
> mottled clouds driven from the
> northeast—a cold wind. Beyond, the
> waste of broad, muddy fields
> brown with dried weeds, standing and falling
>
> patches of standing water
> the scattering of tall trees

It is hard to say who this is reminiscent of if not Clare (although I know of no evidence that Williams read Clare). Any of these visual fragments could have come from one of the Northborough sonnets, and they share the stark matter-of-factness of Clare's descriptions. In their introduction to their edition of *The Northborough Sonnets* (Manchester: Carcanet Press, 1995), Eric Robinson, David Powell and P. M. S. Dawson make a similar observation about how 'the sonnets are often impressively focussed on their subject', and how 'each subject seems isolated from everything else' (pp. ix–x).

25. *Biographia Literaria*, ed. James Engell and W. Jackson Bate, 2 vols (Princeton: Princeton University Press, 1983), p. 133. All citations from *Biographia Literaria* are taken from this edition and will be noted in parentheses.

26. *Oxford Authors*, p. 278.

27. Also see his journal entry for 29 October 1824 where he admires many of Wordsworth's poems, but ends on a note of disappointment: 'there is some of the sweetest poetry I ever met with tho full of his mysterys', 'The Journal', *By Himself*, p. 190.

28. 'Letter to C. A. Elton', 18 December 1824, *Letters*, pp. 309–11. Also witness this poignant entry from 'The Journal', 26 November 1824: 'Went to see if the old hazel tree in lea close was cut down & found it still standing...the Inclosure has left it desolate its companions of oak and ash being gone' *By Himself*, p. 199.

    Emphasis on the feelings of the tree marks the extent of Clare's sympathy and reiterates the intimate relationship between his poetry and his social and environmental concerns. For a discussion of further implications of this and other entries on trees in 'The Journal', and of Clare's efforts to associate his sympathy for these natural 'subjects' with his sympathy for human 'subjects', see the section on 'Botanizing' in Chapter 7, pp. 154–8.

29. *Lyrical Ballads and Other Poems*, ed. James Butler and Karen Green (London: Cornell University Press, 1992), pp. 744–5. All citations from the Preface are taken from this edition and will be noted in parentheses.

30. The decision by Wordsworth and Coleridge to 'retire' to Somerset is often misconstrued as a conservative retreat from the political world. It is as easily understood as a radical political gesture, particularly in relation to Coleridge's correspondence with his friend John Thelwall (hardly a conservative).

31. 'Autobiographical Fragments', *Autobiographical Writings*, p. 129.

32. *Oxford Authors*, p. 20.

33. 'Autobiographical Fragments', *Autobiographical Writings*, p. 53.
34. *The Idea of Landscape and the Sense of Place*, p. 188.

2 Viewing and Reviewing

1. 'Romanticism' is a vexed term, and the history of its use and development is outside the scope of this discussion. In the context of Wordsworth and Coleridge, critics have employed the term to refer to poetry that emphasises philosophical reflection in relation to the natural world. Romanticism of that kind develops from Georgic taste, which shared a sense of the country as a place of calm restoration, by de-emphasising classical allusions to an ideal, bucolic golden age in favour of 'the language of real men'. The aesthetic value of rural speech became a crucial debate between Coleridge and Wordsworth, and the theory of Romanticism that followed from that debate placed special emphasis on the inwardness of the poet, the philosophical product of the poetry rather than its materials (nature, rural life and speech, and so on).
2. *Poems Descriptive of Rural Life and Scenery* (London: Taylor & Hessey, 1820), p. ix.
3. Clare is in a long line of peasant poets taken up and promoted by the gentry. Such patronage was often competitive, as discriminating gentlemen vied with one another to discover and champion the next literary sensation. Writing about the conditions of the patronage extended to Stephen Duck, E. P. Thompson trenchantly commented: 'Patronage of this order is simply a form taken by the conspiracy of the polite against the poor.' *The Thresher's Labour by Stephen Duck and The Woman's Labour by Mary Collier*, ed. E. P. Thompson and Marian Sugden (London: Merlin Press, 1989), p. iv.
4. *Lectures on Rhetoric and Belles Lettres*, 3 vols. 2nd edn (London: W. Strachan & T. Cadell, 1785), vol. 2, pp. 114–36. Subsequent references will appear in parentheses in the text.
5. Clare had probably not read Blair's lecture before he composed the poems in *Poems Descriptive* and most of those in *The Village Minstrel*, but Blair's *Lectures* was among the first books given to him by his patron Lord Radstock in February 1820. He had read it by 1824, as entries in his journal make clear. He employed Blair's terms, for example, in dismissing Pope's efforts at pastoral: 'the Pastorals are nick[n]amed so for daffodils breathing flutes beachen bowls silver crooks and purling brooks and such like everlasting sing song does not make pastorals', 'The Journal', 26 October 1824, *By Himself*, p. 189. The influence of Blair's lecture can be heard as an echo in Wordsworth's use of the word 'disgust' in his *Preface*, and in Coleridge's attack on Wordsworth's philosophical 'pedlar'.
6. See Clare's letter to Hessey of 10 July 1820 where he complains of 'false delicasy's seriousness', and the social presumption that demands that 'poor Dolly' 'have her artless lamentations shut out', *Letters*, p. 83.
7. Jeffrey attacked Wordsworth's 'The Excursion', for example, because it confused the simplicity of the lower classes and philosophical pretension. He ridiculed the portrait of the Pedlar on precisely those grounds: 'A man

who went selling flannel and pocket-handkerchiefs in this lofty diction, would soon frighten away all his customers.' *Edinburgh Review* vol. 24, 1814, pp. 1–30. Coleridge, as indicated in Chapter 1, took a similar line in *Biographia Literaria* when he challenged Wordsworth's claims for the superiority of rural subject matter and diction.

8. Bloom's phrase.

9. 'Letter to Markham Sherwill', 12 July 1820, *Letters*, pp. 85–7, and 'Letter to John Taylor', 6 December 1821, *Letters*, p. 221.

10. Quoted in *Early Poems*, p. 158.

11. The *OED* definition of 'deficient' emphasises the condition of lack: 'Present in less than the proper quantity; not sufficient of force; wholly or partly wanting or lacking; insufficient, inadequate.' The examples of usage, however, indicate how fickle matters of taste are in determining the poetic qualities that the poet must have in sufficient quantity. The example closest in time (1856) to Clare's career is taken from Emerson's estimation of Hallam's poetic gifts: 'Hallam is uniformly polite, but with deficient sympathy.' This is a complete reversal of the notions of poetic 'deficiency' used to patronise Clare in the previous 35 years, *The Compact Edition of the Oxford English Dictionary*, vol. 1, p. 135.

12. Taylor did not confine his shaping of public reception to his introduction. He had a piece by his friend, the critic and journalist Octavius Gilchrist, placed in the January 1820 edition of the *London Magazine* in advance of publication. Despite having read only a few of the poems, Gilchrist introduced Clare to the literary world by sharing anecdotes about the poet's struggle against extreme poverty, and offering cautious aesthetic judgements of the sort that Taylor was to employ. Clare was judged capable of being 'an acute observer of nature, aided by genius', but whose 'genius [was] not framed for sustained or lofty flights'. This strategy created the same double bind (the delimited genius) as Taylor's more elaborate aesthetic claims. Reprinted in *Critical Heritage*, pp. 39–40.

13. *Poems Descriptive*, p. 9. Subsequent references to 'Helpstone' will appear in parentheses in the text.

14. There has been some confusion in Clare studies concerning which printing of the book Radstock wanted cut. Critics variously have referred to the third edition, the third printing and the fourth edition when identifying the book. It was in fact the third edition. I am grateful to Bob Heyes for this useful clarification.

15. *The British Critic*, June 1820, pp. 662–7. I have noted the original publication because the excerpts from the review in *Critical Heritage* do not include the texts of the poems or the note on 'The Village Funeral'.

16. *Antijacobin Review*, June 1820, pp. 348–53, reprinted in *Critical Heritage*, pp. 105–6. The phrase, 'and astonished the neighbouring villages with the brilliancy of his song', contains considerable unintended irony. The comparison of Clare's poetry to birdsong followed the general pattern of condescension (the unconscious peasant), but birdsong was one of the natural beauties most under threat from the enclosing of land. Bird habitat disappeared as woodlands and thickets were pulled up. Clare was particularly sensitive to this loss, as witnessed by the stanza from 'The Village Minstrel' in which the 'woodlark's song is hush'. I discuss this stanza in detail below.

17. *Monthly Review*, March 1820, pp. 296–300, excerpted in *Critical Heritage*, pp. 73–4.
18. This critical view also follows Coleridge's reservations about Wordsworth's claims about rustic speech. See *Biographia Literaria*, ch. 17, vol. 2, pp. 52–7.
19. *The Guardian*, 28 May 1820, reprinted in *Critical Heritage*, pp. 100–1.
20. *Blackwood's Edinburgh Magazine*, June 1820, reprinted in *Critical Heritage*, pp. 102–3.
21. Mark Storey speculates that the reviewer was almost certainly the poet Josiah Conder who owned and edited the *Eclectic* from 1814–1837. Comparison with Conder's identified prose of the period bears this contention out on both stylistic and cultural grounds. See *Critical Heritage*, pp. 7 and 202.
22. *Eclectic Review*, April 1820, pp. 327–40, reprinted in *Critical Heritage*, pp. 88–92.
23. *Eclectic Review*, January 1822, pp. 31–45, reprinted in *Critical Heritage*, pp. 168–71.
24. *The Village Minstrel* (London: Taylor & Hessey, 1821), p. 50.
25. I use the word 'enclose' here because Clare's resistance to efforts to define him as a simple peasant followed from his resistance to the economic logic of agricultural enclosure. The calls to remove the vulgar language of the rustic from the poems, or the calls to be more philosophical, were efforts to 'enclose' Clare by pulling up his aesthetic weeds and 'improving' his figural landscape. These calls were the aesthetic equivalent to the calls of his conservative patrons to be 'content' in the new economic dispensation of the countryside.
26. Letter to Taylor, 16 May 1820, *Letters*, p. 69.
27. Letter to Clare, 6 June 1820, *Letters*, p. 69.
28. Letter to Clare, 27 September 1820, *Letters*, p. 98.
29. *Letters*, p. 98, n. 2.
30. 'Clare's Politics', p. 175.
31. *The Village Minstrel*, p. 51. As I have indicated above the explicit political critique in these stanzas was clear enough that the *Eclectic Review* referred to them as 'political economy'.
32. Enclosure was a complex upheaval, and often entailed the removal of ancient hedges and small woodlands and the planting of new ones. As such, Clare decries both the construction and destruction of hedges at various points in the poems.
33. At an early stage, Taylor had been willing to take Radstock's views into account despite his own inclinations. In a letter to Clare of 12 February 1820, Taylor noted that: 'Lord Radstock writes that this poem & Dolly's Mistake also both be omitted next time—So have several other Pastors. For my own part I am not so fastidious', Egerton MS 2245, fol. 37. Taylor was still concerned enough with sales to consider allowing Radstock to censor the bawdy poems from the first volume as he makes clear at the end of the letter: 'When you write your name in Blair's Sermons say "the gift of Admiral Lord Radstock." He has taken the greatest pains in promoting the sale of the Poems.' By early 1822, Taylor no longer cared about Radstock's opinions and the two had formed antagonistic camps vying to influence Clare. A letter to Clare from Mrs Emmerson (Radstock's friend and ally) of 5 February 1822 shows how far things had deteriorated, to the point where she and Radstock were attempting to persuade Clare to switch publishers for the third volume: 'the conduct of certain persons [Taylor], has so thoroughly displeased Lord

R. that he cannot take one step to serve you, without feeling he is at the same time serving those who have acted most unbecoming to him—this reflection necessarily abates the ardor of his Lordships exertions', Egerton MS 2246, fol. 18. Clare resisted these veiled threats, and, given the unhappy publication history of *The Shepherd's Calendar*, perhaps this was to his detriment.
34. *The Village Minstrel*, p. xx.
35. The actual letter is lost, so Taylor's printed excerpt in the introduction is the only record we have.

3   'Grammer in learning is like Tyranny in government'

1. Roughly 1816–1820.
2. Tom Paulin, 'John Clare in Babylon', in *Minotaur: Poetry and the Nation State* (London: Faber & Faber, 1992), p. 53.
3. Zachary Leader, 'John Taylor and the Poems of Clare', in *Revision and Romantic Authorship* (Oxford: Clarendon Press, 1996), pp. 206–20.
4. *Letters*, p. 231.
5. See, for example, the letters from Taylor to Clare of 16 December and 29 December 1820, and 1 January and 6 January 1821, *Letters*, pp. 117–19, 126–7, 129–30, and 134–5. The 6 January letter is particularly interesting because it shows Taylor's pragmatic resolve that he must omit the 'offending stanza' from 'Helpstone' when he prints the 3rd edition of *Poems Descritive*, and it also expresses his ongoing resistance to such political interference: 'Lord R. has put his Mark 'This is radical Slang' against 2 of the best stanzas . . .—Are these to be omitted also?—If so, others will be offensive next, & your Poem will be like the Man who had 2 Wives.'
6. This conclusion is based on a review of the Taylor letters in print, and those in Egerton MSS 2245 and 2246.
7. *Letters*, p. 145.
8. *Letters*, p. 149.
9. *Revision and Romantic Authorship*, pp. 231–2.
10. I do not mean to suggest that the editorial direction of the Clarendon editions is unjustified. There are abundant scholarly reasons to produce an accessible manuscript edition of a major writer much of whose work was unpublished. But that does not justify moralising about Taylor and the printed editions of Clare's poetry. As Hugh Haughton and Adam Phillips indicate in their introduction to *Clare in Context*, Geoffrey Summerfield expressed reservations about such judgements in his decision to publish the Penguin *Selected Poems* (Harmondsworth: Penguin, 1990) in which he decided to 'modify' spelling, punctuation and capitalisation in the service of readability, *Clare in Context*, pp. 20–1.
11. Letter to Taylor, 21 February 1822, *Letters*, p. 231.
12. *Lectures on Rhetoric and Belles Lettres* (Edinburgh, 1820), 2 vols. i. p. 121. Quoted in Smith's *The Politics of Language: 1791–1819* (Oxford: Clarendon Press, 1984), p. 21. Clare was presented with a three-volume edition of Blair's treatise by Lord Radstock in February 1820. Radstock clearly intended the gift as a means of instruction. He typically presented Clare with volumes on grammar and language along with books of religious instruction. For a full

discussion of Radstock's efforts to shape Clare's mind through an active programme of instruction, see the analysis of their relationship in Chapters 4 and 5 below.

13. *Politics of Language*, pp. 26–8.
14. Letter from Taylor, 12 February 1820, Egerton MS 2245, fol. 37.
15. From Clare's unpublished journal of 1824–1825, Northampton MS 15, reprinted in Margaret Grainger's edition of *The Natural History Prose Writings of John Clare* (Oxford: Clarendon Press, 1983), p. 197.
16. *A Dictionary of the English Language to which is Prefixed a Grammar of the English Language*, 14th edn (London: F. C. & J. Rivington, 1815). This is item 263 in the Northampton Library collection of Clare's books.
17. *The Evidences of the Christian Religion to which are added Several Discourses against Atheism and Infidelity and in Defence of Christian Revelation* (Oxford: Clarendon Press, 1809).
18. Addison's treatise is Northampton item 91. Radstock's handwriting can be difficult to decipher, and I have placed parenthetical question marks next to words of which I cannot be sure. I have followed a policy of making the best guess in the context of the passage as a whole, and in cases where the sense of the passage may be affected by any conjecture I have left a gap in the transcription rather than run the risk of distortion.
19. *Politics of Language*, pp. 29–34.
20. In a recent review of Robin Jarvis's *Romantic Writing and Pedestrian Travel* (Basingstoke: Macmillan – now Palgrave Macmillan, 1997), Peter Larkin admonishes the author, claiming 'special pleading' 'tempts us to over-read Clare, or load him with 'virtues' which were the outcome of a lack of cultural choice'. *Coleridge Bulletin*, Spring, 1998, p. 70. As Chapter 2 makes clear, such critical views are inevitable once Clare is understood as primarily a passive victim of social circumstances. Far from passive, Clare's defence of dialect was part of a deliberately conceived poetics, finely integrated into his social and political beliefs, and based not on naïvety but on careful analyses of social conditions and literary taste.
21. *On the Rudiments of the English Language*, 1761, p. 56. Quoted in *The Politics of Language*, p. 10. Emphasis on 'correctness' does not always bring improvement as Priestly's over-punctuation of this passage demonstrates. The commas have the effect of confusing predication.
22. Horne Tooke dedicated the second volume of his treatise to the jury that acquitted him during his treason trial and to his legal counsel. *The Diversions of Purley*, Part II (London: Joseph Johnson, 1805) p. A2. Horne Tooke continued to enlarge and improve the treatise following the appearance of Part I in 1798.
23. Clare was also given a copy of Lowth's *A Short Introduction to English Grammar*, 2nd edn, (London: A. Millar, 1763) by one of his patrons, Mrs Emmerson. However, her gift, unlike the other books of instruction Clare received, was given for a different reason—the copy of the book had belonged to William Cowper. Mrs Emmerson enthused about this fact in a flyleaf inscription. Her sentimentalising of genius, the aura she perceived in Cowper's book, is typical of her distinct mode of patronage. Whatever the motivation of the gift, Clare was also familiar with the Lowth treatise. This is item 288 of the Northamptom Library collection of Clare's books.
24. *Diversions of Purley*, Part I, p. 15.

25. *Diversions of Purley*, Part II, p. 5.
26. *Diversions of Purley*, Part II, p. 9.
27. *Diversions of Purley*, Part II, p. 407.
28. J. W. and Anne Tibble note that Clare often amused Lamb and the other London wits with whom he socialised with his 'imprecations on the pedantic Lindley Murray', *John Clare: A Life*, p. 274.
29. *A Grammar of the English Language in a Series of Letters* (London: Thomas Dolby, 1819).
30. The 'Blanketeers' were a group of 5000 Manchester weavers who met at St Peter's Field on 10 March 1817 to organise a march on London in order to present a petition to the Prince Regent seeking redress. Cavalry dispersed most of them, but some 300 got as far as the Stockport bridge before being turned back by the army. They got their name from the blankets and rugs they carried with them on their journey, *The Oxford Companion to British History*, ed. John Cannon (Oxford: Oxford University Press, 1997), p. 108. Cobbett wrote in order to assist groups like the 'Blanketeers' who, lacking the franchise, had only the power of petition as a political tool. This tool was being systematically taken from them on the grounds that their appeals were grammatically 'vulgar' and thus beneath notice. They could be 'legally' dispersed because of the suspension of habeas corpus in early 1817, and the need to have a magistrate approve any meeting of more than 50 people. The suspension of habeas corpus had also led to Cobbett's prudent decision to revisit America from where he continued to produce the *Political Register*.
31. *Cobbett's Weekly Political Register*, vol. 34, no. 9, pp. 253–4. Further references to vol. 34, no. 9 of the *Political Register* will appear in the text as *PR*.
32. Reprinted in *Oxford Authors*, p. 481.
33. *Revision*, pp. 216–17.

4 'The Cottager's Friend'

1. Quoted in *Critical History*, p. 58.
2. *Poems Descriptive*, p. 9.
3. See Robert Reid, *Land of Lost Content: The Luddite Revolt, 1812* (London: Cardinal, 1986), especially the chapter 'Radical Reformers', pp. 140–6. Reid demonstrates the power Burdett had as a figure in the popular imagination, and laments the misplacement of popular hope.
4. William Cobbett, *Cottage Economy* (Oxford: Oxford University Press, 1979), p. 6.
5. William Paley, *Reasons for Contentment Addressed to the Labouring Part of the British Public* by William Paley, Archdeacon of Carlisle (Newcastle: Edward Walker, 1819).
6. *The Works of Charlotte, Emily and Anne Brontë in Twelve Volumes, Vol. VIII, Poems of Currer, Ellis, and Acton Bell with Cottage Poems by Patrick Brontë* (London: J. M. Dent, 1893), p. 197.
7. It is difficult to know whether Brontë had read *Lyrical Ballads*, but the similarity in poetic assumptions is striking. The faith in the transformative power of nature and the resulting religious connotations provide the perfect poetic resource for the ambitious young churchman.

8. See Reid's description in ch. 4, 'A Man of the People', *Lost Content*, pp. 31–7.
9. *Lost Content*, especially chapters 5 to 18. Reid shows how Brontë was dependent on the largesse of both the Rev. Hammond Roberson and William Cartwright, the owner of Rawfold's Mill. The posthumous effort to vindicate Brontë's part in the events through the filter of Charlotte Brontë's *Shirley* is too often taken at face value as an historical account, rather than as an instance of a charismatic father's ability to awe his children through imaginative self-aggrandisement.
10. *Poems Descriptive*, p. 9.
11. *DNB*, vol. 18, pp. 473–81. The Radstock coat of arms was attached to the end-paper of Hannah More's *The Spirit of Prayer*, 2nd edn (London: T. Cadell, 1825), and is adjacent to a religious homily by his Lordship on the flyleaf that instructs the poet to 'study them and seek the truth' (emphasis his), item 312 in Clare's library in the Northampton Public Library.
12. The British Library copy of Radstock's pamphlet is bound with a pamphlet entitled: *A Dialogue Between a Christian and a Reformer* (Newcastle, 1819). The distinction in the title does much of the polemicist's work; no one professing to favour reform could be a Christian because such a person was in direct violation of God's will. Rivington & Hatchard, the publishers of Radstock's pamphlet, sold the pamphlet in London.
13. See for example: 'Lord Radstock was my best friend   it was owing to him that the first poems succeeded   he introduced them into all places were he had connections got them noticed in newspapers . . .', Peterborough MS B6, fol. 84, quoted in *Autobiographical Writings*, p. 43. I have followed Eric Robinson's transcription.
14. *Letters*, pp. 39, 34 and 47.
15. Radstock to Sherwill, 20 February 1820, Northampton MS 45. I am grateful to Bob Heyes for the use of his transcription of this letter.
16. While Radstock's inspired 'effusion' seems out of character at first blush, confirmation of the quality of one's feelings was a staple reward of patronage, a subject I will take up in detail in Clare's relationship with Mrs Emmerson.

5   'Medlars'

1. *Letters*, pp. 68–70.
2. See Storey's footnote, *Letters*, p. 69.
3. Taylor to John Clare, 6 January 1821, *Letters*, p. 135.
4. *Letters*, pp. 139–40.
5. *Letters*, p. 122.
6. *Letters*, pp. 83–4.
7. Letter to Taylor, 16 January 1821, *Letters*, p. 141. Clare continued to produce 'specimen(s) of rural courtship' (*Letters*, pp. 100–2), which described human sexuality in frank and natural terms.
8. *Letters*, p. 55. The final sentence of this passage seems over-generous given the extreme paternalism Radstock and Sherwill brought to their project of providing for Clare without spoiling him with unnecessary luxury.
9. Cited in *Letters*, p. 71, n. 5.

10. *Letters*, pp. 70–1.
11. A letter to Taylor of 23 January 1821 (*Letters*, p. 143) indicates that despite Clare's efforts Radstock remained maddeningly obtuse: 'Lord R[adstock] is meneuvering uncommonly   now he has written to D[rury] & to Lord Milton about me being ill   he fancies such flummery pleases me but hes mistaken for I wish all such bother far enough & am glad Lord M[ilton] has learnd to disregard paper kites & pass over trifles without notice'. Radstock tried everyone's patience, and his 'flummery' caused constant concern with its potential to disrupt Clare's important relationships with Lord Milton, Earl Fitzwilliam and with Taylor.
12. *Letters*, pp. 117–19.
13. Taylor quotes directly from Radstock's extant letter of 8 December 1820, Pforzheimer MS Misc. 1369, fol.52.
14. The agreement would grant half of all profits from sales to Clare with the other half to be divided between Taylor & Hessey and Drury.
15. *Letters*, pp. 119–21.
16. From Clare's perspective, the agreement would have the added benefit of clarifying the relationship between Taylor & Hessey and Drury, an ongoing source of irritation (*Letters*, p. 120). Woodhouse was not only a friend, but also a joint trustee with Taylor of the fund money held for Clare, and thus the obvious choice to draw up the agreement. Storey comments that despite this declaration, 'no "agreement" seems to have been forthcoming at this stage'. Given that the impetus of the undertaking was the elimination of Radstock's interference, perhaps the appearance of *The Village Minstrel* removed any sense of urgency, especially remembering that the two main parties worried that any change might damage their working relationship.
17. *Letters*, pp. 121–2.
18. *Letters*, p. 125.
19. Murray's address.
20. Letter to Taylor, 21 March 1821, *Letters*, p. 168.
21. Such critical views are common, if not quite universal, and too numerous to list. A typical example, chosen for its brevity, will serve. Eric Robinson's note on Radstock in his edition of Clare's autobiographical writing ends: 'He was an ardent evangelical and a very kindly man.' *Autobiographical Writing*, p. 168, n. 13. Radstock's tract demonstrates that, in his case, the two assertions in this sentence are mutually exclusive.
22. Letter to Clare, 5 February 1822, Egerton MS 2246, fol. 17–18.
23. To Clare, 14 March 1823, Egerton MS 2246, fol. 161–3. Taylor employed a calm respectful tone in his response to Mrs Emmerson, and correctly pointed out that a long enthusiastic review of Clare in a magazine to which he regularly contributed poems would be counter-productive. Nonetheless, given the level of interference during the previous two years, he doubtless also objected to the essay's title: *Four Letters from the Rev. Allen, to the Right Hon. Admiral Lord Radstock, on the Poems of John Clare, the Northamptonshire Peasant*. There is little to reason to doubt Taylor's sincerity in praising the 'taste' and 'judgement' of Allen's 'Critique'. The essay contains perceptive readings of Clare's poems and poetic goals, and a keen appreciation for the cultural conditions from which the work emerged. Indeed, Allen's praise of 'simplicity and feeling' (p. 3), and his admiration of the accuracy of Clare's

poetic eye when he states, 'he [Clare] makes his twigs bend when they ought. He discovers, in almost every page, an exact attention to the minutiae of landscape circumstances' (pp. 15–16), are every bit as thoughtful as either Gilchrist's introduction to Clare or Taylor's introductions to the first two volumes, *Four Letters* (London: Hatchard & Son, 1823). The problem with Allen's appreciation is not that it is an embarrassing hagiography, but rather its timing. The critical views he expressed were apt, but they had already been stated by others, and could only have been read as partisan puffing had they appeared in the *London Magazine*. Radstock presented a copy to Clare with flyleaf inscriptions from himself and Mrs Emmerson, and dated 18 June 1823. This is item 98 of Clare's books at the Northampton Central Library.

24. Letter to James Augustus Hessey, circa 28 June 1823, *Letters*, p. 273. Clare's prophecy proved accurate, and again highlights the ironic juxtaposition of the unschooled peasant put in the position of having to worry about the naïve enthusiasms of his 'simple' aristocratic 'friends'.

25. Letter to Hessey, 11 September 1823, *Letters*, p. 285. The reviewer was Earl Grey, and Clare's reference to 'politics' referred to the fact that, as a Whig grandee, Grey could hardly have been expected to produce a review free of a gratuitous attack on a self-important Tory like Radstock (see n. 2, *Letters*, p. 285).

26. 'The Journal', 21 August 1825, Northampton MS 15, cited in *Natural History*, p. 254 (Margaret Grainger's transcription).

27. In an entry from the previous October, Clare put it succinctly: 'he is one of my best friends & not of much kin with the world.' 'The Journal', 30 October 1824, *Natural History*, p. 197.

28. This is not to say that following Radstock's death Mrs Emmerson became a better friend, simply a different kind of friend. Anyone who has read her letters to Clare recognises that she was an extraordinarily demanding correspondent, and emotionally needy past the point that most friends would tolerate. She came to Clare through Radstock because her intercession on Clare's behalf with her powerful friend authorised their relationship in her mind. Throughout their friendship she wanted Clare to confirm the value of her artistic sensibility, in the beginning as a sensitive admirer of 'natural genius', but ultimately as a poet. Prior to Radstock's death she had trapped herself in the gravitational force of his lordship's ego, and her own needs become primary upon her release.

29. *Autobiographical Writings*, p. 117. The offer provides rich irony when considered in light of the fact that Clare had left a position in the gardens at Burghley Park, having considered it preferable to make his living first in the fields, and then, once his father's infirmity made it necessary, as a lime-burner, rather than work under the tyrannical head kitchen gardener. See 'Sketches in the Life of John Clare' in *Autobiographical Writings*, pp. 10–18.

30. *Letters*, p. 153.

31. Egerton MS 2246, fol. 197. I will elaborate on Clare's relationship to Milton House in the next chapter.

32. Clare's relationship with Earl Spencer is missing from this brief discussion of his main benefactors because not as much has been known. Taylor offered typical advice in thanking Spencer 'in a *very simple* note' (emphasis his), *Letters*, p. 129. Whether or not he ignored Taylor's cautious advice, as he so

often did in mediating the various disputes that arose among his friends, can now be investigated with the recent discovery of 30 previously unknown letters to Earl Spencer. I have yet to be able to consult this new MS resource at the British Library. See Paul Chirico, 'Writing for money: the correspondence of John Clare and Earl Spencer', *TLS*, no. 5094, 17 November 2000, 14–15.

6   The Marketplace

1. *Letters*, p. 348.
2. Egerton MS 2247, fol. 77–8.
3. Cited in *Letters*, p. 348, n. 1. Mrs Emmerson's subsequent advice is also noted by Storey, n. 2.
4. Letter to Clare from Charles Hodgson, 28 November 1825, Egerton MS 2247, fol. 108–9.
5. Clare's letter to Hodgson has not survived, but the enthusiastic reply of 27 February 1826 makes it clear that he understands and accepts the terms of Clare's 'proposition'. Only his absence from London had prevented him from responding sooner. Egerton MS 2247, fol. 148–9.
6. *Letters*, p. 85.
7. *Letters*, p. 85.
8. Storey describes these circumstances in *Letters*, p. 85, n. 9.
9. Storey cites Mrs Emmerson's agitated question: 'What is the importance of 100 Songs compared to your 2nd Volm of Poems?' *Letters*, p. 85, n. 9.
10. The editor proved to be Samuel Carter Hall who finally revealed his identity to Clare in a letter the following year, Egerton MS 2247, fol. 222–3. Hall was an acquaintance of Taylor's, and extremely active in the business of literary annuals. His association with Clare continued until 1834, evidenced by the inclusion of a Clare poem in another of his annuals, *The Literary Souvenir*, for 1835. For a complete list of Clare's contributions to that annual, see Grainger's note in *Natural History*, p. 256, n. 1. Grainger's note occurs in response to a mysterious entry in Clare's *Journal*, dated Sunday 6 February 1828, but included in the space for 6 February 1825. Grainger notes that the 1828 entries interspersed with the 1825 entries are in darker ink suggesting that they were inserted later rather than the less likely possibility that they were misdated (Robinson and Powell simply reiterate Grainger's note in *By Himself*). The note has proved puzzling because Clare records the 'Bankrupt of W. Baynes & Son' and with it the £5 he was 'to have had for writing for the "Amulet"', 'The Journal', *Natural History*, p. 256. As Grainger's note makes clear, Hall's editorial activity and Clare's participation in his projects long outlasts this news. The simply solution to the mystery may be that Hall had employed Baynes & Son as publishers and booksellers and made alternative arrangements before their demise. *The Amulet* may have died with that venture but Hall could offer Clare other outlets for his verse.
11. Letter from Baynes & Son, 20 August 1825, Egerton MS 2247, fol. 57–8.
12. Coincidentally, Clare was corresponding with Montgomery at this time and had submitted his poem, 'The Vanities of Life' to his newspaper. I will

discuss Clare's relationship to Montgomery, and Montgomery's relationship with the Fitzwilliams, later in the chapter.

13. Letter from the Editor of *The Amulet*, Egerton MS 2247, fol. 101.
14. Letter from S. C. Hall (editor of *The Amulet*), 11 November 1826, Egerton MS 2247, fol. 222–3.
15. Hall acted as Clare's contact with other publishers as well. In May 1828, Clare wrote to say that he had acted on Hall's advice and sent 'a Poem within 3 days of Publication' to the magazine, the *Spirit and Manners of the Age*. Clare feared that such a rushed job would displease the publishers, Westley & Davis, so sent a 'corrected copy with a desire they would cancel the other', *Letters*, p. 433. In the end he placed both poems. Hall may have had an ulterior motive. The following year he wrote that he had assumed control of *Spirit and Manners of the Age* and would pay the extraordinary sum of 8 guineas a sheet, Letter from S. C. Hall, 4 March 1829, Egerton MS 2250, fol. 201 (cited in *Letters*, p. 458, n. 1). Clare's letter of 7 March suggests that Hall continued to produce *The Amulet* and that his wife Anna Maria Hall had charge of the *Juvenile-Forget-Me-Not*. He published his poetical version of the tale, 'The Grasshopper', a poem he had written for his children, in her magazine. Children's verse presented another poetic opportunity for Clare at a time when frustrations with Taylor were at a head. He had been writing in several new veins for some time in a deliberate effort to expand his poetic range beyond the 'peasant poet' that was his staple existence. Clare clearly intended to continue to write for all these outlets, and expressed confidence that Hall would make good on the 'little money for my trifles according to agreement' with Westley (*Letters*, p. 458). This letter voices Clare's dissatisfaction with the business of publishing in annuals. Westley & Davis owed Clare 6 guineas, and had promised to pay a guinea a month for the submission of a single page. Hall made good on these debts and increased Clare's rate of payment. Hall's business efficiency and ethics impressed Clare at the moment when he 'almost came to the resolution of never writing any thing of the kind again but for those who paid me punctually'.
16. John Savage, the editor, lived in Surfleet near Spalding. Then as now, Spalding was an important agricultural town on the edge of the fens. Spalding news appeared in the Stamford newspapers and vice versa, and Clare noted that they were 'neighbours'.
17. *By Himself*, p. 192.
18. 'The Journal', 8 January 1825, in *By Himself*, p. 206.
19. Letter from Savage, 3 November 1824, Egerton MS 2247, fol. 404.
20. *Letters*, p. 306.
21. *By Himself*, p. 219.
22. Letter from Savage, 20 March 1825, cited in *Letters*, p. 306, n. 1.
23. Clare recorded his plan in his journal entry of 19 January 1825, *By Himself*, p. 207.
24. *A Life*, p. 196.
25. See 'Clare and Community: The "Old Poets" and the *London Magazine*' in *John Clare: New Approaches*, eds John Goodridge and Simon Kovesi (Peterborough: The John Clare Society, 2000), pp. 47–63. Despite her central thesis, Gorji follows the general pattern of the 'poor Clare' tradition: 'His fame peaked in the early 1820s, buoyed up by the enthusiastic reception of

Poems Descriptive of Rural Life and Scenery, and from then began the decline, and Clare's detachment from the literary world. His growing loneliness in these years perhaps made his desire for a sociable poetic community stronger than ever' (p. 59). This strikes me as counter-intuitive. Surely his engagement with Lamb and with the general enthusiasm for these writers at the *London* marks his participation in 'a sociable poetic community', and his playful use of pseudonyms and accounts of the provenance of these 'lost' works demonstrate his adeptness at a form of literary wit popular at the time (see for example, Thomas Moore's hilarious introduction to his novel *The Epicurean* where he presents the work as a 'translation' of a manuscript discovered in an obscure Greek monastery). As Gorji argues the elevation of Harrington, Suckling, Marvel, Herrick, and the rest represented the recovery of a poetic counter-tradition based on the value of conviviality and sociability, and the *London Magazine* circle represented a contemporary literary practice based on those values. Perhaps Gorji's most important contribution to Clare studies in her essay occurs in her observation that this taste represented a democratic poetics. This insight provides an important corrective to John Barrell's over-valuation of the 'local' in Clare's poetry: 'Clare's efforts to involve himself in poetic communities – to open out of his solitude into company – was perhaps a response to the disintegration of the local community he attributed to the enclosure of Helpston: that his intertexuality, rather than his originality, was a response to enclosure' (p. 61).

26. Letter from Hessey, 14 July 1823, Egerton MS 2246, fol. 220–1.
27. *Letters*, pp. 196–8. See especially n. 1.
28. *Letters*, pp. 314–19, n. 7.
29. *Letters*, p. 314.
30. Letter from Henderson, 2 March 1825, Egerton MS, 2247, fol. 454–5. Henderson was perhaps Clare's most important friend in this period, and also provided him with a broad network sympathetic readers and intellectuals. I will develop Clare's relationship to Henderson later in the chapter. For more on Henderson, see the essay by Bob Heyes, 'Writing Clare's Poems: "The Myth of Solitary Genius"', in *New Approaches*, pp. 33–45.
31. The *Sheffield Iris* of 4 August 1829 contained a long tribute to Earl Fitzwilliam praising his dedication and service to the cause of parliamentary reform, and leadership of the radical Whigs. Montgomery referred to his Lordship as 'our venerable neighbour' (p. 4), and encouraged unqualified admiration of a long and illustrious career. Like Drakard, Montgomery reprinted Cobbett, and reported on Cobbett's numerous campaigns and agitations. See the *Sheffield Iris*, 18 August, 8 September, and 24 November 1829 for continuing coverage of one such campaign. Page 4 of the 18 August edition gives the flavour of the newspaper, and makes clear the deep commitment of its politics. Under the headline, 'The King's Answer to the Weavers' Petition', run not only the text, but an account of its being read to 'a very numerous Meeting of unemployed weavers' and their venting 'their feelings of disappointment'. Immediately below, under the headline, 'Shooting a Baillif' (a title that sounds suspiciously like a 'how to' guide), there is an account of an 'aged couple' arrested in Nottingham for shooting a Bailiff who was in the process of evicting them from their house. These two stories provide the immediate context for the largest piece on

the page, an account of Cobbett's speech to 'The Friends of Radical Reform' under the heading, 'Cobbett's Reasons for a Reformed Parliament'. In researching the *Sheffield Iris*, I hoped to find a reprint of Clare's essay 'Apology for the Poor'. It has long been assumed that it appeared in Drakard's *Stamford Champion*, but regrettably no complete run of the *Champion* has been located. It was my hope that Montgomery might have reprinted the essay because of his relationship to Clare, Drakard and the wider Fitzwilliam circle. Alas, the extant runs of the *Iris* at the Sheffield Public Library, the University of Sheffield archives, and the Colindale Newspaper Collection of the British Library contain similar gaps, especially in the most promising period, 1829–31. Nevertheless, the reprint culture of the radical press of the day makes it possible that Clare's 'lost' essay may finally resurface.

32. *By Himself*, p. 213.

33. *Letters*, p. 314, n. 1.

34. Letter to James Montgomery, 10 December 1827, *Letters*, p. 408.

35. The Tibbles relate the strange afterlife of this affair. Despite the fact that the poem was reprinted in *The Rural Muse*, establishing Clare's authorship, the poem continued to appear in collections of the 'old poets' throughout the nineteenth century. In 1857 R. Bell included it in his collection, *Ancient Ballads and Songs of the Peasantry of England* along with a retelling of Clare's original provenance story. J. H. Dixon wrote to *Notes and Queries* in 1873 defending the authenticity of the poem, which he had included in a similar collection. Dixon went so far as to argue that Clare's authorship showed evidence of 'mental aberration' (*A Life*, p. 234). The richness of the irony inherent in these events hardly needs noting, but the presumption that a 'peasant', Clare, was incapable of composing a poem that was a staple of collections of poems of the 'Peasantry of England' almost defies belief. Historical distance appears to have been a key determinant of whether or not the work of the 'peasantry' was worthy of consideration. This shows another side of the revival of the 'old poets' – a nostalgic attachment to a presumably more settled time when rural pleasures were unencumbered of the taint of 'discontent'.

36. Letter to Montgomery, 8 May 1826, *Letters*, p. 375.

37. See Gorji, pp. 53–5. For the history of the radical associations of Ritson and other collections, see Nicholas Roe, *John Keats and the Culture of Dissent* (Oxford: Clarendon Press, 1997), especially pp. 111–59.

38. See, Letter to William Hone, 15 May 1823, *Letters*, p. 270.

39. In 1832 Clare hoped to interest Cruikshank in producing engraved illustrations for his own satire, 'The Hue & Cry'. I will discuss this work, including Clare's publication plans for it, at length in Chapter 8.

40. Letter to Hone, 23 June 1825, *Letters*, p. 335.

41. The Spalding Gentleman's Society still very much exists. Among the items in their possession of interest to Clare scholars is a complete run of the Stamford Tory newspaper *The Bee*, and its successor the *Lincolnshire Herald*. I am indebted for their generosity in allowing me access to their collection.

42. *Letters*, p. 335, n. 3.

43. Letter to Hone, 2 August 1825, *Letters*, pp. 340–1.

44. Letter to Hone, 2 August 1825, *Letters*, pp. 341–2.

45. Letter to Hone, *c.* 1825–6, *Letters*, p. 345.

46. I will discuss Clare's 'natural history' writings and relationship to Henderson at length in the next chapter.
47. Letter to Hone, 29 February 1828, *Letters*, p. 417.
48. Cited in *Letters*, p. 344, n. 3.
49. Letter from Joseph Henderson, 9 February 1826, Egerton MS 2247, fol. 138–9.
50. Egerton MS 2247, fol. 138.
51. Letter to Hessey, 8 December 1825, *Letters*, pp. 349–50.
52. Letter to Taylor, 20 August 1827, *Letters*, p. 394.
53. Letter to Taylor from 'Percey Green', 19 October 1822, *Letters*, pp. 248–9.
54. *Letters*, pp. 248–9.
55. *Letters*, p. 249.
56. Letter to Hessey, 12 December, 1822, *Letters*, p. 251.
57. Letter to Taylor from 'Stephen Timms', 14 June 1821, *Letters*, pp. 196–8.
58. Letter from Hessey, 14 July 1823, Egerton MS 2246, fol. 220–1.
59. An untypical but illuminating example dates from July 1823. Clare had written to Hessey responding to the allusions to and quotations from his poems that appeared in Elizabeth Kent's *Flora Domestica*. Taylor & Hessey were the publishers, and Hessey published Clare's response, without prior permission, in the next issue of the magazine. Clare's published response had two effects; it confirmed Kent's taste and authorised her use of his poems as verbal illustrations. The letter contained beautiful natural history observations based on local scenery: 'The Author is mistaken about the Cowslip, as it is a very favoured flower, and no cottager's garden is without it, nor farmer's neither: it is as great a favourite as the single Daisy, and the Dwarf Buttercup—the 'little Celandine' of botanists. All spring flowers are beloved with us; but the summer ones seem hardly to claim notice, their names are lost in their number.' *Letters*, pp. 279–80. The gentle correction in this passage rests on local knowledge, something Kent lacked. Clare's response, Kent's book, and Hessey's decision to publish the response combined to encourage Clare to new kinds of writing. In *Flora Domestica* he saw the possibility of a genre we might call poetic natural history. The appearance of his critical judgements of Kent's work in the pages of the *London Magazine* caused Clare to imagine other prose works and genres, and established him as an authority on the local flora of Northamptonshire. I will discuss his various plans for natural history projects, and the constellation of Clare, Kent, Hessey and Joseph Henderson in the next chapter. Admiration of specific pieces, dismissal of others and complaints about the editing of his verse were more typical responses. His journal entry for 11 September 1824 provides a good example: 'Read the september No of the London Mag: only 2 good articles in it— 'Blakesmore in H——shire' by Elia and review of 'Goethe' by De Quincey these are exelent and sufficient to make a bad No interesting', 'The Journal', *By Himself*, pp. 172–3. As the quality of the magazine declined, Clare was unsparing in his journal entries, even indicting Taylor's editorial leadership: 'Blackwood has had a hard hit on Taylor   there is no more Editor Scotts at present to check them', 'The Journal', *By Himself*, p. 185. Lamenting Taylor's lack of physical courage, he also wished that 'Dequincey had better subjects for his genius' than a 30-page review of *Walladmor*. Clare's participation in the *London Magazine* entailed a variety of literary contributions (he hoped to

write more prose), and, perhaps as importantly, provided him with a literary community.

60. 30 October 1822.
61. Cited in *Letters*, pp. 253–4, n. 1 on the Letter to Hessey, 4 January 1823.
62. Letter to Hessey, 7 April 1823, *Letters*, pp. 267–9. Clare's frustrations with his publishers took many forms. The notorious delay in publishing the *Shepherd's Calendar* represented one in a series of complaints. Problems began with the delay in publishing the second edition of the *Village Minstrel*. Clare wanted to present copies to his friends at the *London Magazine*, but delay followed delay (indecision about the frontispiece, etc.): 'I shall expect to see the second Edit. out directly for I imagine New title pages & a wood engraving will not take long doing—my anxiety increases with the delay—I shall as soon as they are out want to make presents to your London contributors Hood Reynolds Cunningham Weathercock Carey &c.', *Letters*, p. 257. Looking back on that delay in the context of the many delays in receiving the proofs for the third book, Clare remembered in his journal: 'in the bringing out the second Edit of the Minstrel they was a twelvmonth in printing a title page', 'The Journal', 25 November 1824, *By Himself*, p. 199. By the end, he had even lost faith in Taylor's editorial ability – a primary reason that he had remained with them when urged by Radstock and Emmerson to let them secure a more 'worthy' outlet: 'I am weary of writing for the *London Magazine* these recent refinings are petty and trifling at best', 'The Journal', 23 January 1825, *By Himself*, p. 208. What Clare could not know because Taylor himself could not was that in assuming the editorship of the *London Magazine*, the firm of Taylor & Hessey was doomed. Completely overextended, Taylor could not delegate tasks efficiently enough to survive. In order to produce the magazine, authors were neglected, editing became haphazard, the quality of their titles declined, the quality of the magazine declined. Inevitably Taylor's editorship ended and Taylor & Hessey dissolved. Clare was not the only victim of this collapse, and Taylor's collapse was total: financial, professional, physical, emotional, and psychological. Elizabeth Kent, for example, acting in good faith, worked with Hessey to produce a study of English birds. Her book died with the dissolution of the firm. Taylor made some flip comment about the market and the poor sales of her previous book, but he had hardly shown himself to be a shrewd judge of the literary marketplace.
63. Letter to Hessey, 4 January 1823, *Letters*, pp. 254–5.
64. *New Approaches*, pp. 33–45, especially pp. 38–42.
65. Letter from Henderson, 12 May 1823, Egerton MS 2246, fol. 196–7.
66. 'Writing Clare's Poems', p. 41.
67. Letter to Taylor, 19 March 1820, *Letters*, p. 38.
68. 'Writing Clare's Poems', p. 42. Heyes's connection of the surviving evidence of editorial collaboration, whether informal familial responses or the inserted critical annotations Henderson provided, to the broader issue of 'authorship' represents a critical step forward in understanding the nature of literary work in the period. In referencing Jack Stillinger's central argument from *Multiple Authorship and the Myth of Solitary Genius* (New York: Oxford University Press, 1991), he aligns his work with a general reconsideration of Romantic authorship as represented by works such as Zachary Leader's *Romantic Revisions*.

Challenging the misimpression of Clare as an isolated and vulnerable genius is one of the main goals of this chapter.

69. Letter from Henderson, 21 May 1823, Egerton MS 2246, fol. 198–9.
70. Evidenced by current interest in Clare as a folklorist, this was indeed a substantial loss. See George Deacon's *John Clare and the Folk Tradition* (London: Sinclair Brown, 1983), for the best introduction to the subject.

7 The Natural Histories of Helpstone

1. Letter from Hessey, 6 May 1823, Egerton MS 2246, fol. 195.
2. 'The Journal', 11 September 1824, *Natural History*, p. 175.
3. Letter from Hessey, 7 September 1824, Egerton MS 2246, fol. 377–8.
4. This title is Grainger's invention, as is the collection of the letters as a cohesive work. The intrinsic value of *The Natural History Prose Works of John Clare* cannot be overstated, but the book exists as a work of editorial imagination coupled with extraordinary scholarship.
5. *Natural History*, pp. 36–40.
6. Letter from Hessey, 13 October 1823, Egerton MS 2246, fol. 245–6.
7. For example, see the letter of 6 March 1824 which included a copy of the will Taylor & Hessey had had Woodhouse draft, Egerton MS 2246, fol. 302–3. Clare's sense of urgency in the completion of this project had to do with a growing morbidity brought on by his illness, but it also doubtless followed from the material details surrounding the death of Bloomfield the previous autumn. Hessey had contributed to his alarm with the details and tone of his account in a letter of 6 September 1823: 'You will have seen in the newspapers that poor Bloomfield is dead—his lot has latterly been a very unhappy one. He suffered his brothers & relations to get from him the money which he obtained in the days of his popularity, and had the mortification of finding that he had outlived his powers and his prosperity. I fear his family are but poorly provided for'. Egerton MS 2246, fol. 237–8. Clare spent much of the following year thinking about Bloomfield and his fate, and his 1824 illness became the physical backdrop for his ruminations. His reflections culminated in his plan to write a critical biography of Bloomfield as he noted in his journal on 12 October 1824, *By Himself*, p. 185.
8. Cited in *A Life*, p. 200.
9. 'The Journal', 10 October 1824, By *Himself*, p. 184.
10. Letter from Taylor, 3 April 1824, Egerton MS 2246, fol. 322.
11. Letter from Hessey, 6 May 1824, Egerton MS 2246, fol. 340–1.
12. Letter from Hessey, 5 October 1824, Egerton MS 2246, fol. 395–6.
13. Letter from Hessey, 31 March 1823, Egerton MS 2246, fol. 173–4.
14. Letter from Hessey, 6 October 1823, Egerton MS 2246, fol. 243–4.
15. Letter from Hessey, 1 November 1823, Egerton MS 2246, fol. 247–8.
16. 'The Journal', 11 September 1824, *By Himself*, p. 172.
17. Letter from Hessey, 5 October 1824, Egerton MS, fol. 395–6.
18. Letter from Hessey, 3 November 1824, Egerton MS 2246, fol. 405–6.
19. I have argued at length against this critical view and its descendents in Romantic studies in 'Clare's Minorness' above. Taylor's demand for a quasi-Wordsworthian poetics of reflection probably led to the composition of

several poems roughly dated to late 1824 and early 1825, especially 'Pastoral Poesy'. That poem, so utterly unlike most of Clare's poetry, concerns the artistic creation of the poem out of the materials of the natural world rather than the objects of that world. Not surprisingly, 'Pastoral Poesy' remains one of the most anthologised of Clare's poems because of its superficial resemblance to a Wordsworth poem. See my detailed discussion in the 'Preface'.

20. 'The Journal', 7 November 1824, *By Himself*, p. 193.
21. Letter from Hessey, 22 November 1824, Egerton MS 2246, fol. 407–8.
22. 'The Journal', 25 November 1824, *By Himself*, p. 199.
23. Letter from Hessey, 29 January 1825, Egerton MS 2246, fol. 432–4.
24. 'The Journal', 12 February 1825, *By Himself*, p. 212.
25. Letter from Hessey, 13 October 1823, Egerton MS 2246, fol. 245–6.
26. 'The Journal', 17 April 1825, *By Himself*, p. 223.
27. 'The Journal', 30 March 1825, *By Himself*, p. 220.
28. 'The Journal, 15 April 1825, *By Himself*, p. 222.
29. Letter to Hessey, 17 April 1825, *Letters*, p. 325–6.
30. Letter from Henderson, 11 May 1825, Egerton MS 2247, fol. 25–6.
31. Letter from Taylor, 18 April 1825, cited in *Letters*, pp. 326–7.
32. Letter from Hessey, 10 May 1825, Egerton MS 2247, fol. 23–4.
33. Letter from Hessey, 30 May 1825, Egerton MS 2247, fol. 32–3.
34. Letter from Hessey, 30 June 1825, Egerton MS 2247, fol. 40–1.
35. Letter from Hessey, 9 July 1825, Egerton MS 2247, fol.42–3. It is difficult not to hear irony in this letter. Taylor's assumption of the *London* was the root cause of the neglect of the *Shepherd's Calendar* project. Hessey helped whenever Taylor was incapacitated, but never had authority to take the project forward. In the end Hessey survived the rigours of producing the magazine, but Taylor was completely, rather than 'almost', 'wore out'.
36. 'The Journal', 11 March 1825, *By Himself*, p. 217.
37. 'The Journal', 18 April 1825, *By Himself*, p. 223.
38. 'The Journal', 28 April 1825, *By Himself*, p. 225. Clare recorded observations on most days in April and May, many with the same detail as the 'Garden snail' entry. For example on 26 May he wrote: 'I watched a Blue cap or Blue Titmouse feeding her young whose nest was in a wall close to an Orchard   she got caterpillars out of the Blossoms of the apple trees and leaves of the plumb—she fetchd 120 Caterpillars in half an hour'.
39. I discuss the fate of Elizabeth Kent's book of 'English Birds' below.
40. Letter from Taylor, 15 June 1825, cited in *Letters*, pp. 331–2.
41. 'The Journal', 19 June 1825, *By Himself*, p. 235.
42. 'The Journal', 29 July 1825, *By Himself*, p. 238. Critics have universally echoed Clare's view that the new plan for the manuscript was a travesty. Critics take as given that *The Shepherd's Calendar* was an inadequate and unrepresentative selection of Clare's poetry from the first half of the 1820s. If anything, this critical view continues to grow in vehemence.
43. Letter from Hessey, 6 September 1825, Egerton MS 2247, fol. 65–6. This letter coincidentally reported the death of Lord Radstock from a 'stroke of Apoplexy'.
44. Letter from Hessey, 5 September 1826, Egerton MS 2247, fol. 210–1.
45. 'The Journal', 3 June 1825, *Natural History*, pp. 244–5.
46. Letter from Henderson, 12 July 1823, Egerton MS 2246, fol. 196–7.

47. Letter from Henderson, 27 November 1824, Egerton MS 2246, fol. 409–10.
48. 'The Journal', 1 November 1824, *Natural History*, p. 197.
49. 'The Journal', 2 November 1824, *Natural History*, p. 198.
50. 'The Journal', 3 November 1824, *Natural History*, p. 198.
51. 'The Journal', 19 November 1824, *Natural History*, p. 204.
52. 'The Journal', 8 November 1824, *Natural History*, p. 209.
53. Margaret Grainger includes a list of natural history books in the Milton Library in *Natural History*, Appendix Vc, p. 365. Some of the listed volumes were sold in 1918, and she correctly indicates that Clare may well have used them nonetheless. More troubling is the fact that at some point there was a collation of the books from the Milton Library and the Wentworth Library at the huge northern Fitzwilliam estate. Even if some of the listed books had been housed at Wentworth Woodhouse, it does not mean that Clare had no access to them. The family and their retainers, including Henderson and Artis, circulated between the two locales and communication between houses was ongoing. Henderson could easily arrange to have books sent to Milton House, as he and Clare needed them. This may have been the source, for example, of Henderson's temporary possession of *The English Botany* in 30 volumes in March 1827. See Letter from Henderson, 14 March 1827, Egerton MS 2247, fol. 276.
54. 'The Journal', 15 December 1824, *Natural History*, p. 210.
55. 'The Journal', 16 December 1824, *Natural History*, p. 210.
56. Letter from Henderson, 11 March 1825, Egerton MS 2246, fol. 467–8.
57. 'The Journal', 24 October 1824, *Natural History*, p. 195.
58. See Heyes's description of Henderson's scientific career in 'Writing Clare's Poems', *New Approaches*, pp. 38–9 and p. 45, n. 12 and n. 13. Heyes reminds us that Earl Fitzwilliam 'was the first president of the British Association for the Advancement of Science', an avid botanist and a collector of rare orchids.
59. See G. G. Yearsley, 'Earl Fitzwilliam and His Gardener, J. Cooper: 18th–19th Century Orchid Growers', *American Orchid Society Bulletin*, 45 (1976), 484–5. Cited in Heyes, p. 45, n. 12.
60. Letter from Hessey, 26 January 1827, Egerton MS 2247, fol. 303.
61. Isaac Emmerton, *The Culture & Management of the Auricula, Polyanthus, Carnation, Pink, and the Ranunculus* (London: Printed for the Author, 1819). This is item 198 in the Northampton Library collection of Clare's books. There are no marks on the book to date Clare's acquisition of it, or identify a donor, but it seems reasonable to assume that it came into his possession during his interest in collecting orchids (circa 1827) and may have been the gift of either Henderson or Earl Fitzwilliam. Clare may have been using it to identify specific flowers in his expeditions, accounting for the appearance of the list on the flyleaf. However, Clare's list of common names makes this less likely, given that the Emmerton uses Latin names and Linnaean classification exclusively.
62. 'The Journal', 29 September 1824, *Natural History*, p. 183.
63. 'The Journal', 8 June 1825, *Natural History*, p. 246.
64. See Sara Lodge, 'A Life Outside: Clare's Mole-Catcher', *John Clare Society Journal*, 2001, pp. 5–18. Lodge brilliantly isolates Clare's emotional investment in the poems describing Coz. Day, carefully situates them in the contexts of enclosure

and the workhouse, and forcefully argues that his poetic treatment of others avoids the pitfalls of Wordsworthian self-aggrandisement.

65. 'The Journal', 20 October 1824, 7 December 1824, 3 June 1825, *Natural History*, pp. 179–80, 209 and 245.
66. 'The Journal', 2 February 1825, *Natural History*, p. 220.
67. 'The Journal', 25 October 1824, *Natural History*, p. 195.
68. Such moments are so common in *The Prelude*, that a specific citation seems superfluous.
69. 'The Journal', 5 December 1824, *Natural History*, p. 209.
70. 'The Journal', 26 November 1824, *Natural History* p. 207.
71. On the other hand, the Fitzwilliams doubtless profited financially from local enclosures, and from those throughout their vast agricultural holdings in England and Ireland, and Henderson's fortune was tied to theirs.
72. Letter from Hessey, 14 July 1823, Egerton MS 2246, fol. 220–1.
73. 'The Journal', 24 October 1824, *Natural History*, p. 195.
74. Hessey presented Clare with a copy of the book in 1828, but it is clear that he knew the format, probably from reading the copy in the Milton House library. The copy that Hessey presented was a new edition from 1825, and testifies to the continued popularity of the work. Indeed, its popularity endures – the book has never been out of print. Clare's copy, item 395 of his books at the Northampton County Library, is inscribed 'from his sincere friend, JA Hessey', and was published by C. & J. Rivington, London, 1825.
75. *Flora Domestica, or the Portable Flower-Garden, with Directions for the Treatment of Plants in Pots; and Illustrations from the Works of the Poets* (London: Taylor & Hessey, 1823), p. xxii.
76. Letter to Hessey, July 1823, *Letters*, pp. 279–80.
77. Letter to Elizabeth Kent, August 1823, *Letters*, pp. 283–4. Clare began the letter, 'Dear Sir', thinking the anonymous author of the volume was a man.
78. *Flora Domestica*, p. xv.
79. *Flora Domestica*, p. xix. For a good discussion of Kent's place in 'Cockney Culture', see Elizabeth Jones, 'Keats in the Suburbs', *Keats-Shelley Journal*, 1996 (vol. 45).
80. For full discussions of 'Cockney Politics' see Nicholas Roe's *Keats and the Culture of Dissent* and Jeffrey Cox's *Poetry and Politics in the Cockney School* (Cambridge: Cambridge University Press, 1998). Kent praised Shelley for his sensibility, his politics and his sociability. Shelley was transformed by nature and then acted on that transformation in his associations with others. Clare shared those values, as evidenced by his participation in the ideal community of writers associated with the *London Magazine*, and in the taste for the 'old poets' and their radical associations. As Keats famously put it in the 3 May 1818 letter to Reynolds: 'Let us have the old poets and Robin Hood!'
81. 'The Journal', 6 March 1825, *Natural History*, p. 227.
82. Letter from Hessey, 2 March 1825, Egerton MS 2246, fol. 456–7.
83. 'The Journal', 11 March 1825, *Natural History*, p. 228.
84. Hessey's enthusiasm for *Sylvan Sketches*, based on its merits as a book, would soon be tempered by Taylor's response to poor sales.
85. Letter to Taylor, 5 May 1825, *Letters*, p. 331.
86. Letter from Hessey, 10 May 1825, Egerton MS 2247, fol. 23–4. Taylor may have alerted Hessey to Clare's frustration over the lack of word on his offer.

Taylor was of course nervous about losing Clare altogether, and while hectoring him about loyalty on one hand may have hoped news from Hessey would be some compensation for the ongoing disaster that was the *Shepherd's Calendar* MS.

87. 'The Journal', 14 May 1825, *Natural History*, p. 239.
88. If Kent left papers, I have been unable to find them.
89. Letter from Elizabeth Kent, 19 January 1826, Egerton MS 2247, fol. 128.
90. Letter from Kent, 16 February 1826, Egerton MS 2247, fol. 144–5.
91. As Hessey was no longer a partner in Taylor & Hessey, this detail did not bode well for Clare's 'Natural History of Helpstone'.
92. Letter from Taylor, 20 May 1826, Egerton MS 2247, fol. 176–7.
93. Letter to Taylor, 11 April 1826, *Letters*, p. 374.
94. Letter from Taylor, 7 August 1826, Egerton MS 2247, fol. 202–3.
95. Letter from Hessey, 5 September 1826, Egerton MS 2247, fol. 210–1.
96. Psychological allowances can, of course, be made. Taylor suffered a nervous breakdown, and part of him may have believed he was following through on Hessey's projects. It is impossible to know.
97. Letter to Taylor, 1 December 1826, *Letters*, p. 390.
98. Letter from Taylor, 3 March 1827, Egerton MS 2247, fol. 274–5.

8   Clare, Cobbett and 'Captain Swing'

1. See 'Clare's Politics', *Clare in Context*, pp. 148–77, and 'Common Sense or Radicalism', *Romanticism*, vol. 2, no. 1, 1996, 81–97. Also see my 'Clare and Political Equivocation', *John Clare Society Journal*, no.18 1999, 37–48, and Stephen Colclough, 'Labour and Luxury': Clare's Lost Pastoral and the Importance of the Voice of Labour in the Early Poems', *New Approaches*, 77–91, for more recent forays into the question of Clare's politics.
2. *John Clare: A Champion for the Poor, Political Verse and Prose*, ed. P. M. S. Dawson, Eric Robinson and David Powell (Manchester: Carcanet, 2000), pp. xiv–xv.
3. 'Captain Swing' was the name taken by the instigators of the agricultural riots throughout the country, especially the machine breakers. The title 'Captain' suggested a war was taking place, and the anonymity of those using it struck fear in those who thought themselves targeted much as the name 'Ned Lud' had during the 1811–12 Luddite rebellion. It seemed as if the threat was everywhere and nowhere.
4. *Champion for the Poor*, pp. liii–liv.
5. *Champion for the Poor*, p. 11.
6. *Champion for the Poor*, p. 12.
7. For a more detailed critique of Robinson's Introduction see my Review of *Champion of the Poor* in the *John Clare Society Journal*, no. 20, 2001, 81–5.
8. Peterborough MS A46, fol. 14. There are at least nineteen partial drafts of 'Apology for the Poor' in MS A46, some of which suggest that a version was published, and that Clare responded to published criticism of it with an open letter signed 'A Poor Man'. Neither the original publication nor the published response has, as yet, been discovered. Eric Robinson, P. M. S. Dawson and David Powell have transcribed the texts of the numerous drafts in MS

A46 as well as related fragments from MSS A51, A42, A45 and A53, *Champion for the Poor*, pp. 267–80.

9. 'Common Sense or Radicalism', p. 83.
10. Peterborough MS A45, fol. 31–2.
11. *The Bee*, 17 December 1830, p. 3.
12. Peterborough MS A46, fol. 113.
13. *Letters*, p. 527.
14. From the evidence of the local newspapers, it appears that the letter was written after 19 December, but probably within that week because Clare tells Simpson that if he wants to interview his neighbours about recent events near Helpstone he should do so while 'the facts are fresher on their memorys'. *Letters*, pp. 522–3.
15. The fact that Simpson was a magistrate was incidental to he and Clare's friendship. Clare had long served as his artistic mentor, encouraging the development of his skill as a painter. For example, at one point during the delay over the second edition of *The Village Minstrel* Clare had suggested Simpson as a possible candidate to produce a drawing of his cottage for the title page.
16. *Stamford Mercury*, 23 December 1830.
17. *Stamford News*, 24 December 1830.
18. *The Bee*, 26 November 1830, pp. 2–3.
19. *The Bee*, 30 November, 17 December and 24 December 1830.
20. *Cobbett's Weekly Political Register*, 13 November and 11 December 1830.
21. *The Bee*, 24 December 1830, p. 3.
22. *The Bee*, 26 November 1830, p. 3.
23. *Letters*, p. 544.
24. *Drakard's Stamford Champion*, 11 January 1831.
25. *Drakard's Stamford Champion*, 15 January 1831.
26. *Letters*, p. 560.
27. 'Common Sense or Radicalism', p. 89.
28. *Rural Rides*, pp. 233–4.
29. *Stamford Mercury*, 2 April 1830. The account in Drakard's *Stamford News* is almost identical, but for the addition of the observation that when the proposition of taking church property was introduced, 'the assemblage cheered', *Stamford News*, 2 April 1830.
30. *Stamford Mercury*, 2 April 1830.
31. *The Bee*, 24 December 1830, pp. 2–3.
32. *The Bee*, 31 December 1830, p. 4.
33. *The Bee*, 21 January 1831, p. 4.
34. *Stamford News*, 17 December 1830.
35. The Crown based their case for sedition on attacks on church property, especially tithes, that had appeared in *the Weekly Political Register*. Part of their claim of the seditiousness of Cobbett's rhetoric was based on the 'confession' of Thomas Goodman who had been convicted of hayrick burning, and claimed Cobbett's speech had incited him to his action. Cobbett's attack on the veracity of the 'confession' was fundamental in the failure of the Crown's case. See 'The King against William Cobbett', *Reports of State Trials. New Series. Vol. II. 1823–1831*, ed. John Macdonell (London: 1889), pp. 789–904.

36. The drafts of the open letter from 'A Poor Man' in Peterborough MS A46 seem to bear this out. Clare appears to be responding to having been attacked as a 'radical'.
37. The distinction persists in British political and theoretical discourse, and often takes the form of British scepticism to continental abstraction, an aversion to 'French theory'. Yet, no one would suggest that Louis Althusser was 'radical' and therefore Raymond Williams was not. The distinction describes political method, not political goals.
38. 'Clare's Politics', *Clare in Context*, p. 173.
39. *DNB*, Vol. 36, p. 213.
40. *DNB*, pp. 211–15.
41. Letter from Marianne Marsh, 14 July 1821, Egerton MS 2245, fol. 345.
42. Letter from Marianne Marsh, 7 January 1832, Egerton MS 2249, fol. 3. 'The reference to Mrs Clare adds to the formality of the letter, but Mrs Marsh and Patty Clare became close in subsequent years. For example, Mrs Marsh often included Patty's favorite tea in the packages she sent to Helpstone'.
43. Egerton MS 2247, fol. 408. I have inserted question marks in parentheses where I cannot be certain of a word in the manuscript.
44. Letter from Marianne Marsh, 9 October 1830, Egerton MS 2248, fol. 274.
45. Letter from Marianne Marsh, Egerton MS 2250, fol. 265. The letter is undated, but references to the success of some 'digestive pills' and to the receipt of 'Cobbett's Grammar' strongly suggest January 1832.
46. 'Letter to Frank Simpson', late December 1830, Peterborough MS B5, reprinted in *Letters*, pp. 522–3. Unfortunately, Storey's edition does not include folio numbers. The idea that the troubles were always the actions of strangers does not quite hold throughout the letter. Clare reports another incident where someone rode like 'a madman' through a farm and called out to one of the labourers by name: 'Will you are getting straw whose farm is it'? Will disclaims knowledge of the 'madman', but Clare clearly knows Will. Storey mis-transcribes 'Will' as 'Well'. I am grateful to Eric Robinson for pointing out this transcription error and thus clarifying the passage.
47. In one of his less successful entrepreneurial schemes, Cobbett had purchased Paine's skeletal remains and brought them back to England.
48. 'Letter to Marianne Marsh', 6 July 1831, MS owned by Robert Heyes, reprinted in *Letters*, pp. 543–4.
49. 'Letter to John Clare', Egerton MS 2248, fol. 368.
50. Of the numerous drafts of 'Apology for the Poor' in Peterborough MS A46, the most complete are in folios 14 and 15. The drafts are difficult to date from internal clues because they contain grievances from over a ten-year period. Its tone is sceptical and occasionally bitter. It may date from as early as 1829, which would mean that it could not be related to Mrs Marsh's request. However, there is no evidence that Clare changed his views.
51. *Cobbett's Two-Penny Trash; or Politics for the Poor* (London: William Cobbett, 1831), pp. 121–68.
52. Egerton MS 2248, fol. 413.
53. 'Letter to Marianne Marsh', January 1832, Peterborough MS A46, reprinted in *Letters*, p. 560.

54. Similar disclaimers are frequent in Clare's letters and journal entries and might lead us to conclude that he was apolitical, but for the fact that they, without exception, preface pieces of cogent political analysis.
55. Eric Hobsbawm and George Rudé detail the high number of those punished as rioters, and the severity of their punishment in their *Captain Swing* (London: Lawrence & Wishart, 1969).
56. *The Bee*, 31 December 1830, p. 3.
57. The editors of *Champion for the Poor* include another open letter from Marsh as an Appendix. It appeared the previous week to the letter in *The Bee* in *The Cambridge Chronicle*, 24 December 1830. The letter reported the fire at the Clark farm, quoted the text of threatening 'Swing' documents, and took the opportunity to attack Cobbett and Henry Hunt by association. See pp. 327–30.
58. Whether or not Cobbett was guilty of sedition is still a matter of historical debate. He was acquitted of the charge and on record as opposed to violence, but the riots undoubtedly contributed to the partial success of his political aims with the passage of the Reform Act in 1832.
59. Lucas is not alone in reading conservative politics in the relationship. On the other side of the argument, Eric Robinson attempts to use Clare's relationship with the Bishop to establish Clare's conservatism. Frankly, this judgement is put in doubt by a close examination of the correspondence. See Robinson's Introduction to *Champion for the Poor*, pp. xix–xx.
60. 'Voicing Loss: Versions of Pastoral in the Poetry of John Clare, 1817–1832', (unpublished doctoral thesis, University of Keele, 1996), p. 175. Cited by Robinson in his Introduction to *Champion for the Poor*, p. xlii.
61. *Letters*, pp. 524–5.
62. Letter from Henry Behnes Burlowe, 4 January 1831, Egerton MS 2248, cited in *Letters*, p. 525, n. 4. I have not checked the citation, but from other letters from the period it must be around folio 300.
63. *Letters*, p. 528.
64. Letter to Samuel Wilson, early January 1831, *Letters*, p. 529. Storey conjecturally dates the letter 4 January.
65. *Champion for the Poor*, p. xliii.

Index